LES VRAYES CENTURIES
et
PROPHETIES
de Maistre
MICHEL NOSTRADAMUS

Nostradamus

His Works and Prophecies

First Edition 1.0

Michel Nostradamus (1503-1566)

translation
Theodore Garencieres

front material
Mark McCloud

standard publications, inc.

Front Material and Layout
Copyright ©2001 by Standard Publications, Inc.
Urbana, Illinois 61825

The publisher of this book makes no warranty of any kind, express or implied, as to the fitness of this book for any purpose. The publisher has made every attempt to maintain the accuracy of the original quatrains and translation, however discrepancies may occur.

The publisher offers discounts on this book when ordered in bulk quantities and is available for classroom use.

ISBN 0-9709788-3-9

Printed in the United States of America

Standard Publications, Inc

English Translation from

The True
Prophecies *or* Prognostications
of
Michael Nostradamus,

PHYSICIAN

TO

Henry II. Francis II. and Charles IX,
Kings of France,

And one of the best
ASTRONOMERS that ever were.
A Work full of Curiosity and Learning.

Translated and Commented by *Theophilus de Garencieres,*
Doctor in Physick *Colleg. Lond.*

Printed in London, *1672*

 Forward

from the Publisher

Has Nostradamus predicted the coming Apocalypse along with a thousand other great events? His believers claim that in the *1500*s he predicted historic milestones that have or will alter the course of human history, such as the rise of Napoleon and Hitler. Published here are the hard to find original English translations from *1672* to help you answer that question. Finally, you can look through the actual work of Nostradamus to see if you can solve his riddles. He scribed over a thousand quatrains, which are four line poems that cover events from the *1500*s to the year *3797*. Since these were translated by Theodore Garencieres, before the rise of the first two antichrists, they are untainted with the bias of current events. See if you can unravel the hidden meaning of his quatrains and discover his vision of the future. Plagued by the Inquisition, Nostradamus was notorious for obfuscating his meaning with anagrams, symbolism, and mythological allusions. Study of his work can be a fascinating hobby or intellectual exercise that can be quite enjoyable. What great event will be discovered next in this cryptic text?

The English translation in this book was originally published in *1672*. This means that throughout the text you man find words with old-fashioned spellings, inconsistent spellings, unusual grammar, and odd punctuation. So, we ask the reader to please excuse apparent mistakes. We have made every attempt to maintain true to the original document, mistakes and all.

The motivation behind the publishing of this translation is so that people of the current day may reflect upon the great work of Nostradamus in a more pure form. Many of the more recent translations that we have encountered have been skewed to support the interpretations of the translator. A common example is the infamous quatrain II-24, which may foretell the coming of Hitler. Reference is made to Ister, or Hister, which at the time referred to a part or area of the Danube River. Many recent translations, however, have replaced Hister with Hitler, claiming that Nostradamus was really just playing a word game. Though the intertwining histories of Hitler and the Danube do not preclude him being the intended antichrist this quatrain refers to. Hindu translations may interpret his prophecies to refer to regions of Asia, just as American translations might interpret his prophecies to places or events in America. Even the Nazis used his work in their propaganda. We also did not want to leave out centuries that did not conform to an intended interpretation. Therefore, we have included all of his Centuries in their entirety, or at least those that have not already been lost to the ages.

The work of Nostradamus has transformed over the years, both through conscience effort and subconsciously, through changes in language, new events, and new developments. We searched for the oldest available modern English translation and were able to find an old volume locked away in the archives of a few, select, rare book rooms around the world. The translator was undoubtedly more familiar with the archaic form of French than most modern scholars. This translation is also particularly well suited for study, since it was performed in as direct a manner as possible. This helps to limit the effect of the translator's views.

While some of the problems mentioned here may also be said for this set of translations, it gives the reader an additional perspective that we fear may otherwise have become lost to history.

Biography

Michel de Nôstredame was born in France in *1503* to a Jewish family. He was quite intelligent, and became educated in the art of language, including Latin, Greek, and Hebrew. He appreciated a good conversation, but had little patience for those of low intellect. This was during the time of the Inquisition, and caused the conversion of his family to the Catholic faith. After studying at Avignon, he moved to Montpellier to learn the advanced sciences. He went on to become a much learned and successful physician. He developed his own methods and cures, which gave him more success than the superstitions that abounded during this age. He published several professional volumes describing ways to combat the black plague. In order to practice his medicine, he set out among the populace.

Nostradamus traveled the countryside and attempted to cure the poor souls that had been stricken by the plague. His efforts, and their success, earned him much renown in his time. After a while, he returned to his alma mater at Montpellier to earn his doctoral degree and teach. Some friction arose over his different methods, so he set out yet again.

He met up with the renowned philosopher Julius Caesar Scaliger in Agen, where he decided to settle down. The two shared a great passion for debating such topics as philosophy, medicine, and poetry. He took upon himself for a wife the local woman Adriète de Loubéjac and had two fine sons together. Ironically, the plague then struck Agen, claiming the lives of his wife and both his children. He fell out of favor with both Scaliger, and his late wife's family. To make matters worse, the Inquisition sent word for him to stand trial for heresy for an oft remark made by him earlier. Discouraged by these turn of events, he set out yet again. This time making sure to avoided church authorities.

He traveled as far as Italy, where he is credited with identifying the future Pope. Already becoming known for his ability to foretell future events, he began to scribe his prophecies in Luxemburg, and then later in Marseilles. His cures continued to help many plague victims, but disaster was to strike again. A torrential rain befell Provence and the plague spread anew, as did word of his ability to cure it. His efforts contributed greatly to the area's recovery. He was even summoned to Aix, where he continued his medicinal battle against the plague.

Vying again for the quiet life, he found a small town in Provence called Salonæ, where he again settled down. He married again, this time in 1547 to the wealthy Anne Ponsart Gemelle. They would soon have a son, Cæsar.

He was now able to spend more time developing his prognostications. Beginning in 1550 he started publishing a yearly Almanach to foretell of happenings in the coming year. He continued his study in astrology, divination, and magic. Using these methods, he was able to create quatrains that predicted events to the year 3797. These are what became his claim to fame and are what fascinates scholars to this day. They were written in a variety of languages, though dominantly French and Latin. To avoid being denounced as a witch or practitioner of magic, he claims to have hidden the true meaning and ordering of his quatrains. 1556 marked the first year that his famous quatrains saw print. He originally published around three and a half "Centuries," or collections of one hundred quatrains, though many more soon followed suit.

His work again spread. This time, all the way to the royal family. Queen Catherine de' Medici and King Henri II summoned him to their presence. It is said that Nostradamus and the queen hit it off remarkably well with similar interests in Italy and Astrology. The queen was mostly concerned about a quatrain that foretold of the king's death. A death that came to pass, just as predicted, a few days after injuries incurred during a tournament in 1559 (Century I, 35). He returned to Salonæ, though in 1558 became an official physician-astrologer and counselor to the king.

He continued his life casting horoscopes for nobles and courtiers and publishing his Almanachs and Centuries. He came into the favor of the new King Charles IX and continued in his services for the king of France.

After a time, his gout became worse and his health degraded into dropsy. In the year of 1566 on July 1st he met with his friend and biographer Jean Aymes de Chavigny and on that night proclaimed, *"Demain, au soleil levant, je ne serais plus,"* which means, "Tomorrow, with the rising sun, I shall be no more." On that night, he died.

His son, Cæsar, published the remainder of his work in the year *1568*. His wife buried his remains upright in the walls of the Church of Cordelier at Salonæ. With the marking, "Do not disturb the peace of the dead."

Nobody dared to desecrate his grave under threat of a curse. Until *1700*, when officials decided to move his tomb to a more prominent location. Peering into his coffin at the time, they discovered a medallion hanging around the skeleton's neck inscribed with the year *1700*.

Almost a hundred years later, in *1791*, some drunken soldiers during the French Revolution axed open his grave. They drank from his skull against the warnings of Nostradamus that anyone desecrating his remains would meet a swift demise. As these soldiers returned, they were ambushed in Aix by an uprising of royalists who killed each of the soldiers, hanging the captain, thus fulfilling another of his prophecies. Because of his predictions of the French Revolution he was honored and his ashes were put to rest at the church of St. Laurent where they remain to this day.

We now leave you to ponder his work with your own eyes:

A letter to the Courteous Reader, *from the Translator:*

Reader,

Before thou goest on further to the perusing of this Work, thou art humbly intreated by the Authour, to forgive him his Anglicisme ; for being born a Forreigner, and having had nobody to help him to the polishing of it, for several reasons, it cannot be expected he should please thin Ears, so much as he may perhaps do thy Fancy. Every Exotick Plant can hardly become Domestical under one or two Generations: Besides that, the Crabbedness of the Original in his own Idiome, can scare admit a Polite Eloquency in another. The very Ancient *English* Language in this refined Age, is become both obsolete and unintelligible, as we may see in *Chaucer, Gower,* and others. If you adde to this, that the Authours Nation hath been always famous for its Civility to those that were Strangers to their Language, as not onely to abstain from laughing them charitably to the best of their power. I may probably expect you will measure me with the same measure, as you would be if you were in my case.

As for the Errataes of the Press, I could not help them, being out of Town most part of the time that the Book was a Printing ; when you meet with any, I hope your Chairtable Pen will either mend or obliterate them, and not lay another mans fault upon me, who neither for pride nor ostentation undertook this laborious Work, but that I might give some Satisfaction and Recreation to the Learned and Curious, who have had a longing for it ever since its Birth.

Farewell.

reface

to the Reader

from the Translator

READER,

Before I speak any thing of the Author, or of his Works, I think it convenient to speak something of my self, and of my intention in setting out this Translation, with my Annotations.

The Reputation that this Book hath amongst all the *Europeans*, since its first coming out, which was in the year *1555.* and the curiosity that from time to time the learned have had to see the Mysteries contained in it, unfolded is a sufficient warrant for my undertaking.

Many better Pens (I confess) could have performed this work with better success, but not with greater facility than I, having from my youth been conversant with those that pretended or endeavored to know something to it. Otherwise, it would have been impossible for a man of my profession to wade through it. This Book was the first after my Primmer, wherein I did learn to read it being then the Custom in *France*, about the year in *18.* to initiate Children by that Book, that they might be acquainted with the old and absolute *French*, such as is now used in the *English* Law ; and Thirdly, for the delightfulness and variety of the matter, so that this Book in those days was printed every year like an Almanack, or a Primer for Children. From that time, without any other Study than reading of History, and observing the events of the world, and conversing with those that made it their Study. (some of which were like to run mad about it) I have attained to so much knowledge, as to bring it into a Volume.

The Book is written in the Nature of Prophecies, digested into old *French* Verses, most of which are very hard to understood, and others impossible at all, whether the Author did affect obscurity, or else wanted the faculty to express himself, which is the cause that it could not be rendred into *English* Verses, it being troublesome though to be understood in Prose, as the Reader will find. That's the reason that I have translated it almost word for word, to make it as plain as I could ; as also because the Reader (if curious of it) may benefit himself in the knowledge of the *French* Tongue, by comparing the *English* and

French together. The rest that can be said upon this subject, you shall find either in the Authors Life, or in the Appology made for him.

And because I have told you before, that many have been like to run mad by over-studying these, and other Prophecies, give me leave to give you this advice, that in vain, or at least without any great profit, thou shalt bestow thy time, care, and study upon it : for which I will give thee the chief reasons, that have disswaded me from it.

The first is, that the thing it self, which you may think to understand, is not certain in it self; because the Author disguiseth it in several manners, sometimes speaking a double sense, as that of the ancient Oracle.

Are to Æàcida Romanos vincere posse.

Which is to be understood two ways, and cannot be determined, till the event of it be past.

It is true, that the Author doth mark so many particular Circumstances, that when the thing is come to pass, every one may clearly see that he pretended to Prophecie that particular thing. And besides, he doth sometimes deliver the thing in so obscure terms, that without a peculiar *Genius*, it is almost impossible to understand it.

The second is, that though the Prophecie be true in itself, yet no body knoweth, neither the time, nor how: For example, he plainly foretelleth, that the Parliament of *England* should put their King to death; nevertheless nobody could tell, nor when, nor how, till the thing was come to pass, nor what King it should be, till we had seen it.

The third is, that he marketh the times with Astrological terms, *viz.* when such and such Planets, shall be in such and such Signs ; but as those Planets are often here, and go out of it, and come there again no certain judgement can be made of it.

The fourth is, that many times he giveth some peculiar Circumstances to those he speaketh of, which may be found in others. Thus *the Royal first born* might have been applied to *Lewis* the XIII. to *Lewis* the XIV. to the first born of *Philip* the II. and *Philip* the III. King of *Spain,* and to Kings of *England,* Father and Son. Nevertheless we find that this word *Royal first born,* was intended for *Henry* IV. Grandfather on his Mothers side, as we shall shew hereafter. This being so, it cannot be expounded, but after the event.

The fifth is, that the orders of Gods providence, which cause the several events in all States, will not permit that men should have publick notion of his designs, sometimes he revealeth them to his Servants, or to some particular man as he pleaseth, but he will not have them to be known among the common fort of men.

The seventh, is the experience we have had of many, who pretending to understand the Author, have made a quantity of false Prophecies, expounding the Stanza's according to their fancy, as if God had given them the same understanding that he gave the Author, and what ought to confirm us more in this point, is, that they have expounded some Prophecies, as if they were to come to pass, which were past already, by which to bite into the forbidden fruit of knowledge.

The eighth is, that this knowledge is no way profitable for the Vulgar ; because those things being decreed by God, they shall come to pass without forceing our liberty, nor hindering the contingency of sublunary things, where we must observe that the Prophecies which were revealed to men, are many times conditional, as we see in that of *Jonas* against *Ninive*, but those that they have left in writing for the times that should come after them, are absolutely true, and shall infallibly come to pass, as they have foretold them. This no ways hindereth, but God may reveal some secret of his to private men, for their benefit, and that of their friends, with out imparting it to the Vulgar, who may be, should laugh at them.

The ninth is, that God hath peculiarly reserved to himself the knowledge of times. *Daniel*, by a special favour, knew the end of the *Babylonian* Captivity, and the time of the *Messiah's* birth, of the seventy weeks of *Daniel*, and we see, that since *1600.* years ago, holy men, from age to age, have foretold the proximity of Dooms-day, and the coming of Antichrist.

The tenth is, that the foretelling of future things in this Author, is for the most part included in business of State, and one might be guilty of a criminal temerity, if he would discover things that concern us not, and the concealing of which, is commended by all prudent persons, seeing that we owe respect, love, and submission, to those that bear rule over us.

For these reasons (dear Reader) I would not have thee intangle thy self in the pretentions of knowing future things. If you have light concerning them, keep thine own secret, and make use of it for thy self : Preserve peace, and let the Almighty govern the World : for he can turn all things to his Glory, and may when he pleaseth, raise up some Wits that will make known unto us, what we desire, without any further trouble to our selves. Before I make an end, I cannot but acquaint thee for gratitude face, of my Obligation to several persons, which have lent me Books, to help me towards the finishing of this work, as namely that worthy Gentleman, and the Honour of his profession Mr. *Francis Bernard*, Apothecary to St. *Bartholemews* Hospital, and Mr. *Philip Auberton*, Gentleman, belonging to the Right Honourable the Earl of *Bridgewater*.

Farewell.

reface

to *Mr. Michael Nostradamus* HIS *PROPHECIES*,
Ad Cæsarem Nostradamum Filium vita & Felicitas.

by the hand of Nostradamus

Thy late coming , *Cæsar Nostradamus,* my son , hath caused me to bestow a great deal of time in continual and nocturnal watchings, that I might leave a Memorial of me after my death , to the common benefit of Manking, concerning the things which the Divine Essence hath revealed to me by Astronomical Revolutions ; and since it hath pleased the immortal God, that thou are come late into this World, and canst not say that thy years that are but few, but thy Months are incapable to receive into thy weak understanding, what I am forced to define of futurity, since it is not possible to leave thee in Writing, what might be obliterated by the injury of times , for the Hereditary word of *occult prædictions* shall be lockt up in my best , considering also that the eventsw are definitely uncertain, and that all is governed by the power of God , who inspired us not by a Bacchant fury or Lymphatick motion, but by Astronomical aflections. *Soli numine Divino afflati præsagiunt & Spiritu Prophetico particularia* : Although I have often foretold long before what hath afterwards come to pass, and in particular Regions, acknowledging all to have been done by Divine Vertue and Inspiration , being willing to hold my peace by reason of the injury, not onely of the present time, but also of the future, and to put them in Writing, because the Kingdoms, Sects, and Regions shall be so Diametrically opposed , that if I should relate what shall happen hereafter , those of the present Reign, Sect, Religion and Faith, would find it so disagreeing with their fances , that they would condemn that which future Ages shall find and know to be true ; considering also the saying of our Saviour , *Nolite Sanctum dare canibus ne conculcent pedibus & conversi discumpant vos,* which hath been the cause that I have withdrawn my tongue from the Vulgar , and my Pen from Paper. But afterwards I was willing for the common good to enlarge my self in dark and abstruse Sentences , declaring the future Events, chiefly the most urgent, and those which I foresaw (what ever humane mutation happened) would not offend the hearers, all under dark figures more then Prophetical , for although , *Abscondisti bœc a sapientibus & prudentibus,* i.e.

potentibus & Regibus enucleasti ea exiguis & tenuibus, and the Prophets by means onely of the immortal God and good Angels , have received the Spirit of Vaticination, by which they foresee things, and foretel future events; for nothing is perfect without him, whose power and goodness is so great to his Creatures, that though they are but men, nevertheless by the likeness of our good Genius to the Angels , this heat and Prophetical power draws near us , as it happens by the Beams of the Sun , which cast their influence both on Elementary and not Elementary bodies ; as for us who are men, we cannot attain any thing by our natural knowledge, of the secrets of God our Creator. *Quia non est nostrum nosse tempora a nec momenta,* &c.

Besides, although there is, or may come some persons, to whom God Almighty will reveal by impressions made upon his understanding some secrets of the future, according to the Judicial Astrology, as it hath happened in former times, that a certain power and voluntary faculty possessed them as a flame of fire, so that by his inspiration, they were able to judge of Divine and Humane things : for the Divine works that are absolutely necessary, God will end. But my son, I speak to thee too obscurely ; but as for the secrets that are received by the subtle Sprit of fire , by which the understanding being moved , doth contemplate the highest Celestial Bodies, as being active and vigilant to the very pronunciation without fear, or any shameful loquacity : all which proceeded from the Divine Power of the Eternal God, from whom all goodness floweth. Now my son, although I have inserted the name of Prophet here, I will not attribute to my self so sublime a Title, for *qui Propheta dicitur bodie olim vocabatur videns* , and Prophets are those properly (my Son) that see things remote from the natural knowledge of Men ; but put the cafe, the Prophets by the means of the perfect light of Prophecy, may see as well Divine things as Humane, (which cannot be seeing the effects of future predictions) do extend a great way, for the secrets of God are incomprehensible, and the efficient power moveth afar off the natural knowledge, taking their beginning at the free will , cause those things to appear , which otherwise could not be known , neither by humane auguries , or any hidden knowledge or secret virtue under Heaven, but only by the means of some indivisible Eternal being , or Comitial and Herculean agitation , the causes come to be known by the Cœlestial motion. I say not therefore my Son, that you may not understand me well, because the knowledge of this matter cannot yet me imprinted in thy weak brain, but that future causes afar off are subject to the knowledge of humane Creatures , if (notwithstanding the Creature) things present and future were neither obscure nor hidden from the intellectual feal ; but the perfect knowledge of the cause of things , cannot be acquired without the Divine Inspiration , seeing that all Prophetical Inspiration received, hath its original principle from God the Creator , next, from good Luck, and afterwards from Nature, therefore cases indifferently produced or not produced, the Prophecy partly happens where it hath been foretold , for the understanding being intellectually created, cannot fee occult things, unless it be by the voice coming from the *Lymbo* , by the means of the thin flame , to which the knowledge of future causes is inclined ; and also my Son I intreat thee not to bestow thy understanding on such fopperies, which drie up the Body and damn the Soul , bringing vexation to the Senses ; chiefly abhor the vanity of the execrable Magick, forbidden by the Sacred Scriptures, and by the Canons of the Church; in the first of which is excepted Judicial Astrology, by which, and by the means of Divine Inspiration , with continual supputations, we have put in writting our Prophecies. And although this occult Philosophy was not forbidden, I could never be persuaded to meddle with it, although many Volums concerning that Art, which hath been concealed a great while , were presented to me ; but fearing what might happen , after I had read them, I presented them to *Vulcan*, who while he was devouring them , the flame mixing with the Air, made an unwonted light more bright then the usual flame, and as if it had been a Lightning, shining all the house over, as if it had been all in a flame; therefore that henceforth you might not be abused in the search of the perfect Transformation, as much selene as solar, and to seek in the waters uncorruptible mettal ; I have burnt them all to ashes, but as to the judgement which cometh to be perfected by the help of the Cœlestial Judgement, I will manifest to you, that you may have knowledge of future things , rejecting the fantastical imaginations that should happen by the limiting the particularity of Places ; by Divine inspiration, supernatural, according to the Cœlestial figures , the places, and a part of the time, by an occult, property, and by a Divine virtue, power and faculty , in the presence of which the three times are comprehended by Eternity , revolution being tyed to the cause that is past, present, and future, *Quia omnia sunt Nudi & aperta,* &c. therefore my Son, thou mayst notwithstanding thy tender brain comprehend things that shall happen hereafter, and may be foretold by cœlestial natural lights, and by the Spirit of Prophecy; not that I will attribute to my self the name of a Prophet, but as a mortal man, being no farther from Heaven by my fench, then I am from Earth by my Feet, *possum errare, falli, decipi* ;

I am the greatest Sinner of the World, subject to all humane afflictions, but being supprised sometimes in the week by a Prophetical humour, and by a long Calculation , pleasing by self in my Study, I have made Books of Prophecies, each one containing a hundred Astronomical Stanza's , which I have joyned obscurely, and are perpetual Vaticinations from this year to the year 3797. at which some perhaps will frown, seeing so large an extention of time, and that I treat of every thing under the Moon , if thou livest the natural Age of a Man, thou shalt see in thy Climat , and under the Heaven of thy Nativity the future things that have been foretold , although God only is he who knoweth the Eternity of his Light, proceeding from himself ; and I say freely to those to whom his incomprehensible greatness hath by a long meloncholick inspiration revealed, that by the means of this occult cause Divinely manifested, chiefly by two principle causes, which are comprehended in the understanding of him that is Inspired and Prophecyeth , one is that he cleareth the supernatural Light in the person that foretelleth by the Doctrine of the Planets, and Prophecyeth by inspired Revelation, which is a kind of participation of the Divine Eternity , by the means of which the Prophet judgeth of what the Divine Spirit hath given him by the means of God the Creatour, and by a natural instigation, *viz.* that what is predicted is true , and hat taken its original from above, and such light and small flame is of all efficacy and sublimity, no less then the natural light makes the Philosophers so secure, that by the means of the principles of the first cause, they have attained the greatest depth of the profoundest science, but that I may not wander too far (my Son) from the capacity of thy sense, as also, becaues I find that Learning would be a great loss, and that before the universal Conflagration shall happen so many great Inundations, that there shall scarce be any Land, that shall not be covered with water, and this shall last so long, that except *Ænographies* and *Topographies* all shall perish, also before and after these Inundations in many Countreys there shall be such scarcety of rain, and such a deal of fire, and burning stones shall fall from Heaven, that nothing unconsumed shall be left, and this shall happen a little while before the great conflagration ; for although the Planet Mars makes an end of his course , and is come to the end of his last Period, nevertheless he shall begin it again, but some shall be gathered in *Aquarius* for many years, others in *Cancer* also for many years, and now we are governed by the Moon, under the power of Almighty God ; which Moon before she hath finished her Circuit, the Sun shall come, and then *Saturn*, for according to the Coelestial Signs, the Reign of *Saturn* shall come again, so that all being

Calculated, the World draws near to an Anaragonick revolution, and at this present that I write this before *177.* years , three Months, eleven Days, through Pestilence, Famine, War, and for the most part Inundations , the World between this and that prefixed time, before and after for several times shall be so diminished , and the people shall be so few, that they shall not find enough to Till the Ground, so that they shall remain fallow as long as they have been Tilled ; although we be in the seventh Millenary, which ends all and brings us near the eight, where the Firmament of the eighth Sphere is , which in a *Latitudinary dimention* is the place where the great God shall make an end of the revolution, where the Cœlestial Bodies shall begin to move again. By that Superiour motion that maketh the Earth firm and stable, *non inclinabitur in seculum seculi* , unless his will be accomplished, and no otherwise ; although by ambiguous opinions exceeding all natural reasons by *Mahometical* Dreams , also sometimes God the Creator by the Ministers of his Messengers of fire and flame shows to our external senses , and chiefly to our eyes , the causes of future Predicitons, signifying the future Event , that he will manifest to him that Prophecyeth for the Prophecy that is made by the Internal Light, comes to judge of the thing, partly with and by the means of External Light, for although the party which seemeth to have by the eye of understanding, what it hath not by the Lœsion of its imaginative sense , there is no reason why what he foretelleth should come by Divine Inspiration , or by the means of an Angelical Spirit, inspired into the Phophetick person, annointing him with vaticination, moving the fore part of his fancy , by divers nocturnal apparitions , so that by Astronomical administration , he Prophecyeth with a Divine certitude , joyned to the Holy prediction of the future , having no other regard then to the freedom of his mind. Come now my Son, and understand what I find by my revolutions, which are agreeing with the Divine Inspiration, *viz.* that the Swords draws near to us now, and the Plague and the War more horrid then hath been seen in the Life of three Men before, as also by Famine , which shall return often , for the Stars agree with the revolution, as also he said *visitabo in virgâ ferrea iniquitates eorum & in verberibus percutiam eos* , for the Mercies of God shall not be spead a while, my Son, before most of my Prophecies shall come to pass; then oftentimes shall happen sinister storms, (*Conteram ergo* (said the Lord) *& confringam & non miserebor*) and a thousand other accidents that shall happen by Waters and continual Rains, as I have more fully at large declared in my other Prophecies, written in *solutâ oratione* , limiting the places, times and prefixed terms , that men coming after , may see and know that those accidents are certainly come to pass, as we have marked in other places, speaking more clearly, although the explication be involved in obscurity , s*ed quando submovenda erit ignorantia,* the case shall be made more clear ; making an end here, my Son, accept of this Gift of thy Father *Michael Nostradamus* , hoping to expound to thee every Prophecy of these Stanza's, praying to the Immortal God , that he would grant thee a long Life in Felicity.

From Salon *this* I. *of* March *1555.*

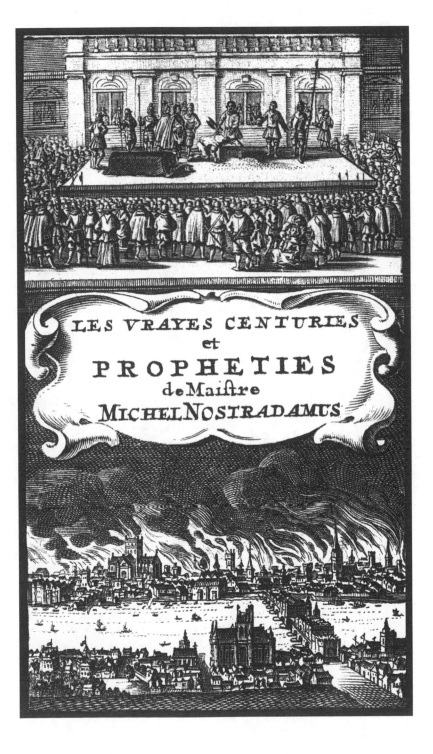

LES VRAYES CENTURIES
et
PROPHETIES
de Maistre
MICHEL NOSTRADAMUS

Century I

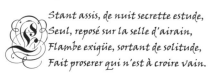

Stant assis, de nuit secrette estude,	1	Sitting by night in my secret Study
Seul, reposé sur la selle d'airain,		Alone, resting upon the Brazen stool,
Flambe exigüe, sortant de solitude,		A slight flame braking forth out of that solitude,
Fait proserer qui n'est à croire vain.		Makes me utter what is not in vain to believe.

La verge en main, mise au milieu des Branches,	2	With Rod in hand, set in the middle of the Branches,
De l'Onde je moüille & le Limbe & le Pied,		With Water I wet the limb and the foot,
En peur j'escris fremissant pas les manches ;		I fear I writ, quaking in my sleeves,
Splendeur divine: le Divine prez s'assied.		Divine splendor! The Devine sitteth by.

Quand la littiere du tourbillon versée,	3	When the litter shall be overthrown by a gust of wind,
Et seront faces de leurs Manteaux couvers,		And faces shall be covered with cloaks,
La Republique par gens nouveaux vexée,		The common-wealth shall be troubled with a new kind of man
Lors blancs & rouges jugeront a l'envers.		Then white and red shall judge amiss.

Par l'Univers sera fait un Monarque,	4	In the world shall be one Monarch,
Qu'en paix & vie ne sera longuement,		Who shall be not long alive, nor in peace,
Lors se perdra la Piscature Barque,		Then shall be lost the Fishing Boat,
Sera regie en plus grand detriment.		And be governed with worse detriment.

Chassez seront sans faire long combat,	5	They shall be driven away without great fighting,
Par les Païs seront plus fort grevez,		The whole of the country shall be more grieved,
Bourg & Cité auront plus grand debat,		Town and City shall have a greater debate,
Carcas, Narbonne auront cœurs esprouvez.		Carcas, Narbonne shall have their hearts, tried.

L'œil de Ravenne sera destitué,	6	The eye of Ravena shall be forsaken,
Quand à ses pieds les aisles failliront ;		When the wings shall rise of his feet,
Les deux de Bresse auront constitué,		The two of Brefcia shall have constituted,
Turin, Verseil, que Gaulois fouleront.		Turin, Verceil, which the French shall tread upon.

Tard arrivé, l'execution faite,	7	One coming too late, the execution shall be done,
Le Vent contrare, Lettres au chemin prinses,		The wind being contrary and Letters intercepted by the way,
Les Conjurez quatorze d'une Secte,		The conspirators fourteen of a sect,
Par le Rousseau seront les entreprinses.		By the Red-hair'd Man the undertaking shall be made.

Combien de fois prinse Cité Solaire	8	How often taken O Solar City,
Seras, changeant ses Loix barbares & vaines,		Shalt thou be? Changing the barbarian and vain Laws,
Ton mal s'approche, plus seras tributaire,		Thy evil groweth nigh, thou shalt be more tributary,
Le grand Adrie recouvrira tes veines.		The great Adria shall recover thy veins.

De l'Orient viendra le cœur punique,	9
Fascher Adrie, & les hoirs Romulides,	
Accompagné de la classe Libique	
Trembler Melites, & proches Isles vuides.	

9

From earth shall come the African heart,
To vex Adria, and the Heirs of Romulus,
Accompanied with the Libian feet,
Melites shall tremble, and the Neighbouring Islands be empty.

Sergens transmis dans la Cage de Fer,
Ou les Enfans septains du Roy sont pris,
Les vieux & Peres sortiront bas d'Enfer,
Ains mourir voir de son fruit mort & cris.

10

Sergeants sent into an Iron Cage,
Where the seven children of the King are,
The old Men and Fathers shall come out of Hell,
And before they die shall see the death and cries of their fruit.

Le mouvement de Sens, Cœur, Pieds, & Mains,
Seront d'accord, Naples, Leon, Sicile,
Glaives, Feux, Eaux, puis au Noble Romains,
Plongez, Tuez, Morts, par cerveau debile.

11

The motion of the Sense, Heart, Feet and Hands
Shall agree. Naples, Leon, Sicily,
Swords, Fires, Waters, then to the noble Romans,
Dipt, Killed, Dead by a weak-brain.

Dans peu ira fauce brute fragile,
De bas en haut eslevé promptement,
Puis en estant desloyal & labile,
Qui de Verone aura gouvernment.

12

Within a little while a false frail brute shall go,
From low to high, being quickly raised,
By reason that shall have the Government of Verona,
Shall be unfaithful and slippery.

Les exiles, par ire, haine intestine,
Feront au Roy grand conjuration,
Secret mettront ennemis par la mine,
Et les vieux siens, contre eux sedition.

13

The banished, by choler, and intestine hatred
Shall make against the King a great conspiracy,
They shall put secret enemies in the mine,
And the old his own against them sedition.

De gens esclave, chansons, chants, & requestes,
Captifs par Princes, & Seigneurs aux prisons,
A l'aduenir par Idiots sans testes,
Seront receus par divins oraisons.

14

From slavish people, Songs, Tunes and requests
Being kept Prisoners by Princes and Lords,
For the future by headless Idiots,
Shall be admitted by divine prayers.

Mars nous menace par la force bellique,
Septante fois fera le sang respandre,
Auge & ruine de l'Ecclesiastique,
Et par ceux qui d'eux rien ne voudront entendre.

15

Mars threatneth us of a Warlike force,
Seventy times he shall cause blood to be shed.
The flourishing and ruine of the clergy,
And by those that will bear nothing from them.

Faux à l'Estang, joint vers la Sagittaire,
En son haut Auge de l'Exaltation,
Peste, Famine, mort de main Militaire,
Le Siecle approcher de renovation.

16

The Sith to the Fish-pond, joined to Sagittarius
In the highest Auge of the Exaltation,
Plagye, Famine, Death by a Military hand,
The age groweth near to its renovation.

Par quarante ans l'Iris n'apparoistra,
Par quarante ans tous les jours sera veu,
La Terre aride en siccité croistra,
Et grand deluge quand sera apparceu.

17 During forty years the Rainbow shall not appear,
During forty years it shall be seen every day.
The parched Earth shall wax dryer and dryer.
And great Flouds shall be when it shall appear.

Par la discorde, negligence Gauloise,
Sera passage à Mahomet ouvert,
De sang trempé la Terre & Mer Senoise,
Le Port Phocen de Voilles & Nefs couvert.

18 Through the discord and negligence of the French,
A passage shall be opened to Mahomet,
The Land and Sea of Sienna shall be bloody,
The Phocen Haven shall be covered with Sails and Ships.

Lors que Serpens viendront circuir l'Air,
Le sang Troien versé par les Espagnes,
Par eux: grand nombre en sera fait tare,
Chef fuit, caché aux Marcts dans les saignes.

19 When Serpents shall come to encompass the Are,
The Trojan blood shall be vexed by Spain.
By them, a great number shall perish,
Chief runneth away, and is hid in the rushes of the Marshes.

Tours, Orleans, Blois, Angers, Renes & Nantes,
Cités vexées par soudain changement,
Par Langues estranges seront tenduës Tentes,
Fleuves, Darts, Rennes, Terre & Mer tremblement.

20 Tours, Orleans, Blois, Angers, Renes, and Nautes,
Cities vexed by sudden change,
By strange languages tents shall be set up,
Rivers, Darts, Rennes, Land, and Sea shall quake.

Profonde argile blanche nourrit rocher,
Qui d'un abysme istra l'acticineuse,
En vain troublez ne l'oseront toucher,
Ignorant estre au fond terre argileuse.

21 A deep white clay feedeth a Rock,
Which clay shall brake out of the deep like milk,
In vain people shall be troubled not daring to teach it.
Being ignorant that in the bottom there is a milky clay.

Ce qui vivra & n'aura aucun sens,
Viendra le Fer à mort son artifice,
Autun, Chalons, Langres & les deux Sens,
La Guerre & la Glasse fera grand malefice.

22 That which shall live, and shall have no sense.
The Lion shall destroy the art of it,
Autun, Chalous, Langres, and both Sens,
The war and the Ice shall do great harm.

Au mois troisiesme se levant le Soleil,
Sanglier, Leopart, aux champs Mars pour cômbatre,
Leopart lassé au Ciel esttend son œil,
Un Aigle autour du Soleil voit sesbatre.

23 In the third month at the rising of the Sun,
The Boar and Leopard in Marth camp to fight;
The Leopard weary, lift his eyes to the Haven,
And seeth an Eagle playing about the Sun.

A Cité neuve pensif pour condamner,
Loisel de proise au ciel se vient offrir,
Apres Victoire a Captifs pardonner
Cremone & Mântoue grânds maux auront souffert.

24 In the new city for to condemn a Prisoner,
The Bird of pray shall offer himself to Heaven,
After the Victory, the Prisoners shall be forgiven,
After Cremonia and Montua have suffered many troubles.

Perdu, trouvé caché de si long siecle,	25

Lost, found again, hidden so great a while,
A Pastor as Deme-God shall be honoured;
But before the Moon endeth her great Age,
By other winds he shall be dishonoured.

Perdu, trouvé caché de si long siecle,
Sera Pasteur demy-Dieu honoré,
Ains que la Lune acheve son grand Siecle,
Par autre vents sera deshonoré.

26

Le grand du Foudre tombe d'heure diurne,
Mal & predit par Porteur populaire,
Suivant presage tumbe d'heure nocturne,
Conflit Reims, Londres, Ettrusque Pestifere.

The great Man falleth by the Lighting in the day time,
An evil foretold by a common Porter;
According to this foretelling another falleth in the night,
A fight at Rhemes, and the Plaque at London and Tuscany.

27

Des soubs le Chesne Guyen du Ciel frappé,
Non loin de la est caché le Thresor,
Qui par long Siecles avoit esté grappé,
Trouvé mourra, l'œil crevé de ressor.

Under the Oak Guyen stricken from Heaven,
Not far from it is the Treasure hidden,
Which hath been many Ages a gathering;
Being found he shall die, the eye put out by a spring.

28

La tour de Boucq craindra fuste Barbare
Un temps, long temps apres barque hesperique,
Bestail, gêns, meubles, tous deux ferônt
grând'tare,
Taurus & Libra quelle mortelle picque.

The tower of Bouk shall be in fear of Barbarian fleet,
For a while, and long after afraid of Spainsh shipping.
Flocks, peoples, goods both shall recive great damage,
Tourus and Libra, O what a deadly feud.

29

Quand le Poisson, Terrestre & Aquatique,
Par forte vague au gravier sera mis,
Sa forme estrange suave & horrifique,
Par Mer aux murs bien tost les Enemies.

When the Fish that is both Terrestrial and Aquatick,
By a strong Wave shall be cast upon the Sand,
With his strange fearful sweet horrid form,
Soon after the enemies will come near to the Walls by Sea.

30

La Nef estrange par le tourment Marin,
Abordera ptes le Port incognu,
Nonobstant signes du rameau palmerin,
Apres mort, pille bon avis tard venu.

The Outlandish ship by a sea storm.
Shall come near unknown Haven,
Notwithstanding the signs given to it with Bows,
It shall die, be plundered, a good advice came too late.

31

Tant d'ans les guerres, en Gaule dureront,
Outre la course du Castulon Monarque,
Victoire incerte trois grands couroneront,
Aigle, Coq, Lune, Lion, Soleil en marque,

So many years the wars shall last in France,
Beyond the course of the Castulon Monarque,
An uncertain Victory three great ones shall Crown,
The Eagle, the Cock, the Moon, the Lion, Spanuza having
sun in its mark.

32

Le grand Empire sera tost translaté
En lieu petit, qui bien tost viendra croistre,
Lieu bien infime d'exique Comté,
Ou au milieu viendra poser son Sceptre.

The great Empire shall soon be translated,
Into a little place which shall soon grow afterwards.
An interior place of a small country,
In the middle of which he shall come to lay down his
Scepter.

Pres d'un grand Pont de plaine spatieuse,
Le grand Lion par force, Cesarées,
Fera abatre hors Cité rigoreuse,
Par effroy portes luy seront reserrées.

33 | A great Bridge near a spacious Plain,
The great Lion by Cæfarean Forces,
Shall cause to be pulled down without rigorous City,
For fear of which, the Gates shall be shut to him.

L'Oiseau de proye volant à la Fenestre,
Avant conflict fait aux François parure,
L'un bon prendra, l'autre ambigue sinistre,
La partie foible tiendra pour bonne augure.

34 | The Bird of Prey flying to the window,
Before Battle, shall appear to the French;
One shall take a good omen of it, the other a bad one,
The weaker part shall hold it for a good sign.

Le Lion jeune le vieux surmontera,
En champ bellique par singulier Duelle,
Dans Cage dor L'œil il lui crevera,
Deux playes une puis mourir mort cruelle.

35 | The young Lion shall overcome the old one,
In Martial field by a single Duel,
In a Golden Cage he shall put out his Eye,
Two wounds from one, then he shall die a cruel death.

Tard le Monarque se viendra repentir,
De navoir mis à Mort son Adversaire,
Mais viendra bien à plus haut consentir,
Que tout son sang par Mort fera deffaire.

36 | The monarque shall too late repent,
That he hath not put to death his Adversary;
But he shall give his consent to a grater thing than that,
Which is to put to death all his Adversaries Kinderd,

Un peu devant que le Soleil sabsconse
Conflict donné, grand peuple dubiteux,
Profligez, Port-Marin ne fait responce,
Pont & Sepulchre en deux estranges lieux.

37 | A little before the sun setteth,
A Battle shall be given, a great people shall be doubtful
Of being failed, the Sea-Port maketh no answer,
A Bridge and Sepulchre shall be in two strange places.

Le Sol & l'Aigle victeur paroistront,
Response vain au vaincu lon asseure,
Par Cor ne cris, harnois narresteront,
Vindicte paix par Mort lacheve a l'heure.

38 | The Sun and the Eagle shall appear to the Victorious,
A vain Answer shall be made good to the vanquished,
By no means Arms shall not be stopped,
Vengeance maketh Peace, by death he then accomplisheth
it.

De nuit dans le lit le supresme estrang'é,
Pour avoir trop suborné blond esleu,
Par trois l'Empire subrogé Exanclé,
A mort mettra, Carte ne Pacquet leu.

39 | By night in the bed the chief one shall be strangled.
For having too much suborned fair Elect,
By three the Empire subrogate Exancle.
He shall put him to death, reading neither Card nor Packet.

La tourbe fausse dissimilant folie,
Fera Bizance un changement de loix,
Istra d'Ægypt qui veus que l'on deflie,
Edict, changant Monnoys & alloys.

40 | The false Troup dissembling their folly,
Shall make in Bizance an alteration of Laws.
One shall come out of Ægypt who will have united
The Edict, changing the coin and allay.

Siege e Cité & de nuit assaille,	41
Peu eschapéz non loing de Mer conflict,	
Femane de joye, retour fils de faillie	
Poison & Lettres caché dedans le plic.	

41   A Siege laid to a City, and assaulted, by night
Few escaped, a fight not far from Sea,
A woman swoundeth for joy to she her son returned;
A poison hidden in the fold of Letters.

Le dix Calendes d'Avril de fait Gothique,
Resuscité encor par gens malins,
Le feu estaint, assemblée Diabolique,
Cherchant les Os de Damant & Psellin.

42   The tenth of the Calends of April, Gothic account,
Raised up again by malitious persons,
The five put out, a Diabolical assembly,
Shall seek for the Bones of Damant and Psellin.

Avant qu'aviene le changement d'Empire,
Il adviendra un cas bien merveilleux,
Le Champ mué, le Pilier de Porphyre,
Mis, translaté sur le Rocher Noileux.

43   Before the Change of the Empire cometh,
There shall happen a strange accident,
A field shall be changed, and a Pillar of Prophyry
Shall be transported upon the Chalky Rock.

En bref seront de retour Sacrifices,
Contrevenans seront mis à Martyre,
Plus ne seront Moines, Abbes, ne Novices,
Le Miel sera beaucoup plus cher que Cire.

44   Within a little while sacrifices shall come again,
Opposers shall be put to Martyrdom;
There shall be no more Monks, Abbots, nor Novices.
Honey shall be much dearer then Wax.

Secteur de Sectes, grand paine au Delateur,
Beste en Theatre, dressé le jeu Scenique,
Du fait antique ennobly l'Inventeur,
Par Sectes, Monde, confus & Schismatique.

45   Follower of Sects, great troubles to the Messenger
A Beast upon the Theatre prepareth the Scenical play,
The Inventor of that wicked fact shall be famous,
By Sects the World shall be confounded and Schismatik.

Tout apres d'Auch, de Lectoure & Mirande,
Grand feu du Ciel en trois nuits tombera,
Cause adviendra bien stupende & mirande,
Bien peu apres la Terre tremblera.

46   Near Auch, Lectoure and Mirande,
A great fire from Heaven shall fall three nights together,
A thing shall happen stupendious and wonderful,
A little while after, the Earth shall quake.

Du Lac Leman les Sermons fascheront,
Des jours seront reduits par des Sepmaines,
Puis mois, puis an, puis tous defailliront,
Les Magistras damneront leurs Loix vaines.

47   The Sermons of the Leman Lake shall be troublesome,
Some days shall be reduced into weeks,
Then into months, then into year, then they shall fail,
The Magistrates shall condemn their vain Laws.

Vingt ans du Regne de la Lune passez,
Sept mil ans autre tiendra sa Monarchie,
Quand le Soleil prendra ses jours laissez,
Lors accomplit & fine ma Prophecie.

48   Twenty years of the Reign of the Moon being past,
Seven thousand years another shall hold his Monarchy,
When the Sun shall reassume his days past,
Then is fulfilled, and endeth my Prophecy.

Beaucoup, beaucoup avant telles menées,	49 A great while before these doings,
Ceux d'Orient par la vertu Lunaire,	Those of the East by virtue of the Moon,
L'An mil sept cens feront grands emmenées,	In the year 1700. shall carry away great droves,
Subjungant presque le coin Aquilonaire.	And shall subdue almost the whole Northern corner.
De l'aquatique triplicité naistra,	50 From the Aquatick triplicity shall be born,
D'vn qui fera le Ieudy pour sa feste:	One that shall make Thursday his Holiday,
Son bruit, loz, regne, sa puissance croistra,	His Fame, Praise, Reign, and Power shall grow,
Par terre & mer aux Oriens tempeste.	By Land and Sea, and a Tempest to the East.
Chef d'Aries, Iupiter, & Saturne,	51 Heads of Aries, Jupiter and Saturn,
Dieu eternel quelles mutations !	O Eternal God, what changes shall there be !
Puis apres long siecle son malin temps retourne,	After a long age his wicked time cometh again,
Gaule & Italie, quelles esmotions.	France and Italy, what commotions ?
Les deux malins de Scorpion conjont,	52 The two malignants of Scorpion being joyned,
Le grand Seigneur meurtry dedans sa salle,	The grand Seignor murdered in his Hall,
Peste a l'Eglise par le nouveau Roy joint,	Plague to the Church by a King newly joyned to it,
L'Europe basse, & Septentrionale.	Europe low, and Septentrional
Las! qu'on verra grand peuple tourmenté,	53 Alas, how a great people shall be tormented,
Et la Loy Sainte en totale ruine,	And the Holy Law in an utter ruine ;
Par autres Loix toute la Chrestienté,	By other Laws, all Christendom troubled,
Quand d'Or, d'Argent trouve nouvelle Mine.	When new Mines of Gold and Silver shall be found,
Deux revolts faits du malin falcigere,	54 Two revolts shall be made by the wicked Link-carrier,
De Regne & Siecles fait permutation,	Which shall make a change of the Reign and the Age,
Le mobil signe à son endroit s'Ingere,	The moveable Sign doth offer it self for it,
Aux deux egaux & d'Inclination.	To the two equals in inclination.
Soubs lopposite climat Babilonique,	55 In the climat opposite to the Babylonian,
Grande sera de sang effusion,	There shall be a great effusion of Blood.
Que Terre, & Mer, Air, Ciel sera inique,	Insomuch that the Land, and Sea, Air and Heaven shall seem unjust
Sectes, Faim, Regnes, Pestes, Confusion.	Sects, Famine, Reigns, Plague, Confusion.
Vous verrez tost ou tard faire grand change,	56 You shall see soon or late great alterations
Horreurs extremes & vindications,	Extreme horrours and revenges,
Que si la Lune conduite par son Ange,	The Moon leaden by her Angel,
Le Ciel sapproche des inclinations.	The Heaven draweth near its inclinations.

Par grand discord la tombre tremblera, *Accord rompu, dressant la teste au Ciel,* *Bouche sanglante dans le sang nagera,* *Au Sol la face ointe le loit & Miel.*	57 By great discord, the Trumpet shall sound, Agreement broken, lifting the head to Heaven, A bloody mouth shall swim in blood, The face turned to the Sun anointed with Milk and Honey.

Tranché le ventre, naistra ave deux testes, *& quatre bras, quel qu'ans entiers vivra,* *Jour qu'Aquilare celebrera era ses festes,* *Fossen, Thurin, chef Ferrare suiera.*	58 Slit in the belly, shall be born with two heads, And four Arms, it shall live some years. The day that Aquilare shall celebrate his Festivals, Foffan, Thurin, chief Ferrare shall run away.

Les exilez deportez dans les Isles, *Au changement d'un plus cruel Monarque,* *Seront meurtris & mis dans les Scintiles,* *Qui de parler ne seront este parques.*	59 They banished that were carried into the Islands, At the change of a more cruel Monarque, Shall be murdered, and put in the sparks of fire, Because they had not been sparing of their tongues.

Un Empereur naistra pres d'Italie, *Qui à l'Empire sera vendu bien cher,* *Diront avec quels gens il se ralie,* *Qu'on trouvera moins Prince que Boucher.*	60 An Emperour shall be born near Italy, Who shall coft dear to the Empire, They shall say, with what people he keepeth company ! He shall be found less a Prince, than a Butcher.

La Republique miserable infelice, *Sera vastée du nouveau Magistrat,* *Leur grand amas de l'exil malefice,* *Fera Sueue ravir leur grand contract.*	61 The miserable and unhappy Common-wealth Shall be wasted by the new Magistrate ; Their great gathering from exiled persons, Shall cause Swedeland to break her Contract.

La grande perte, las que feront les Lettres, *Avant le Circle de Latona parfait,* *Feu, grand Deluge, plus par ignares Sceptres,* *Que de long siecle ne se verra refait.*	62 Alas what a great loss shall learning suffer, Before the Circle of the Moon be accomplished, Fire, great flood, and more by ignorant Scepters, Then can be made good again in a long age.

Les Fleux passez, diminué le Monde, *Long temps la Paix, Terres inhabitées,* *Seur marchera par Ciel, Terre, Mer & Onde,* *Puis de nouveau les Guerres suscitées.*	63 The Scourges being past, the World shall be diminished, Peace for a great while, Lands inhabited, Everyone safe shall go by Heaven, Land and Sea, And then the Wars shall begin a fresh.

De nuit Soleil penseront avoir veu, *Quand le Pourceau demy homme on verra,* *Bruit, Chant, Bataille au Ciel battre apperceu,* *Et bestes brutes à parler on orra.*	64 They shall think to have seen the Sun in the night, When the Hog half a man shall be seen, Noise, Singing, Battles in Heaven shall be seen to fight, And brute beasts shall be heard to speak.

Enfant sans mains, jamais veu si grand Foudre,	65	A child without hands, so great Lightning never seen,
L'Enfant Royal au jeu d'esteuf blessé,		The Royal Child wounded at Tennis,
Au puy brisez, fulgures allant mouldre,		Bruised at the Well, Lightnings, going to grind,
Trois sur les champs par le milieu troussez.		Three shall be struken by the middle.
Celuy qui lors portera les nouvelles,	66	He that then shall carry the news,
Apres un peu il viendra respirer,		A little while after shall draw his breath,
Viviers, Tournon, Montferrand & Pradelles,		Viviers, Tournon, Montferrant, and Pradelles,
Gresle & tempestes le fera souspirer.		Hail and storm shall make them sigh.
La grand famine que je vois approcher,	67	What a great famine do I see drawing near,
Souvent tourner, puis estre universelle,		To turn one way, then another, and then become universal,
Si grande & longue qu'on viendra arracher		So great and long, that they shall come to pluck
Du Vois racine, & l'Enfant de mamelle.		The root from the Wood, and the child from the breast.
O quel horrible & malheureux tourment,	68	O to what a horrid and unhappy torment,
Trois innocens qu'on viendra à livrer,		Shall be put three Innocents !
Poison suspect, mal gardé tradiment.		Poison shall be suspected, evil Keepers shall betray them,
Mis en horreur par Bourreaux enyvrez.		They shall be put to horrour by drunken Executioners.
La grand Montagne ronde de sept Stades,	69	The great Mount in compass seven Stades,
Apres Paix, Guerre, Faim, Inodation,		After Peace, War, Famine, and Innundation,
Roulera loing abisuant grand contrades,		Shall tumble a great way, sinking great Countries,
Mesmes antiques, & grand Fondation.		Yea ancient Buildings, and great Foundation.
Pluye, Faim, Guerre en Perse non cessée,	70	The Rain, Famine, War, in Persia being not ceased,
La foy trop grand trahira le Monarque;		Too great credulity shall betray the Monarque ;
Par la finie en Gaule commencée,		Being ended there, it shall begin in France,
Secret augure pour à un estre parque.		A secret Omen to one that he shall die.
La Tour Marine trois fois prise & reprise,	71	The Sea-tower three times taken and retaken,
Par Espagnols, Barbares, Ligurains,		By Spaniards, Barbarians, and Ligurians,
Marseille & Aix, Arles par ceux de Pise,		Marseilles and Aix, Arles by those of Pisa,
Vast, feu, fer pillé, Avignon des Thurins.		Wast, fire, Iron, plunder, Avignon of Thurins.
Du tout Marseille des habitans changee,	72	Marseille shall wholly change her Inhabitants
Course & poursuite jusqus pres de Lion,		These shall run and be pursued as far as Lion,
Narbon, Tholouze par Bourdeaux outragée,		Narbon, Tholoze shall wrong Bourdeaux,
Tuez, Captifs presque d'un Milion.		There shall be killed and taken prisoner almost a Milion.
France à cinq parts par neglect assaillie,	73	France by a neglect shall be assaulted on five sides,
Tunis, Argier, esmeus par Persiens,		Tunis, Argier shall be moved by the Persians,
Leon, Seville Barcelonne faillie,		Leon, Sevil, Barcelone shall be missed,
N'aura la classe par les Venetiens.		And not be pursued by the Venetians

Apres sejourné vogueront en Empire,	74 After a stay, they shall Sail towards an Empire,
Le grand secours viendra vers Antioche,	The great succours shall come towards Antioch,
Le noir poil crespe tendra fort à l'Empire,	The Black Hair Curled, shall aim much to the Empire,
Barbe d'Airain se rostira en broche.	The Brazen Beard shall be roasted on a Spit.

Le tyran Siene occupera Savone,	75 The Tyrant Sienna shall occupy Savone ;
Le fort gaigné tiendra classe Marine,	The Fort being won, shall hold a Fleet,
Les deux Armees par la marque d'Ancone,	The two Armies shall go in the mark of Ancora,
Par effrayeur le chef sen examine.	By fear the chief shall be examined.

D'un nom farouche tel proferé sera.	76 By a wild name one shall be called,
Que les trois Sœurs auront Fato le nom,	So that the three Sisters shall have the name of Fato,
Puis grand peuple par langue & fait dira,	Afterwards a great people by Tongue and Deeds, shall say,
Plus que nul autre aura bruit & renom.	He shall have fame and renown more than any other.

Entre deux Mers dressera promontoire,	77 Between two Seas shall a Promontory be raised,
Que puis mourra par le mors du Cheual,	By him, who shall die by the biting of a Horse,
Le sier Neptune pliera Voile noire,	The proud Neptune shall fold the black Sail.
Par Calpre & Classe aupres de Rocheval.	Through Calpre, and a fleet shall be near Rocheval

D'un chef vieillard naistra sens hebeté,	78 An old head shall beget an Idiot,
Degenerant par sçavoir & par Armes,	Who shall degenerate in Learning and in Arms,
Le chef de France par sa Sœur redouté,	The head of France shall be feared by his sister,
Champs diuisez, concedez aux Gensdarmes.	The fields shall be divided, and granted to the Troopers.

Bazaz, L'Estoure, Condom, Auch Agine,	79 Bazas, l'Estoure, Condom, Auch, Agen,
Esmeus par Loix, querelle & Monopole,	Being moved by Laws, quarrels and Monopoly,
Car Bourd, Tholose, Bay, mettra en ruine,	For they shall put to ruine Bordeaux, Tholose, Bayonne,
Renouueler voulant leur Tauropole.	Going about to renew their Tauropole,

De la sixiesme claire splendeur Celeste,	80 From the sixth bright Cœlestial splendour,
Viendra Tonnerre si fort en la Bourgongne,	Shall come very great Lightning in Burgundy ;
Puis naistra monstre de treshideuse beste,	After that shall be born a Monster of a most hideous beast,
Mars, Avril, May, Juin, grând charpin & rogne.	In March, April, May, June shall be great quarelling and muttering.

D'humain troupeau neuf seront mis à part,	81 Nine shall be set aside from the human flock,
De Jugement & Conseil separez,	Being divided in Judgement and Counsel,
Leur sort sera divisé en depart,	Their fortune shall be to be divided,
Kappa, Theta, Lambda, mors, bannis egarez.	Kappa, Theta, Lambda, dead, banished, scattered.

Quand les Colomnes de Bois grande tremblée,
D'Auster conduite, couverte de rubriche,
Tant videra dehors grande assemblée,
Tremble Vienne, & le Païs d'Austriche.

82 | When the wooden Columns shall be much shaken,
By Auster, and covered with rubbish,
Then shall go out a great assembly,
And Vienne, and the Land of Austria shall tremble.

L'Agent estrange divisera butins,
Saturne & Mars son regard furieux,
Horrible, estrange, aux Toscans & Latins,
Grees qui seront à frapper curiux.

83 | The stranger Agent shall divide booties,
Saturn in Mars shall have his aspect furious,
Horrid, and strange to the Tuscans and Latines
The Grecians shall be curious to strike.

Lune obscurcie aux profondes tenebres,
Son frere passe de couleur ferrugine,
Le grand caché long temps soubs les tenebres,
Tiedera Fer dans la Pluie sanguine.

84 | The Moon shall be darkned in the deepest darkness,
Her brother shall pass being of a ferrugineous colour,
The great one long hidden under darkness,
Shall make his Iron lukewarm in the bloody Rain.

Par la response de Dame Roy troublé,
Ambassadeurs mespriseront leur vie,
Le grand ses Freres contrefera doublé,
Par deux mourront, haine, ire, & envie.

85 | A King shall be troubled by the answer of a Lady,
Emassadors shall despise their lives,
The great on being double in mind shall counterfeit his
Brothers,
They shall die by two, anger, hatred, and envy.

La grande Roine quand se verra vaincue,
Fera excés de Masculin courage,
Sur le Cheval, Fleuve passera nue,
Suite par Fer: à Foy fera outrage,

86 | When the great Queen shall see her self vanquished,
She shall do a deed of a Masculine courage,
Upon a Horse, she shall pass over the River naked,
Followed by Iron, she shall do wrong to her Faith.

Ennosigee feu du Centre de Terre
Fera trembler autour de Cité Neuve,
Deux grânds Rochers long têmps feront la guerre,
Puis Arethuse rougira nouveau fleuve.

87 | Ennosigee, fire of the Center of the Earth,
Shall make quake about the New City,
Two great Rocks shall a great while War one against the
other,
After that, Arethusa shall colour red a new River.

Le Divin mal surprendra un grand Prince,
Un peu devant aura femme espousée,
Son appuy & credit à un coup viendra mince,
Conseil mourra pour la teste rasée.

88 | The Divine sickness shall surprise a great prince,
A little while after he hath married a woman,
His support and credit shall at once become slender,
Council shall die for the shaven head.

Touts ceux d'Illerde seront dans la Moselle,
Mettant à mort tous ceux de Loire & Seine,
Le course Marin viendra pres d'Hautevelle,
Quand Espagnols ouvrira toute veine.

89 | All those of Illerde shall be in the Mosel,
Putting to death all those of Loire and Seine,
The Sea course shall come new Hautevelle,
When the Spaniard shall open all veins.

Bourdeaux, Poitiers, au son de la Campane,	Bourdeaux, Poitiers, at the sound of the Bell,
A grande classe ira jusqu' à Langon,	With a great Navy shall go as far as Langon,
Contre Gaulois sera leur Tramontane;	Against the French shall their Tramontane be,
Quand Monstre hideux naistra pres de Orgôn.	When an hideous Monster shall be born near Orgon.

90

Les dieux feront aux humains apparence,
Ce quils seront auteurs de grand conflict,
Avant ciel veu serain Espée & Lance,
Que vers main gauche se plus grand affliction.

91 The Gods shall make it appear to Man-kind,
That they are the Authors of a great War;
For the Heaven that was Serene, shall shew Sword and Lance,
Signifying, that on the left hand the affliction shall be greater.

Soubs un la paix, par tout sera clamence,
Mais non long temps, pille & rebellion,
Par refus Ville, Terre & Mer entamée,
Morts & Captifs le liers d'un Million.

92 Under one shall be peace, and every where clemency,
But not a long while, then shall be plundering and Rebellion,
By a denyal shall Town, Land and Sea be assaulted,
There shall be Dead and taken Prisoners the third part of a Million.

Terre Italique de Mons tremblera,
Lion & Coq non trop confederez,
en lieu & peur l'un l'autre saidera,
Seul Catulon & Celtes moderez.

93 The Italian Land of the Mountains shall tremble,
The Lion and the Cock shall not agree very well together,
Shall for fear help one another,
The only Catulon and Celtes shall be moderate.

Au Port Selyn le Tyrant mis à Mort,
La liberté non pourtant recouurée,
Le nouveau Mars par vindict & remort,
Dame par force de frayeur honorée.

94 In the Port Selyn the Tyrant shall be put to death,
And yet the liberty shall not be recovered,
The new Mars by vengeance and remorse,
Lady by excess of fear honoured.

Devant Moustier trouvé enfant besson,
D'Heroik sang de Moine & Vetustique,
Son bruit per Secte, Langue, & puissance Son,
Qu'on dira fort eslevé le Vopisque.

95 Before the Minster shall one twin be found,
From Heroik blood, of a Monk and Ancient,
His fame by Sect, Tongue, and Power shall be sounded,
So that they shall say the Vopisk is much raised.

Celuy qu'aura la charge de destruire,
Temples & Sectes changez par fantasie,
Plus aux Rochers, qu'aux vivans viendra nuire,
Par langue ornée d'oreille rassasie.

96 He that shall have charge to destroy,
Churches and Sects, changed by fancy ;
Shall do more harm to the Rocks, than to the living,
By a smooth tongue filling up the Ears.

Ce que fer, flamme na sçeu paracheuer,
La douce langue au conseil viendra faire,
Par respos, songe, le Roy fera resuer,
Plus l'Ennemy en feu sang militaire.

97 What neither Iron nor Fire could compass,
Shall be done by a smooth tongue in the Councel,
In sleep a dream shall make the King to think,
The more the Enemy in fire and Military blood.

Le Chef qu'aura conduit peuple infiny,
Loin de son Ciel: de mœurs & langue estrange,
Cinq mille en Crete & Thessalie finy,
Le Chef fuiant sauvé en la Marine Grange.

Le grand Monarque qui fera compagnie,
Avec deux Rois unis par amitié,
O quel souspir fera la grand mesgnie,
Enfans, Narbonne alentour, quel pitié!

Long temps au Ciel sera veu gris Oiseau,
Aupres de Dole & de Toscane Terre,
Tenant au Bec un verdoiant rameau,
Mourra tost Grand & finira la Guerre.

98 The Captain that shall lead an infinite deal of people
Far from their Countrey, to one of strange manners and
Language,
Five thousand in Candia and Thessalia finished,
The Head running away, shall be safe in a Barn by the Sea.

99 The great Monarch shall keep company,
With two Kings united in friendship;
O what sights shall be made by their followers!
Children, O what pity shall be about Narbon.

100 A great while shall be seen in the Air a gray Bird,
Near Dola and the Tuscan Land,
Holding in his Bill a green bough;
Then shall a great one die, and the War have and end.

Century II

1

Ers Aquitaine par insults Britanniques,
De par eux mesmes grandes incursions,
Pluyes, Gelees, feront terroirs iniques,
Port Selyn fortes fera invasions.

Towards Gascony by English assaults,
By the same shall be made great incursions,
Rains, Frosts, shall marre the ground,
Port Selyn shall make strong Invasions.

2

La teste gluë fera la teste blanche,
Autant de mal que France à fait leur bien,
Mort à l'Anthene, grand pendu sus la branche,
Quand prins des siens, le Roy dira combien.

The Glue-head shall do the white head
As much harm, as France hath done it good,
Dead at the Sails yard, a great one hang'd on a Tree,
When a King taken by his own, shall say, how much ?

3

Par la chaleur Solitaire sur la Mer,
De Negrepont, les Poissons demy cuits,
Les Habitans les viendront entamer,
Quand Rhode & Genes leur faudra le Biscuit.

By the heat of the Sun upon the Sea
Of Negrepont, The Fishes shall be half broiled,
The Inhabitants shall come to cut them up,
When Rhodes and Genoa shall want Biscake.

4

Depuis Monac jusqu'aupres de Sicile,
Toute la plage demoura desolée,
Il ny aura Fauxbourgs, Cité, ne Ville,
Que par Barbares pillée soit & vollée.

From Monaco as far as Sicily,
All the Sea coast shall be left desolate ,
There shall not be Suburbs, Cities, nor Towns,
Which shall not be pillaged and plundered by Barbarians.

5

Quand dans Poisson, Fer & Lettre enfermée,
Hors sortira qui puis fera la Guerre,
Aura par Mer sa classe bien ramée,
Apparoissant pres de Latine Terre.

When in a Fish, Iron and a Letter shall be shut up,
He shall go out, that afterwards shall make War,
He shall have his Fleet by Sea well provided,
Appearing by the Roman Land.

6

Aupres des Portes & dedans deux Citez,
Seront deux Fleaux & onc n'aperceu un tel,
Faim, dedans Peste, de Fer hors gens boutez,
Crier secours au grand Dieu immortel.

Near the Gates and within two Cities,
Shall be two Scourges, I never saw the like,
Famine, within Plague, people thurst out by the Sword,
Shall cry for help to the great God immortal.

7

Entre plusieurs aux Isles deportez,
L'un estre nay à deux dens en la gorge,
Mourront de Faim, les Arbres esbroutez,
Pour eux neuf Roy, nouvel Edict leur forge.

Among many that shall be transported into the Islands,
One shall be born with two Teeth in his mouth,
They shall die of hunger, the Trees shall be eaten,
They shall have a new King, who shall make new Laws
for them.

8

Temples Sacrez, prime façon Romaine,
Rejetteront les goffes Fondemens,
Prenant leurs Loix premieres & humaines,
Chassants non tout, des Saints le cultement.

Churches Consecrated, and the ancient Roman way,
Shall reject the tottering Foundations,
Sticking to their first humane Laws,
Expelling, but not altogether the worshipping of Saints.

Neuf ans le Regne le maigre en paix tiendra,
Puis il cherra en soif si sanguinaire,
Pour luy peuple sans Foy & Loy mourra,
Tué par un beaucoup plus debonaire.

9

Nine years shall the lean one keep the Kingdom in Peace,
Then he will fall into such a bloody thirst,
That a great people shall die without Faith or Law,
He shall be killed by one milder than himself.

Avant long temps le tout sera rangé,
Nous esperons un siecle bien senestre,
L'Estat des masques & des seuls bien changé,
Peu trouveront qui à son rang vueille estre.

10

Before it be long, all shall be set in order,
We look for a sinister Age,
The state of the Visards and of the alone shall be changed,
They shall find few that will keep their ranks,

Le prochain, fils de l'Aisnier parviendra,
Tant eslevé jusqu'au au Regne des fors,
Son aspre gloire un chasun la craindra,
Mais les enfans du Regne jettez hors.

11

The eldest Son of l'Aisnier shall prosper,
Being raised to the degree of the great ones,
Every one shall fear his high glory,
But his children shall be cast out.

Yeux clos ouverts d'antique faitaisie,
L'habit des seuls sera mis à neant,
Le grand Monarque chastiera leur frenesie,
Ravir des Temples le Thresor par devant.

12

Eyes shut, shall be open by an antick fancy,
The cloths of the alone shall be brought to nothing.
The great Monarck shall punish their frenzy,
For having ravished the Treasure of the Temple before.

Le corps sans ame plus n'estre en sacrifice,
Jour de la mort mis en Nativité.
L'Esprit Divin fera l'ame fælice,
Voiant le Verbe en son Eternité.

13

The body without the soul shall be no more admitted in
Sacrifice,
The day of the death shall be put for the Birth-day,
The Divine Spirit shall make the Soul happy,
By seeing the Word in its Eternity.

A Tours, Gien, gardé seront yeux penetrans,
Descouvriront de long la grand Sereine,
Elle & sa Suite au Port seront entrans,
Combat poussez Puissance Souveraine.

14

At Tours, Gien, Gergeau, shall be piercing eyes,
Who shall discover along the great Syren,
She and her Attendans shall enter into the Port,
By a fight shall be thrust out the Soveraign Power.

Un peu devant Monarque trucidé?
Castor, Pollux, en nef astre crinite,
L'Airain public par Terre & Mer vuidé,
Pisa, Ast, Ferrare, Turin Terre interdite.

15

A little before a Monarch be killed,
Castor, and Pollux shall appear, and a Comet in the Ship ;
The publick brafs, by Land and Sea shall be emptyed,
Pisa, Aft, Ferrare, Turin, Countreys forbidden.

Naples, Palerme, Sicile, Syracuses,
Nouveaux Tyrans, fulgures, feu Cælestes,
Force de Londres, Gand, Bruxelles & Suses,
Grand Hecatombe, Triomphs and Feasts.

16

Naples, Palermo, Sicily, Syracuse,
New Tyrants, Lightnings, Celestial fires,
Army from London, Ghent, Bruxelles, and Suse,
A great Hecatomb, Triumphs, and Feasts.

Le champ du temple de la vierge vestale,
Non esloigné d'Ethne & monts Pyrenées,
Le grand conduit est chassé dans la Male,
North gettez Fleuves, & vignes mastinées.

Nouvelle Pluie, subite, impetueuse,
Empeschera subit deux exercites,
Pierre, Ciel, Feux, faire la Mer pierreuse,
La mort de sept, Terre & Marin subites.

Nouveaux venus, lieu basty sans defence,
Occuper place pour lors inhabitable,
Prez, Maisons, Champs, Villes, prendre à plaisance,
Faim, Peste, Guerre, arpent long labourable.

Freres & Sœurs en divers lieux captifs,
Se trouveront passer pres du Monarque,
Les comtempler ses deux yeux ententifs,
Des plaisant vont, Menton, Frônt, Nez, les marques.

L'Ambassadeur envoié par Biremes,
A my chemin incogneus repoulsez,
De Sel renfort viendront quatre triremes,
Cordes & Chaines en Negrepont troussez.

Le Camp Ascop d'Europe partira,
Sadioignant proche de l'Isle submergée,
D'Arton classe Phalange patira,
Nombril du Monde plus grand voix subrogée.

Palaces, Oiseau, par Oiseau dechassé,
Bien tost apres le Prince parvenu,
Combien qu'hors Fleuve ennemy repoulsé,
Dehors saisy, trait d'Oiseau soustenu,

Bestes farouches de faim Fleuves traner,
Plus part du Champ encontre Ister sera,
En cage de Fer le grand fera traisner.
Quand rien enfant de Germain obseruera.

17
The Camp of the Temple of the Vestal Virgin,
Not far from Ethene and the Pyrenean Mountains,
The great Conduit is driven in the Clock-bag,
Rivers overflown in the North, and the Vines spoiled.

18
A new Rain, sudden, impetuous,
Shall suddenly hinder two Armies,
Stone, Heaven, fire, shall make the Sea stony,
The death of seven shall be sudden upon Land and Sea.

19
New comers shall build a place without fence,
And shall occupy a place that was not then habitable,
They shall at their pleasure take Fields, Houses and Towns.
There shall be Famine, Plague, War, and a long arable field.

20
Brothers and Sisters shall be made slaves in divers places,
And shall pass before the Monarck,
Who shall look upon them with attentive eyes,
They shall go in heaviness, witness their Chin, Forehead and Nose.

21
The Embassadour that was sent in Biremes,
In the midleway shall be repulsed by unknown Men,
From the Salt to his succours shall come four triremes,
Ropes and Chains shall be carried to Negrepont.

22
The Camp Ascop shall go from Europe,
And shall come near the drowned Island;
From Arton shall go an Army by Sea and Land,
By the Navel of the World a greater vice shall be substituted.

23
Palais Birds, driven away by a Bird,
Soon after that, the Prince is come to his own,
Although the enemy be driven beyond the River,
He shall be seased upon without, by the trick of the Bird.

24
Wild Beasts for hunger shall swim over Rivers,
Most part of the field shall be near Ister,
Into an Iron Cage he shall cause the great one to be drawn,
When the Child of German shall observe nothing.

La Garde estrange trahira Forteresse,	
Espoir & umbre de plus haut mariage,	
Garde deçeüe Fort prins dedans la presse,	
Loire, Saone, Rosne, Gar, à Mort oultrage.	

25 The Garrison of strangers shall betray the Fort,
Under the hope and shadow of a higher Match,
The Garrison shall be deceiued, and the Fort taken in the crowd,
Loire, Saone, Rhosne, Gar, shall do harm to Death.

Pour la faveur que la Cité fera,
Au grand qui tost perdra Camp de Bataille,
Le sang d'ans Pau Thesin versera,
De sang feux, mors, noyez de coup de taille.

26 Because of the favour the City shall show,
To the great one, who soon after shall loose the Battle,
The Thesin shall pour blood into the Pau,
Of blood, fire, dead, drowned, by Edgeling.

Le Divin Verbe sera du ciel frappé
Qui ne pourra proceder plus auant,
Du reseruant le secret estoupé,
Quon marchera par dessus & devant.

27 The Divine Word shall be struck by Heaven,
So that he shall proceed no further,
The secret of the close Keeper, shall be so closed up,
That people shall tread upon, and before it.

Le penultiesme de Surnom de Prophete,
Prendra Diane pour son jour & repos
Loing vaguera par Frenetique teste,
En delivrant un grand peuple d'Impos.

28 The last, but one of the Sirname of the Prophet,
Shall take Diana for his day and his rest,
He shall wander far by reason of his Frenetick head,
Delivering a great people from impositions.

L'Oriental sortira de son Siege,
Passer les Monts Apennins, voit la Gaule
Transpercera le Ciel, les Eaux & Neige,
Et un chacun frappera de sa Gaule.

29 The Oriental shall come out of his Seat,
Shall pass over the Apennine Mountains, and see France,
Shall go over the Air, the Waters and Snow,
And shall strike every one with his Rod.

Un qui les Dieux d'Annibal infernaux,
Fera renaistre, effrayeur des Humains,
Onc plus d'horreur ne plus dire journaux,
Qu'avint viendra par Babel aux Romains.

30 One that shall cause the infernal Gods of Hannibal
To live again, the terror of Mankind,
There was never more horror, not to say ill dayes,
Did happen, or shall, to the Romans by Babel.

En Campanie le Cassilin fera tant,
Quon ne verra que d'Aux les Champs couvers,
Devant apres la pluye de long temps,
Hormis les arbres rien lon verra de verts.

31 In Campania the Cassilin shall so behave himself,
That nothing shall be seen but Fields covered with Garlick,
Before, and after it, shall not Rain for a good while,
Except the Trees, no Green shall be seen.

Lait Sang, Grenovilles, escouldre en Dalmatie
Conflict donné preste pres de Balene,
Cry sera grand par toute Esclauonie,
Lors naistra Monstre pres & dedans Ravenne.

32 Milk, Blood, Frogs shall reign in Dalmatia,
A Battle fought, the Plague near Balene,
A great wail shall be though all Sclavonia,
Then shall be born a Monster, near and within Ravenna.

Dans le torrent qui descent de Verone,	**33**
Par lors qu'au Pau quidera son entrée.	
Vn grand Naufrage, & non moins en Garonne,	
Quand ceux de Gênes Marcherônt leur contrée.	

33 In the torrent which cometh down from Verona,
About the place where it falleth into the Pau,
A great Shipwrack, and no less in Garonna,
When those of Genoa shall go into their Countrey.

L'Ire insensée du Combat furieux,
Fera à Table par Freres le Fer luire,
Les departir, blessé, curieux,
Le fier duel viendra en France nuire.

34 The mad anger of the furious fights,
Shall cause by Brothers the Iron to glister at the Table,
To part them one wounded, curious,
The fierce Duel shall do harm after in France.

Dans deux Logis de nuit le feu prendra,
Plusieurs dedans estoufez & rostis,
Pres de deux Fleuves pour seul il adviendra,
Sol, l'Arc, & Caper, tous seront amortis.

35 The fire shall take by night in two Houses,
Many shall be stifled and burnt in it ;
Near two Rivers it shall for certain happen,
Sun, Arc, Caper, they shall all be mortified.

Du grand Prophete les Lettres seront prinses,
Entre les Mains du Tyran deviendront,
Frauder son Roy seront ses entreprinses,
Mais ses rapines bien tost le troubleront.

36 The Letters of the great Prophet shall be intercepted,
They shall fall into the hands of the Tyrant,
His undertakings shall be to deceive his King,
But his extortions shall trouble him soon.

De ce'grand nombre que l'on enuoiera,
Pour secourir dans le fort assiegez,
Peste & Famine tous les deuorera,
Horsmis septante qui seront profligez.

37 Of that great number which shall be sent,
To succour the besieged in the Fort,
Plague and Famine shall devour them all,
Except seventy that shall be beaten.

Des Condamnez sera fait un grand nombre,
Quand les Monarques seront conciliez,
Mais l'un d'eux viendra si mal encombre,
Que quere ensemble ne seront raliez.

38 There shall be a great number of condemned men,
When the Monarchs shall be reconciled,
But one of them shall come to such misfortune,
That their reconciliation shall not last long.

Un devant le conflict Italique,
Germains, Gaulois, Espagnols pour le Fort,
Cherra l'Escole maison de republique,
Où, horsmis peu, seront suffoquéz morts.

39 One year before the Italian fight,
Germans, French, Spaniards for the Fort,
The school-house of the Common-wealth shall fall,
Where, except few, they shall be suffocated, and dead.

Un peu apres non point long intervalle,
Par Mer & Terre sera fait grand tumulte,
Beaucoup plus grande sera pugne Navalle,
Feux, Animaux, qui plus feront d'Insulte.

40 A little while after, without any great distance of time,
By Sea and Land shall a great tumult be made,
The Sea fight shall be much greater,
Fire and Beasts which shall make greater insult.

La grand Estoile par sept jours bruslera,
Nuce fera deux Soleils apparoir,
Le gros mastin toute nuit hurlera,
Quand grand Pontife changera de terroir.

41

The great Star shall burn for the space of seven days,
A Cloud shall make two Suns appear,
The big Mastif shall houl all night,
When the great Pope shall change his Countrey.

Coq, Chiens & Chats de sang seront repeus,
Et de la playe du Tyran trouvé Mort,
Au lict d'un autre, Jambes & Bras rompus,
Qui n'avoit peu mourir de cruele Mort.

42

A Cock, Dogs, and Cats shall be fed with Blood,
And with the wound of the Tyrant found dead
In the bed of another, with Legs and Arms broken,
Who could not die before by a cruel Death.

Durant l'estoile chevelue apparente,
Les trois grand Princes seront faits ennemis,
Frappez du Ciel, Paix, Terre tremulente,
Arne, Timbre, undans Serpent sur le bord mis.

43

During the hairy apparent Star,
The three great Princes shall be made Enemies,
Struck from Heaven, Peace, quaking Earth,
Arne, Tyber, full of Surges, Serpent cast upon the Shore.

L'Aigles poussée entour de Pavillons,
Par autre oiseaux d'Entour sera chassée,
Quand bruit de Timbres, Tubes, & Sonaillons,
Rendront lesens de la Dame insensee.

44

The Eagle flying among the Tents,
By other Birds shall be driven away,
When noise of Cymbals, Trumpets, and Bells,
Shall render the sense to the Lady that was without it.

Trop le Ciel pleure l'Androgyn procrée,
Pres de Ciel sang humain respandu,
Par mort trop tard grand peuple recrée,
Tard & tost vient le secours attendu.

45

The Heaven bemoaneth too much the Androgyn born,
Near Heaven humane blood shall be spilt,
By death too late a great people shall be refreshed,
Late and soon cometh the succours expected.

Apres grând troche humain, plus grând sapreste,
Le grand Moteur les siecles renouvelle,
Pluye, Sang, Lait, Famine, Fer & Peste,
Au Ciel veu feu courant longue estincelle.

46

After a great humane change, another greater is nigh at hand,
The great Motor reneweth the Ages,
Rain, Blood, Milk, Famine, Sword, Plague,
In the Heaven shall be seen a running fire with long sparks.

L'Ennemy grand viel, duelt, meurt de poison,
Les Souverains par infinis subjiuguez,
Pierres pleuvoir cache soubs la Toison,
Par mort Articles en vain sont alleguez.

47

The great and old Enemy grieveth, dieth by Poison,
An infinite number of Soveraign's conquered,
It shall rain stones, they shall hide under Rocks,
In vain shall death alledge Articles.

La grand Copie qui passera les Monts,
Saturne, Aries, tournant au Poisson Mars,
Venins cachez sous testes de Moutons,
Leur chef pendu à fil de Polemars.

48

The great Army that shall pass over the Mountains,
Saturn, Aries, Mars, turning to the Fishes,
Poisons hidden in Sheeps heads,
Their Captain hang'd with a thread of Polemars.

Les conseillers du premier Monopole.	49 The advisers of the first Monopoly,
Les Conquerans seduits par la Melite,	The Conquerors seduced by the Melite,
Rhodes, Bisance pour leur exposant pole,	Rhodes, Bizance, for exposing their Pole,
Terre faudra les pour-suivans de fuite.	The ground shall fail the followers of runaways.

Quând ceux d'Hainault, de Gând, & de Bruxelles,
Verront à Langres le Siege devant mis,
Derrier leur flancs seront guerres cruelles,
La playe antique fera pis qu'Ennemis.

50   When these of Hainault, of Gand, and of Bruxelles,
Shall see the Siege laid before Langres,
Behind their sides shall be cruel Wars,
The old wound shall be worse then Enemies.

Le sang du juste à Londres fera faute,
Bruslez par feu de vingt & trois, les Six
La Dame antique cherra de place haute,
De mesme secte plusieurs seront occis.

51   The blood of the just shall be wanting in London,
Burnt by fire of three and twenty, the Six,
The ancient Dame shall fall from her high place,
Of the same Sect many shall be killed.

Dans plusieurs nuits la Terre tremblera,
Sur le printemps deux efforts feront suitte,
Corinthe, Ephese aux deux Mers nagera,
Guerre sesmeut par deux vaillants de Luitte.

52   During many nights the Earth shall quake,
About the Spring two great Earth-quakes shall follow one another,
Corinth, Ephesus shall swim in the two Seas,
War shall be moved by two great Wrestlers.

La grande Peste de cité maritime,
Ne cessera que Mort ne soit vengée,
Du juste sang par prix damné sans crime,
De la grand Dame par feinte noutragée.

53   The great Plague of the Maritime City,
Shall not cease till the death be revenged
Of the just blood by price condemned without crime,
Of the great Dame not fainedly abused.

Par gent estrange & Nation lomtaine,
Leur grand Cité, apres eau fort troublée,
Fille sans trop different domaine,
Prins chef, ferreure navoir esté riblée.

54   By a strange people and remote Nation,
The great City near the water shall be much troubled,
The Girl without great difference for a portion,
Shall take the Captain, the Lock having not been pick.

Dans le conflit le grand qui peu valoit,
A son dernier fera cas merueilleux.
Pendant qu'Adrie verra ce qu'il falloit,
Dans le Banquet poignarde l'orgueilleux.

55   In the fight the great one who was but little worth,
At his left endeavour shall do a wonderful thing.
While Adria shall see what was wanting,
In the Banquet he shall stabb the proud one.

Que Peste & Glaive n'a sceu definer,
Mort dans les plutes, sommet du Ciel frappé,
L'Abbé mourra quand verra ruiner,
Ceux du Naufrage, l'Escueil voulant graper.

56   He whom neither Plague, nor Sword could destroy,
Shall die in the Rain being stricken with Thunder,
The Abbot shall die when he shall see ruined,
Those in the Shipwrack, striving to catch hold of the Rock,

Avant conflit le grand tombera,	57	Before the Battle the great one shall fall,
Le grand à mort trop subite & plainte,		The great one to death too sudden and bewailed;
Nay miparfait, la plus part nagera,		One shall be born half perfect, the most part shall swim,
Aupres du Fleuve, de sang la Terre teinte.		Near the River the Earth shall be dyed with blood.

Avant conflit le grand tombera,
Le grand à mort trop subite & plainte,
Nay miparfait, la plus part nagera,
Aupres du Fleuve, de sang la Terre teinte.

57 Before the Battle the great one shall fall,
The great one to death too sudden and bewailed;
One shall be born half perfect, the most part shall swim,
Near the River the Earth shall be dyed with blood.

Sans pied ne main, dent aique, & forte,
Par Globe au fort de Port & laifné nay,
Pres du portail desloial le transporte,
Seline luit, petit grand emmené.

58 Without foot or hand, sharp and strong tooth,
By a Globe, in the middle of the Port, and the first born,
Near the Gate shall be transported by a Traitor,
Seline shineth, the little great one carried away.

Classe Gauloise par appuy de grand Garde,
Du grand Neptune & ses tridens Soldats,
Ronger Provence pour soustenir grand bande,
Plus Mars, Narbon, par Javelots & Dards.

59 The French Fleet by the help of the great Guard,
Of great Neptune and his Tridentary Soldiers,
Shall gnaw Provence by keeping great company,
Besides, Mars shall plague Narbon by Javelins and Darts.

La foy Punique en Orient rompue,
Grand Jud. & Rosne, Loive & Tag changeront,
Quand du Mulet la faim sera repeue,
Classe espargie, Sang & Corps nageront.

60 The punick faith broken in the East,
Great Jud. and Rhosne, Loire and Tag. shall be changed,
When the Mules hunger shall be satisfied,
The Fleet scattered, Blood and Bodies shall swim.

Agen, Tonneins, Gironde & la Rochelle,
O sang Troien mort au Port de la fleche,
Derrier le fleuve au Fort mise leschelle,
Pointes, feu, grand meurtre sus la bresche.

61 Agen, Tonneins, Gironde and Rochelle,
O Trojan blood death is at the harbour of the Arrow,
Beyond the River the Ladder shall be raised against the Fort,
Points, fire, great murder upon the breach.

Mabus pluis tost alors mourra, viendra,
De gens & bestes un horrible desfaite,
Puis tout à coup la vengeance on verra,
Sang, Main, Soif, Faim, quand courra la Comete,

62 Mabus shall come, and soon after shall die,
Of people and beasts shall be an horrible destruction,
Then on a sudden the vengeance shall be seen,
Blood, Hand, Thirst, Famine, when the Comet shall run.

Gaulois, Ausone bien peu subiugera,
Pau, Marne & Seine fera Perme l'Vrie,
Qui le grand Mur contre eux dressera,
Du moindre au Mur le grand perdra la vie.

63 The French shall a little subdue Ausonne,
Pau, Marne, and Seine shall make Perme l'Urie,
Which shall raise a great Wall against them,
From the less to the Wall the great one shall loose his life.

Secher de faim, de soif, gent Genevoise,
Espoir prochain viendra au defaillir,
Sur point tremblant sera Loy Gebenoise,
Classe au grand Port ne se peut accueillir.

64 Those of Geneva shall be dried up with hunger and thirst,
A near hope shall come when they shall be fainting,
The Gebenna Law shall be upon a quaking point,
The Navy shall not be capable to come into the Port.

Le park enclin grande calamité,
Par l'Hesperie & Insubre fera,
Le Feu en Nef, Peste, & Captivité,
Mercure en l'Arc, Saturne fenera.

65 | The Park enclineth to great calamity,
Which shall be through Hesperia and Insubria,
The Fire in the Ship, Plague, and Captivity,
Mercury in Aries, Saturn shall wither.

Par grand dangers le Captif eschapé,
Peu de temps grand a fortune changée,
Dans le Palais le peuple est attrapé,
Par bonne augure la Cité assiegée.

66 | The Prisoner escaped through great danger,
A little while after shall become great, his fortune being changed,
In the Palace the people shall be caught,
Aud by a good Sign the City shall be besieged.

Le blond au nez forche viendra commettre,
Par la Duel & chassera dehors,
Les exiles dedans fera remettre,
Aux lieux marins commettans les plus forts.

67 | The fair one shall fight with the forked Nose,
In Duel, and expel him out,
He shall re-establish the banished,
Putting the stronger of them in Maritime places.

De l'Aquilon les efforts seront grands,
Sus l'Occean sera la Porte ouverte,
Le Regne en l'Isle sera reintegrand.
Tremblera Londres par voiles descouvertes.

68 | The endevours of the North shall be great,
Upon the Ocean the gate shall be open,
The Kingdom in the Island shall be re-established,
London shall quake, for fear of Sails discovered.

Le Roy Gaulois par la Celtique dextre,
Voiant discorde de la grand Monarchie,
Sur les trois parts fera fleurir son Sceptre,
Contre ta Cappe de la grand Hierarchie.

69 | The French King, by the Low-Countreys right hand,
Seeing the discord of the great Monarchy,
Upon three parts of it, will make his Scepter to flourish,
Against the Cap of the great Hierarchy.

Le Dard du Ciel fera son estendue,
Morts en parlant, grande execution,
La pierre en larbre la fiere gent rendue,
Brait Humain, Monstre purge expiation.

70 | The Dart of Heaven shall make his circuit,
Some die speaking, a great execution,
The stone in the tree, the fierce people humbled,
Humane noise, a Monster purged by expiation.

Les exiles en Sicile viendront,
Pour delivrer de faim la gent estrange,
Au point du jour les Celtes luy faudront,
La vie demeure à raison Roy se range.

71 | The banished persons shall come into Sicily,
To free the forrain Nation from hunger,
In the dawning of the day the Celtes shall fail them,
Their Life shall be preserved, the King shall submit to reason.

Armée Celtique en Italie vexée,
De toutes partes conflit & grande perte.
Romains fuis, ô Gaule repoussée,
Pres du Thesin, Rubicon pugne incerte.

72 | The French Army shall be vexed in Italy,
On all sides fighting, and great loss,
The Romans run away, and thou France repulsed,
Near the Thesin, by Rubicon the fight shall be doubtful,

Au lac Fucin de Benac Rivage,	73	At the Fucin Lake of the Benacle Shore,
Pres du Leman au port de Lorguion,		Near the Leman, at the Port of Lorguion,
Nay de trois Bras prædit Bellique Image,		Born with three Arms, a Warlike Image,
Par trois courones au grand Endymion.		By three Crowns to the great Endimion.

De Sens, d'Autun viendront jusques au Rhosne,	74	They shall come from Sens and Autun, as far as the Rhosne,
Pour passer outre vers les Monts Pyrenée,		To go further to the Pyrenean Mountains,
La gent sortir de la Marque d'Ancone,		The Nation come from the Mark of Ancona,
Par Terre & Mer Suivra à grand trainées.		By Land and Sea shall follow speedily after.

La voix ouïe de l'Insolit oiseau,	75	The noise of the unwonted Bird having been heard,
Sur le Canon du respiral estage,		Upon the Canon of the highest story,
Si haut viendra du froment le boisteau,		The Bushel of Wheat shall rise so high,
Que l'homme d'homme sera Antropophage.		That man of man shall be Antropophage.

Foudre en Bourgongne avec cas portenteux,	76	Lightning in Burgundy, with marvellous accidents,
Que par engin oncques ne pourroit faire,		Which could never have been done by art,
De leur Senat Sacriste fait boiteux,		Of their Senate Sacrifice being lamed,
Fera Sçavoir aux ennemis l'affaire.		Shall make known the business to the enemies.

Par Arcs, Fœux, Poix, & par feux repoussez,	77	Being repulsed with Bows, Fires, and Pitch,
Cris hurlemens sur la minuit ouys,		Cries and howlings shall be heard about midnight,
Dedans sont mis par les rampars cassez,		They shall get in through the broken Walls,
Par Canicules les Traditeurs fuis.		The betrayers shall run away through the Conduits.

Le grand Neptune du profond de la Mer,	78	The great Neptune in the middle of the Sea,
De sang punique & sang Gaulois meslé,		Having joyned African and French blood,
Les Isles à sang pour le tardif ramer,		The Islands shall be put to the Sword, and the slow rowing
Puis luy nuira que l'occult mal celé.		Shall do them more prejudice, than the concealed evil.

La Barbe crespe & noire par engin,	79	The frizled and black Beard by fighting,
Subjuguera la gent cruelle & fiere,		Shall overcome the fierce and cruel Nation,
Le grand Cheyren ostera du longin,		The great Cheyren shall free from Bands,
Tous les Captifs par Seline Baniere.		All the Captives made by Selyne Standard.

Apres conflit du læsé l'Eloquence,	80	After the Battle, the eloquency of the wounded man,
Par peu de temps se trame Saint repos,		Within a little while shall procure a holy rest,
Point l'on admet les grands à delivrance.		The great ones shall not be delivered,
Des ennemis sont remis à propos.		But shall be left to their Enemies will.

Par feu du Ciel la Cité presqu'aduste,
L'Urne menace encor Deucalion,
Vexée Sardaigne par la punique fuste,
Apres que Libra lairra son Phaëton.

81 | By fire from Heaven the City shall be almost burnt,
The Waters threatens another Deucolion,
Sardaigne shall be vexed by an African Fleet,
After that Libra shall have left her Phaeton.

Par faim la proye fera Loup prisonier,
L'Assaillant lors en extreme detresse,
Lesnay ayant au devant le dernier,
Le grand neschape au milieu de la presse.

82 | By hunger, the prey shall make the Wolf prisoner,
Assaulting him then in a great distress.
The eldest having got before the last,
The great one doth not escape in the middle of the crowd.

Le gros Traffic d'un grand Lion changé,
La pluspart tourne en pristine ruine,
Proye aux Soldats par playe vendangé,
Par Jura Mont, & Sueve bruine.

83 | The great Trade of a great Lion alter'd,
The most part turneth into its former ruine,
Shall become a Prey to Soldiers and reaped by wound,
In Mont-Jura, and Suaube great Foggs.

Entre Campagne, Sienne, Pise & Ostié,
Six mois neuf jours ne pleuvra une goute,
L'Estrange Langue en Terre Dalmatie,
Courira sus, vastant la Terre toute.

84 | Between Campania, Sienna, Pisa and Ostia,
For six Months and nine days there shall be no rain,
The strange Language in Dalmatia's Land,
Shall overrun, spoiling all the Countrey.

Le vieux plein barbe soubs le statut severe,
A Lion fait dessus l'Aigle Celtique,
Le petit grand trop outre persevere,
Bruit d'Arme au Ciel, Mer rouge Ligustique.

85 | The old plain beard under the severe Statute,
Made at Lion upon the Celtique Aigle,
The little great persevereth too far,
Noise of Arms in the Skie, the Ligustrian Sea made red.

Naufrage à classe pres d'Onde Adriatique,
La Terre tremble emeuë sur l'Air en Terre mis
Ægypt tremble augment Mahometique,
L'Heraut sov rendre à crier est commis.

86 | A Fleet shall suffer Shipwrack near the Adriatick Sea,
The Earth quaketh, a motion or the Air cometh upon the Land,
Ægypt trembleth for fear of the Mahometan increase.
The Herald surrendring shall be appointed to cry.

Apres viendra des extremes Contrées,
Prince Germain dessus Throsne d'Oré,
La servitude & les Eaux rencontrées,
La Dame serve son temps plus n'adoré.

87 | After that shall come out of the remote Countreys,
A German Prince upon a gilded Throne,
The slavery and waters shall meet,
The Lady shall serve, her time no more worshipped.

Le Circuit du grand fait ruineux,
Le nom septiesme du cinquiesme sera,
'Dun tiers plus grand l'estrange belliqueur,
De Ram, Lutece, Aix ne garentira.

88 | The circumference of the ruinous buildings,
The seventh name shall be that of the fifth,
From a third, one greater, a Warlike man,
Aries shall not preserve Paris nor Aix.

Un jour seront amis les deux grands Maistres,	89	One day the two great Masters shall be friends,
Leur grand pouvoir se verra augmenté,		Their great power shall be increased,
La Terre neufue sera en ses hauts estres,		The new Land shall be in a flourishing condition,
Au sanguinaire le nombre racompté.		The number shall be told to the bloody person.

Par vie & mort changé Regne d'Hungrie,	90	By Life and Death the Kingdom of Hungary shall be changed.
La loy sera plus aspre que service,		The Law shall be more severe than the service.
Leur grand Cité d'Urlemens plaine & crie,		Their great City shall be full of howling and crying,
Castor & Pollux ennemis dans la Lice.		Castor and Pollux shall be enemies in the Lift.

Soleil levant ungrand feu lon verra,	91	At the rising of the Sun a great fire shall be seen,
Bruit & clarté vers Aquilon tendans,		Noise and light tending towards the North,
Dedans le rond mort & cris lon orra,		Within the round death and cries shall be heard,
Par Glaive, Feu, Faim, mort les attendans.		Death by Sword, Fire, Hunger watching for them.

Feu couleur d'or, du Ciel en terre veu,	92	A fire from Heaven of a Golden colour shall be seen,
Frappé du haut nay, fait cas merveilleux,		Stricken by the high born, a wonderful case,
Grand meurtre humain, prinse du grand Neveu,		Great murder of Mankind, the taking off the great Neveu,
Morts de spactacles, eschapé lorgueilleux.		Some dead looking, the proud one shall escape.

Aupres du Tybre bien prese la Lybitine,	93	Near the Tyber, going towards Lybia,
Un peu devant grand Inondation,		A little before a great Innundation,
Le chef du nef prins, mis à la sentine,		The Master of the Ship being taken shall be put into the Sink.
Chasteau, Palais en conflagration.		And a Castle and Palace shall be burnt.

Grand Pau, grand mal par Gaulois recevra,	94	Great Pau shall receive great harm by the French,
Vaine terreur au Maritin Lion,		A vain terrour shall seize upon the Maritine Lion,
Peuple infiny par la Mer Passera,		Infinite people shall go beyond Sea,
Sans eschaper un quart d'un Million.		Of which shall not escape a quarter of a Million.

Les lieux peuplez seront inhabitables,	95	The populous places shall be deserted,
Pour Champs avoir grande division,		A great division to obtain Fields,
Regnes livrez à prudents incapables,		Kingdoms given to prudents incapable,
Lors les grands Freres mort & dissension.		When the great Brothers shall die by dissention.

Flambeau ardant au Ciel soir sera veu,	96	A burning shall be seen by night in Heaven,
Pres de la fin & principe du Rhosne,		Near the end and beginning of the Rhosne,
'Famine, Glaive, tard le secours pourveu,		Famine, Sword, too late succours shall be provided,
La Perse tourne envahir Macedoine.		Persia shall come against Macedonia.

Century II - 56

Romain Pontife garde de taprocher,
De la Cité que deux fleuves arrouse,
Ton sang viendras aupres de la cracher,
Toy & les tiens quand fleurira la Rose.

Celuy du sang reperse le visage,
De la Victime proche du Sactifice,
Venant en Leo, augure par presage,
Mis estre à mort alors pour la fiance.

Terroir Romain qu'interpretoit Augure,
Par gent Gauloise par trop sera vexée,
Mais Nation Celtique craindra l'heure,
Boreas, classe trop loing l'avoit poussée.

Dedans les Isles si horrible tumulte,
Rien on n'orra qu'une bellique brique,
Tant grand sera de predareurs l'Insult,
Qu'on se viendra ranger à la grand ligue.

97 | Roman Pontife take heed to come near
To the City watered with two Rivers,
Thou shall spit there thy blood,
Thou and thine, when thee Rose shall blossom.

98 | He that shall have his face bloody,
With thee blood of the Victim near to be sacrificed,
The Sun coming into Leo shall be an Augury by presage,
That then he shall be put to death for his confidence.

99 | The Roman Countrey in which the Augur did interpret,
Shall be too much vexed by the French Nation,
But the Celtique Nation shall fear the hour,
The Northwind had driven the Navy in too far.

100 | In the Islands shall be so horrid tummults,
That nothing shall be heard but Warlike surprise,
So great shall be the insult of the Robbers,
That every one shall shelter himself under the great League.

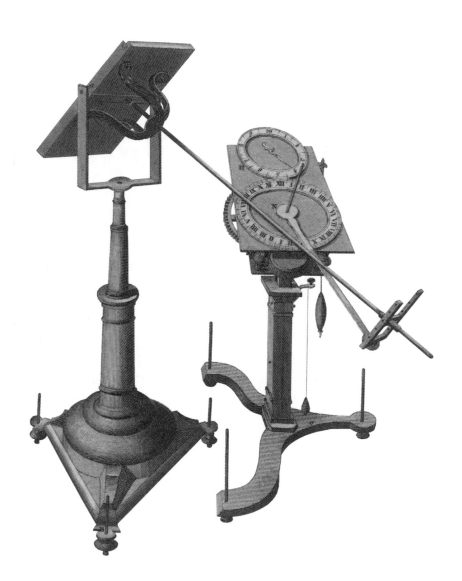

Century III

Pres Combat & Bataille Navale, *Le grand Neptune à son plus haut* *beffroy,* *Rouge adversaire de peur de peur viêndra* *pasle,* *Mettant le grand Occean en effroy.*	*1*	After the fight and Sea Battle, The great Neptune in his highest Steeple, The red adversary shall wax pale for fear, Putting the great Ocean in a fright.
Le Divin Verbe donra à la substance, *Cômpris Ciel, Terre, or occult au lait mystique,* *Corps, Ame, Esprit, ayant toute puissance,* *Tant sous ses pieds comme au Siege Celique.*	*2*	The Divine Word shall give to the substance, Heaven and Earth, Gold hid in the mystical milks, Body, Soul, Spirit, having all power, As well under his feet, as in the Heavenly Seat.
Mars & Mercure, & Largent joint ensemble, *Vers le Midy extréme siccité,* *Au fond d'Asie on dira Terre tremble,* *Corinthe, Ephese lors en perplexité.*	*3*	Mars and Mercury, and Silver joyned together, Towards the South a great drought, In the bottom of Asia shall be an Earth-quake, Corinth and Ephesus shall then be in perplexity.
Quand seront proches le defaut des Lunaires, *De l'un à lautre ne distant grandement,* *Froid, siccité, danger vers les frontieres,* *Mesme où l'Oracle à pris commencement.*	*4*	When the want of the Luminaries shall be near, Not being far distant one from another, Cold, drought, danger towards the Frontiers, Even where the Oracle had his beginning.
Pres le de defaut des deux grands luminaires, *Qui surviendra entre l'Avril & Mars,* *O quel cherté! mais deux grands debonnaires,* *Par Terre & Mer secourront toutes parts.*	*5*	Near the Ecclipses of the two great Luminaries, Which shall happen between April and March, O what a dearth ! but two great ones bountiful, By Land and Sea shall succour them on all sides.
Dans Temples clos le foudre y entrera. *Des Citadins dedans leurs fort grevez,* *Chevaux, Bœufs, Hômmes, l'Onde mur touchera,* *Par faim, soif, soubs les plus foibles armez.*	*6*	Into a close Church the lightning shall fall, The Citizens shall be distressed in their Fort, Horses, Oxen, Men, the Water shall touch thee Wall, By hunger, thirst, down shall come the worst provided.
Les fugitifs, feu du Ciel sur les Piques, *Conflit prochain des Corbeaux s'esbatans,* *De Terre on crie, aide, secours Celiques,* *Quand pres des murs seront les combatans.*	*7*	The runaways, fire of Heaven upon the Pikes, A fight near hand, the Ravens sporting, They cry from the Land, succours O Heavenly powers ! When near the walls shall be the fighting men.
Les Cimbres joints avecques leurs voisins, *Depopuler viendront presque en l'Espagne,* *Gens ramassez, Guienne & Limousins* *Seront en ligue & leur feront Compagne.*	*8*	The Cimbres joyned with their neighbours, Shall come to depopulate almost all Spain, People gathered from Guienna and Limosin, Shall be in league with them, and keep them Company.

Bourdeaux, Roüan & la Rochelle joints,	9

Bourdeaux, Rouan, and Rochel joyned together,
Will range about upon the great Ocean,
English Brittans, and Flemings joyned together,
Shall drive them away as far as Rouane.

Bourdeaux, Roüan & la Rochelle joints,
Tiendront autour de la grand Mer Occeane,
Anglois, Bretons, & les Flamans conjoints,
Les chasseront jusque aupres de Roüane.

10

De sang & faim plus grand calamité,
Sept fois s'apreste à la Marine plage,
Monech de faim, lieu pris captivité,
Le grand, mené Croc enferré en cage.

Of blood and famine, what a great calamity !
Seven times is ready to come upon the Sea Coast,
Monech by hunger, the place taken, captivity,
The great one carried away, Croc, shut up in a Cage,

11

Les Armées battre au Ciel longue saison,
L'Arbre au milieu de la Cité tombé,
Vermine, Rogne, Glaive en face tison,
Lors le Monarque d'Adrie succombé.

Armies shall fight in the Air a great while,
The Tree shall fall in the middle of the City,
Vermin, Scabs, Sword, fire-brand in the face,
When the Monarck of Adria shall fall.

12

Par la tumeur du Heb. Po. Tag. Tibre de Rome,
Et par l'estang Leman & Aretin,
Les deux grands chefs, & Citez de Garonne,
Prins, Morts Noiez, partir humain butin.

By the swelling of Heb. Po. Tag. Tiber of Rome,
And by the Lake Leman and Aretin,
The two great Heads, and Cities of Garonne,
Taken, Dead, Drowned. The human booty shall be divided.

13

Par Foudre en Arche Or & Argent fondu,
De deux Captifs l'un l'autre mangera,
De la Cité le plus grand estendu,
Quand submergée la Classe nagera.

By Lightning shall gold and silver be melted in the Arch,
Of two Prisoners one shall eat up the other,
The greatest of the City shall be laid down,
When the Navy that was drowned shall swim.

14

Par le Rameau du vaillant personage,
De France infirme, par le Pere infelice,
Honeurs, Richesses, travail en son vieil Age,
Pour avoir creu le conseil d'homme nice.

By the Bow of the valliant men,
Of weak France, by the unfortunate Father,
Honours, Riches, labour in his old age,
For having believed the councel of a nice man.

15

Cœur, vigueur, gloire, le Regne changera,
De tous points contre, ayant son adversaire,
Lors France enfance par mort subjugera,
Un grand Regent sera lors plus contraire.

Heart, vigour, and glory shall change the Kingdom
In all points, having an adversary against it,
Then shall France overcome Childhood by death,
A great Regent shall then be more adversary to it.

16

Un Prince Anglois Mars à son cœur du Ciel,
Voudra poursuivre sa fortune prospere,
Des deux duelles l'un percera le fiel,
Hay de luy, bien aymé de sa Mere.

An English Prince Mars hath his heart from Heaven,
Will follow his prosperous fortune,
Of two Duels one shall pierce the gall,
Being hated of him, and beloved of his Mother.

Mont Aventin brusler nuit sera veu,	17	Mount Aventine shall be seen to burn in the night.
Le Ciel obscur tout a un coup en Flandres,		The Heaven shall be darkned upon a sudden in Flanders,
Quand le Monarque chassera son Neveu,		When the Monarch shall expel his Neveu,
Lors gens d'Eglise commettrônt les esclandres.		The Churchmen shall commit scandals.
Apres la pluye de lait assez longuette,	18	After a pretty long rain of Milk,
En plusieurs lieux de Rheims le Ciel touche,		In many places of Rhemes the lightning shall fall,
O quel conflit de sang pres deux sappreste,		O what a bloody fight is making ready near them,
Pere & Fils Rois, noseront approché.		Father and Son, both Kings, shall not dare to come near.
En Luques sang & lait viendra pleuvoir,	19	In Luca it shall rain Blood and Milk,
Un peu devant changement de Preteur,		A little before the change of the Magistrate,
Grand Peste & Guerre, Faim & soif fera voir,		A great Plague, War, Hunger and Thirst shall be seen,
Loin ou mourra leur Prince Recteur.		A great way off, where their Prince Ruler shall die.
Par les contrées du grand flevue Betique,	20	Through the Countreys of the great River Betis,
Loin d'Ibere, au Royaume de Grenade,		Far from Iberia, in the Kingdom of Granada,
Croix repoussées par gens Mahometiques,		Crosses beaten back by Mahometan people,
Un de Cordube trahira a la fin Contrade.		One of Corduba shall at last betray the Countrey.
Au Crustamin pres Mer Adriatique.	21	In the Crustamin near the Adriatick Sea,
Apparoistra un horrible poisson,		An horrid Fish shall appear,
De face humaine & de corps aquatique,		Having a mans face, and a fishes body,
Qui se prendra dehors de l'Hameçon.		Which shall be taken without a hook.
Six jours lassaut devant Cité donné,	22	Six days shall the assault be given to the City,
Livrée sera forte & aspre Bataille,		A great and fierce Battle shall be fought,
Trois la rendront & a eux pardonné,		Three shall surrender it, and be pardoned,
Le reste a feu & sang trauche taille.		The rest shall be put to fire and Sword, cut and slasht.
Si France passe outre Mer Liquistique,	23	If France goeth beyond the Ligustick Sea,
Tu te verras en Isles & Mers enclos,		Thou shalt see thy self inclosed with Islands and Seas.
Mahomet contraire plus Mer l'Adriatique,		Mahomet, against thee besides the Adriatick Sea,
Chevaux & Asnes tu rongeras les os.		Of Horses and Asses thou shat gnaw the bones.
De l'Entreprise grande confusion,	24	From the undertaking great confusion,
Perte de gens Thresor innumerable,		Loss of people and innumerable Treasury,
Tu ny doibs faire encore tension,		Thou oughtest not yet to tend that way,
France a mon dire fais que sois recordable.		France endeavour to remember my saying.

Qui au royaume Navarrois parviendra,	25 He that shall obtain the Kingdom of Navarre,
Quand le Sicile & Naples seront joints,	When Sicily and Naples shall be joyned,
Bigorre & Landes par fois larron tiendra,	Bigorre and Landes then by Foix shall behold
D'un qui d'Espagne sera par trop conjoints.	Of one who shall too much be joyned to Spain.

Des Rois & Princes dresseront simulachres,
Augures, creux eslevez aruspices :
Corne, victime dorée, & d'Azur & de Nacre,
Intrepretez seront les extispices.

26 Some Kings and Princes shall set up Idols,
Divinations, and hollow raised Divinators,
Victim with gilded Horns, and set with Azur and Mother of Pearl
The looking into the Entrals shall be interpreted.

Prince Libique puissant en Occident,
François d'Arabe viendra tant enflammer,
Sçavant aux Lettres fera condescendent,
La Langue Arabe en François translater.

27 A Libian Prince being powerful in the West,
The French shall love so much the Arabian Language,
That he being a Learned man shall condescend,
To have the Arabian tongue translated into French,

De terre foible & pauvre parentelle
Par bout & paix parviendra dans l'Empire,
Long temps regner une jeune femelle,
Qu'oncq, en regne n'en survint un si pire.

28 One weak in Lands and of poor Kindred,
By thrusting, and peace shall attain to the Empire,
Long time shall Reign a young woman,
Such as in a Reign was never a worse.

Les deux Neveux en divers lieux nourris,
Navale pugne, Terre peres tombez,
Viendront si haut eslevez aguerris,
Venger l'Injure ennemis succombez.

29 The two Nephews brought up in divers places,
A Sea fight, fathers fallen to the Earth,
They shall come highly educated, and expert in Arms,
To avenge the injury, their enemies shall fall down under them.

Celuy qu'en luitte & fer au fait Bellique,
Aura porté plus grand que luy le prix,
De nuit au lit six luy feront la pique,
Nud sans harnois subit sera surprins.

30 He who in Wrestling and Martial affairs,
Had carried the prize before his better,
By night Six shall abuse him in his bed,
Being naked, and without harness, he shall suddenly be surprised.

Aux champs de Mede, d'Arabe, & d'Armenie,
Deux grands Copies trois fois sassembleront,
Pres du Rivage d'Araxes la mesgnie,
Du grand Soliman en Terre tomberont,

31 In the fields of Media, Arabia, and Armenia,
Two great Armies shall meet thrice,
Near the Shore of Araxes, the people
Of great Solyman shall fall down.

Le grand sepulchre du peuple Aquitanique,
S'aprochera aupres de la Toscane,
Quand Mars sera pres du coin Germanique,
Et au terroir de la gent Mantuane.

32 The great grave of thee Aquitanick people,
Shall come near Tuscany,
When Mars shall be in the German corner,
And in the Territory of the Mantuan people.

En la Cité où le loup entrera, *Bien pres de là les ennemis seront,* *Copie estrange grand pais gastera,* *Aux Monts des Alpes les amis passeront.*	33 In the City wherein the Wolf shall go, Near that place the enemies shall be, An Army of strangers shall spoil a great Countrey, The friends shall party over the Mountains of the Alpes.
Quand le defaut du Soleil lors sera, *Sur le plein jour le Monstre sera veu,* *Tout autrement on l'Interpretera,* *Cherté na garde, nul ny aura pourveu.*	34 When the Ecclipse of the Sun shall be At noon day, the Monster shall be seen, It shall be interperted otherways, Then for a dearth, because no body hath provided against it.
Du plus profond de l'Occident d'Europe, *De pauvre gens un jeune enfant naistra,* *Qui par sa langue seduira grande troupe,* *Son bruit au Regne d'Orient plus croistra.*	35 Out of the deepest part of the West of Europe, From poor people a young child shall be born, Who with his tongue shall seduce many people, His fame shall increase in the Eastern Kingdom.
Ensevely non mort Apoplectique, *Sera trouvé avoir les mains mangees,* *Quand la Cité damnera l'Heretique,* *Qu'avoit leur Loix ce leur sembloit changees.*	36 One buried, not dead, but Apoplectical, Shall be found to have eaten up his hands, When the City shall blame the heretical man, Who as they thought had changed their Laws.
Avant l'assault l'Oraison prononcée, *Milan prins l'Aigle, par embusche deceus,* *Muraille antique par Canons enfoncée,* *Par feu & sang à mercy peu receus.*	37 Before the assault the Prayer shall be said, An Eagle shall take a Kite, they shall be deceived by an Embuscado. The ancient wall shall be beaten down with Canons, By fire and blood, few shall have quarter.
La gens Gauloise & Nation estrange, *Outre les Monts, morts pris & profligez,* *Au mois contraire & proche de vendange,* *Par les Seigneurs en accord redigez.*	38 The French Nation, and another Nation, Being over the Mountains, shall die, and be taken, In a month contrary to them, and near the vintage, By the Lords agreed together.
Les sept en trois Mois en concorde, *Pour subjuger les Alpes Apenines,* *Mais la tempeste & Ligure coüarde,* *Les profligent en subites ruines.*	39 The seven shall agree together within three Months, To conquer the Apennine Alpes, But the tempest, and coward Genoese, Shall sink them into sudden ruines.
Le grand Theatre se viendra redresser, *Les dez jettez & les rets ia tendus,* *Trop le premier en glaz viendra lasser,* *Pars arc prostrais de long temps ia fendus.*	40 The great Theatre shall be raised up again, The Dice being cast, and the nest spread, The first shall too much in Glass. Beaten down by Bows, who long before were split.

Bossu sera esleu par le Conseil,	41	Crook-back shall be chosen by the Councel,
Plus hideux Monstre en Terre napperceu,		A more hideous Monster I never saw upon Earth.
Le coup volant luy crevera un œil,		Thy flying blow shall put out one of his eyes,
Le traistre au Roy pour fidele receu.		The Traitor to the King, shall be admited as faithful.

L'Enfant naistra à deux dents en la gorge,	42	A Child shall be born with two Teeth in his mouth,
Purres en Tuscie par pluie tomberont,		It shall rain stones in Tuscany,
Peu d'ans apres ne sera Bled ny Orge,		A few years after there shall be neither Wheat nor Barley
Pour saouler ceux qui de faim failleront.		To feed those that shall faint for hunger.

Gens d'alentour du Tar, Lot, & Garonne,	43	People that live about the Tar, Lot, and Garonne,
Gardez les Monts Apenines passer,		Take heed to go over the Apennine Mountains,
Vostre tombeou pres de Rome & d'Ancone,		Your Grave is near Rome and Ancona,
Le noir poil crespe fera Trophée dresser.		The black frisled hair shall dress a Trophy of you.

Quand l'Animal à l'homme domestique,	44	When the Beast familiar to Mankind,
Apres grands peines & sauts viendra parler,		After great labour, and leaping shall come to speak,
Le foudre à vierge sera si malefique,		The Lightning shall be so hurtful to a Virgin,
De terre prinse & suspenduë en l'air.		That she shall be taken from the Earth, and suspended in the Air.

Les cinq estranges entrez dedans le temple,	45	The five strangers having come into the Church,
Leur sang viendra la Terre prophaner,		The blood shall prophane the ground,
Aux Tholosains sera bien dur exemple,		It shall be a hard example to those of Thoulouse,
D'un qui viendra ses loix exterminer.		Concerning one that came to break their Laws.

Le Ciel (de Plancus la Cité) nous presage,	46	The Heaven foretelleth concerning the City of Plancus,
Par clers insignes & par estoiles fixes,		By famous Clerks, and fixed Stars,
Que de son change subit s'approche l'age,		That the time of her sudden change is near hand,
Ne pour son bien, ne pour ses malefices.		Neither because of her goodness, or wickedness.

Le vieux Monarque dechasé de son regne	47	The old Monarch being expelled out of his Kingdom,
Aux Oriens son secours ira querre,		Shall go into the East to get succours,
Pour peur des Croix ploiera son Enseigne,		For fear of the Crosses he shall fold up his Colours,
En Mitylene ira par port & Terre.		He shall go into Mitylene by Sea and Land.

Sept cens Captifs attachez rudement,	48	Seven hundred prisoners shall be tied together,
Pour la moitié meurtrir, donné le sort,		To murder half of them, the lot being cast,
Le proche espoir viendra si promptement,		The next hope shall come quickly,
Mais non si tost qu'une quinziesme mort.		And not so quickly, but fifteen shall be dead before.

Regne Gaulois tu seras bien changé,	49 French Kingdom thou shalt be much changed,
En lieu estrange est translaté l'Empire,	The Empire is translated in another place,
En autre mœurs & Lois seras rangé,	Thou shalt be put into other manners and Laws,
Roman & Chartres te feront bien du pire.	Rouan and Chartres shall do the worse they can to thee.

La republique de la grande Cité,	50 The Common-wealth of the great City,
A grand rigueur ne voudra consentir,	With great hardness shall not consent,
Roy sortir hors par trompette Cité,	That the King should go out being summoned by a Trumpet,
L'Eschelle au Mur la Cité repentir.	The Ladder shall be put to the Wall, and the City repent.

Paris conjure un grand meurtre commettre,	51 Paris conspireth to commit a great murder,
Blois le fera sortir en plein effect,	Blois will cause it to come to pass,
Ceux d'Orleans voudront leur Chef remettre,	Those of Orleans will set up their head again,
Angers, Troyes, Langres leur feront un mes fait.	Angers, Troyes, Langres will do them a mischief.

En la Campagne sera si longue pluye,	52 In Campania shall be so long a rain,
Et en l'Apoville si grande siccité,	And in Apulia so great a drought,
Coq verra l'Aigle l'aisse mal accomplie,	The Cock shall see the Eagle with his wing disordered,
Par Lion mise sera en extremité.	And by the Lion brought to extremity.

Quand le plus grand emportera le prix,	53 When the great one shall carry the prize,
De Nuremberg, d'Ausbourg, & ceux de Basle,	Of Nuremberg, Ausbourg, and Basil,
Par Agipine Chef de Frankfort repris,	By Agrippina the Chief of Frankfort shall be taken,
Traverseront par Flandres juseu en Gale.	They shall go through Flandes as far as France.

L'un des plus grands fuira aux Espagnes,	54 One of the greatest shall run away into Spain,
Qu'en longue playe apres viendra seigner,	That shall cause a wound to bleed long,
Passant Copies par les hautes Montaines,	Leading Armies over the high Mountains,
Devastant tout, & puis apres regner.	Destroying all, and afterwards shall Raign.

En l'an qu'un œil en France Regnera,	55 In the year that one eye shall Reign in France,
La Cour sera en un bien fascheux trouble,	The Court shall be in a very hard trouble,
Le grand de Blois son amy tuera,	The great one of Blois shall kill his friend,
Le Regne mis en mal & doubte double.	The Kingdom shall be in an ill case, and double doubt.

Montauban, Nismes, Avignon & Besier,	56 Montauben, Nismes, Avignon and Besier,
Peste, Tonnerre, & Gresle à fin de Mars,	Plague, Lightning and Hail at the end of March,
De Paris Pont, de Lion Mur, Monpelier,	The Bridge of Paris, the Wall of Lion, and Monpelier, shall fall,
Depuis six cens & sept vingt, trois parts.	From six hundred and seven score, three parts.

Sept fois changer verrez gens Britanique,	57 Seven times you shall see the English to change,
Taints en sang en deux cens nonante an,	Died in blood, in two hundred ninety year,
France non point par appuy Germanique,	Not France, by the German support,
Aries double son Pope Bistarnan.	Aires doubleth his Bastarnan Pole.

Aupres du Rhin des Montagnes Noriques,   58 Near the Rhine, out of the Norick Mountains,
Naistra un grand de gens trop trard venu,   Shall be born a great one, though too late come,
Qui defendra Sarmates & Pannoniques,   Who shall defend the Polonians and Hungarians,
Qu'on ne sçaura quil sera devenu.   So that it shall not be known what is become of him.

Barbare Empire par le tiers usurpé,   59 A Barbarian Empire shall be usurped by a third person,
La plus grand part de son sang mettre àmort,   Who shall put to death the greatest part of his Kindred,
Par mort senicle par luy le quart frappé,   By death of old age, the fourth shall be stricken by him,
Pour peur que sang par le sang ne soit mort.   For fear that blood should not die by blood.

Par toute Asia grande proscription,   60 Through all Asia shall be a great proscription,
Mesme en Mysie, Lydie, & Pamphilie,   Yea in Mysia, Lydia, and Pamphilia,
Sang versera par dissolution,   Blood shall be spilled by the debauchness
D'un jeune noir remply de felonie.   Of a young black man, full of felony.

La grande bande & secte Crucigere,   61 The great troop and sect wearing a Cross,
Se dressera en Mesopotamie,   Shall rise up in Mesopotamia,
Du proche Fleuve compagnie legere,   Near the next River shall be a light company,
Qui telle Loy tiendra pour ennemie.   Which shall hold that law for enemy.

Proche del Duero par Mer Cyrene close,   62 Near the Duero closed by the Cyrenian Sea,
Viendra percer les grands Monts Pyrenees,   Shall come to pierce the great Pyrenean Mountains,
La main plus courte & sa percée gloses,   The shorter hand and his pierced glose,
A Carcasonne conduira ses menées.   Shall in Carcassone lead his plot.

Romain pouvoir sera du tout à bas,   63 The Roman power shall be quite put down,
Son grand Voisin imiter les vestiges,   His great Neighbour shall follow his steps,
Occultes haines civiles, & debats,   Secret and civil hatreds and quarrels,
Retarderont aux boufons leur folies.   Shall stop the Buffons folly.

Le Chef de Perse remplira grand Olchade,   64 The Head of Persia shall fill a great Olchade,
Classe Trireme contre gent Mahometique,   A Fleet of Galleys against the Mahometan Nation,
De Parthe, & Mede, & piller les Cyclades,   From Parthia and Media they shall come to plunder the Cyclades,
Repos long temps au grand Port Jonique.   A long rest shall be on the Jonique Port.

Quand le Sepulchre du grand Romain trouué,	65	When the Sepulcher of the great Roman shall be found,
Le jour apres sera esleu Pontife,		The next day after a Pope shall be elected,
Du Senat queres il ne sera prouué,		Who shall not be much approved by the Senate,
Empoisonné, son sang au Sacré Scyphe.		Poisoned, his blood in the Sacred Scyphe.
Le grand Ballif d'Orleans mis à mort.	66	The great Bailif of Orleans shall be put to death,
Sera par un de sang vindicatif,		But one of a revengeful blood,
De mort merite ne montra, ne par sort,		He shall not die of a deserved death, nor by chance,
Des pieds & mains mal, le faisoit captif.		But the disease of being tied hand and foot, hath made him prisoner.
Une nouvelle Secte de Philosophes,	67	A new Sect of Philosophers shall rise,
Mesprisant mort, or, honneurs & richesses,		Despising Death, Gold, Honours and Riches,
Des Monts Germains seront fort limitrophes,		They shall be near the Mountians of Germany,
A les ensuivre auront appuy & presses,		They shall have abundance of others to support and follow them.
Peuple sans Chef d'Espagne & d'Italie,	68	A people of Spain and Italy without a Head,
Morts, profligez dedans le Cheronese,		Shall die, being overcome in the Cheronese,
Leur dict trahy par legere folie,		Their saying shall be betrayed by a light folly,
Le sang nager par tout à la traverse.		The blood shall swim all over at random.
Grand exercite conduit par jouvenceau,	69	A great Army led by a young man,
Se viendra rendre aux mains des ennemis		Shall yield it self in the hands of the enemies,
Mais le vieillard nay au demy pourceau,		But the old man born at the sign off the halfe-Hog,
Fera Chalon & Mascon estre amis.		Shall cause Chalon and Mascon to be friends.
La grand Bretagne comprise d'Angleterre,	70	Great Britany comprehended in England,
Viendra par eaux si haut à inondre,		Shall suffer so great an Inundation by Waters,
La Ligue nevue d'Ausone fera gerre,		The new League of Ausone shall make Wards,
Que contre eux ils se viendront bander.		So that they shall stand against them.
Ceux dans les Isles de long temps assiegez,	71	Those in the Islands that have been long besieged,
Prendront vigueur force contre ennemis,		Shall take vigour and force against their enemies,
Ceux par dehors morts de faim profligez,		Those without shall die for hunger ; being overcome,
En plus grand faim que jamais seront mis.		They shall be put in greater famine than they were before.
Le bon Vieillard tout vif Ensevely,	72	The good old man shall be buried alive,
Pres du grand Fleuve par faux soupçon,		Near the great River by a false suspicion,
Le nouveaux vieux de richesse ennobly,		The new old one made noble by his riches,
Prins en chemin tout l'or de la Rançon.		The gold of his ransom shall be taken in the way.

Quand dans le Regne parviendra le boiteux, *Competiteur aura proche Bastard,* *Luy & le Regne viendront si fort rogneux,* *Qu'ains quil guerisse son fait sera bien tard.*	73	When the lame man shall attain to the Kingdom, He shall have a Bastard for his near competitor, He, and his Kingdom shall be so scabby, That before he be cured it will be late.

Naples, Florence, Fayence, & Imole,
Seront en termes de telle fascherie,
Que pour complaire au malheureux de Nole,
Plaint d'avoir fait à son Chef moquerie.

74 Naples, Florence, Fayenza, and Imola,
Shall be put into so much distress,
For being complaisant to the unhappy one of Nola,
Who was complained of for having mocked his Superiour.

Pau, Verone, Vicence, Saragousse,
De Glaive attents, Terroirs de sang humides,
Peste si grande viendra à la grand gousse,
Proche secours & bien long les remedes,

75 Pau, Verona Vicenza, Saragossa,
Shall be hit by the Sword, the Countrey shall be moist with blood,
So great a plague and so vehement shall come,
That thought the succours be near, the remedy shall be far off.

En Germanie naistront diverses Sectes,
S'aprochant fort de l'heureux Paganisme,
Le cœur captif & petites receptes,
Feront retour à payer le vray disme.

76 In Germany shall divers Sects arise,
Coming very near the happy Paganisme,
The heart captivated and small receivings,
Shall open the gate to pay the true Tithes.

Le tiers climat soubs Aries comprins,
L'An mil sept cens vingt sept en Octobre,
Le Roy de Perse par ceux d'Ægypte prins,
Conflict, mort, perte, à la Croix grand opprobre.

77 The third Climat comprehended under Aries,
In the year 1700. the twenty seven of October,
The King of Persia shall be taken by those of Ægypt,
Battle, death, loss, a great shame to the Christains.

Le Chef d'Escosse avec six d'Allemagne,
Par gents de mer Orientaux captif,
Traverseront le Calpre & Espagne,
Present en Perse au nouveau Roy craintif.

78 The Chief of Scotland with fix of Germany,
Shall be taken prisoners by Seamen of the East,
They shall go through the Calpre and Spain,
And shall be made a present in Persia to the new fearful King.

Le grand criard fans honte audacieux,
Sera esleu Governeur le d'Armée,
La hardiesse de son contentieux,
Le pont rompu, Cité de peur pasmeé

79 The great bawler proud without shame,
Shall be elected Governour of the Army,
The stoutness of his Competitor,
The Bridge being broken, the City shall faint for fear.

Erins, Antibe, villes auteur de Nice,
Seront vastées fort par Mer & par Terre,
Les Sauterelles Terre & Mer vent propice,
Prins, morts, troussez, pillez, sans loy de guerre.

80 Erins, Antibe, and the Towns about Nices,
Shall be destroyed by Sea and Land,
The Grashopers shall have the Land, the Sea, and Wind favourable,
They shall be taken, killed, thrust up, plundered, without Law of War.

L'Ordre fatal sempiternal par chaisne,	
Viendra tourner par ordre consequent,	
Du Port Phocen sera rompue la chaine,	
La Cité prinse, l'ennemy quant & quant.	

81 The fatal and eternal order by chain,
Shall come to turn by consequent order,
Of Port Phocen the chain shall be broken,
The City taken, and the enemy presently after.

Du Regne Anglois le digne dechasse,
Le Conseiller par ire mis a feu,
Ses adherans iront si bas tracer,
Que le bastard sera demy receu.

82 From the English Kingdom the worthy driven away,
The Councellor through anger shall be burnt,
His partners shall creep so low,
That the bastard shall be half received.

Les longs cheveux de la Gaule Celtique,
Accompagnez d'Estranges Nations,
Mettront captif l'Agent Aquitanique,
Pour succomber à leurs intentions.

83 The long hairs of the Celtian France,
Joyned with forrain Nations,
Shall put in prison the Aquitanick Agent,
To make him yield to their intentions.

La grand Cité sera bien desolée,
Des habitans un seul n'y demoura,
Mur, Sexe, Temple, & Vierge violée,
Par Fer, feu, Peste, Canon, peuple mourra.

84 The great City shall be made very desolate.
Not one of the Inhabitants shall be left in it,
Wall, Sex, Church, and Virgin ravished,
By Sword, Fire, Plague, Canon, people shall die.

La Cité prinse par tromperie & fraude,
Par le moyen d'Un bean jeune attrapé,
Assault donné, Raubine pres de Laude,
Luy & touts morts pour avoir bien trompé.

85 The City shall be taken by cheat and deceit,
By the means of a fair young one caught in it,
Assault shall be give, Raubine near Laude,
He, and all shall die, for having deceived.

Un chef d'Ausonne aux Espagnes ira,
Par Mer, fera arrest dedans Marseilles,
Avant sa mort un long temps languira,
Apres sa mort on verra grand merveille.

86 A chief man of Ausone shall go into Spain
By Sea, he shall stay at Marseilles,
He shall languish a great while before his death,
After his death great wonders shall be seen.

Classe Gauloise naproche de Corsegne,
Moins de Sardaigne, tu ten repentiras,
Trestous mourrez frustrez de laide Greigne,
Sang nagera, captif ne me croiras.

87 French Fleet do not come near unto Corsica,
Much less to Sardinia, thou shalt repent of it,
All of you shall die frustrate of the help Greigne,
Blood shall swim, being Captive thou shalt not believe me.

De Barcelone par Mer si grande Armée,
Toute Marseille de frayeur tremblera,
Isles saisies; de Mer aide fermée,
Ton traditeur en Terre nagera.

88 There shall come from Barcelona by Sea so great a fleet,
That Marseilles shall quake for fear,
The Islands shall be seized, the help by Sea shut up,
Thy Traitor shall swim to Land.

En ce temps la sera frustreé Cypre,
De son secours, de ceux de Mer Ægée,
Vieux trucidez mais par Mesles & Lipre,
Seduit leur Roy, Roine, plus outragée.

89 | At that time Cyprus shall be frustrated
Of its succours, of those of thee Ægean Sea,
Old ones shall be killed, but by Mesles and Lipre,
Their King shall be seducted, and the Queen more wronged.

Le grand Satyre & Tygre d'Hircanie,
Don presenté à ceux de l'Occean,
Un chef de Classe istra de Carmanie,
Qui prendra Terre au Thyrren Phocean.

90 | The great Satyr and Tyger of Hircania,
Shall be a gift presented to those of the Ocean,
An Admiral of a fleet shall come out of Carmania,
Who shall Land in the Thyrren Phocean.

L'Arbre qu'estoit par long temps mort seiché,
Dans une nuit viendra à reverdir,
Son Roy malade, Prince pied estaché,
Criant d'ennemis fera Voiles bondir.

91 | The Tree that had been long dead and withered,
In one night shall grow green again,
His King shall be sick, his Prince shall have his foot tied,
Being feared by his enemies, he shall make his Sails to rebound.

Le monde proche du dernier periode,
Saturn encor sera tard de retour,
Tanslat Empire devers Nation brode,
L'œil arraché à Narbon par Autour.

92 | The world being near its last period,
Saturn shall come yet late to his return,
The Empire shall be translated into brode Nationosss,
Narbon shall have her eye pickt out by a Hawk.

Dans Avignon tout le Chef de l'Empire,
Fera arrest, pour Paris desolé,
Tricast tiendra l'Annibalique ire,
Lion par change sera mal consolé.

93 | In Avignon all the Chief of the Empire,
Shall stay, by reason of Paris being desolate,
Tricast shall stop the Annibalik anger,
Lion by change shall be ill comforted.

De cinq cens ans plus compte lon tiendra,
Celuy qu'estoit l'ornement de son temps,
Puis à vn coup grande clarté donra,
Qui pour ce Siecle les rendra tres-contens.

94 | For five hundred years no account shall be made,
Of him who was the ornament of his time :
Then on a sudden he shall give so great a light,
That for that age he shall make them to be most contented.

Lu Loy Moricque on verra defaillir,
Apres un autre beducoup plus seductive,
Boristhenes premier viendra faillir,
Par dons & langue une plus attractiue,

95 | We shall see the Morish Law to decline,
After which, another more seducing shall arise,
Boristhenes shall be the first that shall fall.
By gifts and tongue that Law shall be most seducing.

Chef de Fossan aura gorge coupee,
Par le Ducteur du Limier & L'curier,
Le fait patré ceux du Mont Tarpée,
Saturne en Leo 13. de February.

96 | The Chief of Fossan shall have his throat cut,
By the Leader of the Hunt and Greyhound,
The fact committed by those of the Tarpeian Mountain,
Saturn being in Leo the 13. of February.

Nouvelle Loy, Terre neuve occuper,
Vers la Syrie, Judée & Palestine,
Le grand Empire, Barbare corruer,
Auant que Phebé son Siecle determine.

97 | A new Law shall occupy a new Countrey,
Towards Syria, Judea and Palestina,
The great Barbarian Empire shall fall down,
Before Phœbe maketh an end of her course.

Deux Royal Freres si fort guerroieront,
Qu'entreux sera la guerre si mortelle,
Qu'un chacun places fortes occuperont,
De Regne & vie sera leur grand querelle.

98 | Two Royal Brothers shall War so much one against the other,
That the War between them shall be mortal,
Each of them shall seize upon strong places,
Their quarrel shall be concerning Kingdom and Life.

Aux Champs Herbes d'Alein & du Varneigre,
Du Mont Lebron proche de la Durance,
Camps des deux parts conflict sera si aigre,
Mesopotamie defaillira en France.

99 | In the Meadow Fields of Alein and Varneigre,
Of the Mountain Lebron near the Durance,
Armies on both sides, the first shall be so sharp,
That Mesopotamia shall be wanting in France.

Entre Gaulois le dernier honoré,
D'homme ennemy sera victorieux,
Force & terreur en moment exploré,
D'un coup de trait quand mourra l'envieux.

100 | He that is the least honoured among the French,
Shall be Conqueror of the man that was his Enemy,
Strength and terrour shall in a moment be tried,
When the envious shall be killed with an Arrow.

Century IV

Ela du reste de sang non espandu,
Venice quiert secours estre donné,
Apres avoir bien lon têmps attendu,
Cité livrée au premier Cer sonné.

1 There shall be a remnant of blood unspilt,
Venice shall seek for succours,
After having long waited for it,
The City shall be surrendred at the first sound of the
Trumpet.

Par mort la France prendra voiage à faire,
Classe par Mer, marcher Monts Pyrenées,
Espagne en trouble marcher gent militaire,
Des plus grands Dames en France emmenées.

2 By reason of a death, France shall undertake a Journey,
They shall have a Fleet at Sea, and march towards the
Pyrenes,
Spain shall be in trouble by an Army,
Some of the greatest Ladies in France carried away.

D'Arras & Bourges, de Brodes grans enseignes,
Un plus grand nombre de Gascons battre à pied,
Ceux long du Rhosne saigneront les Espaignes,
Proche du Mont où Sagonte sassied.

3 From Arras and Bourges many colours of black men shall
come,
A greater number of Gascons shall go on foot,
Those along the Rhosne shall let Spain blood,
Near the Mountain where Saguntus is seated.

L'Impotent Prince faché, plaint & querelles,
De rapts & pillé par Coqs & par Libiques,
Grands & par Terre, par Mer infinies Voiles,
Seule Italie sera chassant Celtiques.

4 The considerable Prince vexed, complaineth and
quarellth,
Concerning rapes and plunderings done by the Cocks and
Libiques
Great trouble by Land, by Sea infinite Sails.
Italy alone shall drive away the French.

Croix, Paix, soubs un accomply Diuin Verbe,
L'Espagne & Gaules seront unis ensemble,
Grand clade proche & combat tresacerbe,
Cœur si hardy ne sera qui ne tremble.

5 The Cross shall have peace, under an accomplished
Divine Word
Spain and France shall be united together,
A great Battle near hand, and most sharp fight,
No heart so stout but shall tremble.

D'Habits nouveaux apres faite la treuve,
Malice trame, & machination,
Premier mourra qui en fera la preuve,
Couleur Venise, Insidiation.

6 After the new Cloaths shall be found out,
There shall be malice, plotting and machination,
He shall die the first that shall make trial of it,
Under colour of Venice, shall be a conspiracy.

Le fils mineur du grand & hay Prince,
De Lepre aura à vingre ans grande tache,
De dueil mourra triste & mince,
Et il mourra là où tombe cher lache.

7 The younger Son of the great and hated Prince,
Being twenty years, old shall have a great touch of
Leprosie,
His mother shall die for grief, very sad and lean,
And he shall die of the disease loose flesh.

La grand Cité dassaut prompt repentin,	8
Surpris de nuit, gardes interrompus,	
Les Excubies & veilles Saint Quentin,	
Trucidez gardes, & les Portails rompus.	

8   The great City shall be taken by a sudden assault,
Being surprised by night, the Watch being beaten,
The Court of Guard and Watch of Saint Quentin
Shall be killed, and the Gates broken.

Le Chef du Camp au milieu de la presse,
D'un coup de fleche sera blessé aux cuisses,
Lors que Geneve en larmes & detresse,
Sera trahie par Lozanne & Souisses.

9   The Chief of the Camp in the middle of the crowd,
Shall be wounded with an Arrow through both his thighs,
When Geneva being in tears and distress,
Shall be betrayed by Lozane and the Switzers.

Le jeune Prince accusé faucement,
Mettra le camp en trouble & en querelles,
Meurtry le chef par le souslevement,
Sceptre appaiser, puis querir escroüelles.

10   The young Prince being falsely accused,
Shall put the Camp in trouble, and in quarrele,
The Chief shall be murdered by the tumult,
The Scepter shall be appeased, and after cure the Kings-
evil.

Celuy quavra couvert de la grand Cappe,
Sera induict à quelque cas patrer,
Les douze rouges viendront soüiller la nappa,
Soubs meurtre, meurtre se viendra perpetrer.

11   He that shall be covered with a great Cloak,
Shall be induced to commit some great fact,
The twelve red ones shall Soil the Table-cloth,
Under murder, murder shall be committed.

Le Champ plus grand de route mis enfuite,
Gueres plus outre ne sera pourchassé,
Ost recampé & legion reduicte,
Puis hors, des Gaules du tout sera chassé

12   The greatest Camp being in disorder, shall be routed,
And shall be pursued not much after,
The Army shall incamp again, and the Troops set in order
Then afterwards, they shall be wholly driven out of France

De plus grand perte nouvelles rapportées,
Le rapport le camp s'estournera.
Bandes unies encontre revoltées,
Double Phalange, grand abandonnera.

13   News being brought of a great loss,
The report divulged, the Camp shall be astonished,
Troops being united and revolted,
The double Phalange shall forsake the great one.

La mort subite du premier personage,
Aura changé & mis un autre au Regne,
Tost, tard venu à si haut & basage,
Que Terre & mer faudra que lon le craigne.

14   The sudden death of the chief man,
Shall cause a change, and put another in the Raign,
Soon, late come to so high a degree, in a low age,
So that by Land and Sea he must be feared.

D'où pensera faire venir famine,
De là viendra le rassasiement,
L'œil de la Mer par avare canine,
Pour de l'un lautre donra Huile, Froment.

15   Whence one thought to make famine to come,
Thence shall come the fulness,
The eye of the Sea through a doggish covetousness,
Shall give to both Oyl and Wheat.

La Cité franche de liberté fait serue,	16
Des profligés & resueurs fait azyle,	
Le Roy changé à eux non si proterue,	
De cent seront deuenus plus de Mille.	

The free City from a free one shall become slave,
And of the banished and dreamers shall be a retreat,
The King changed in mind, shall not be so forward to them
Of one hundred they shall become more then a thousand.

Changer à Banne, Nuis, Chalons, & Dijon, 17
Le Duc voulant amender la barrée
Marchât pres Fleuve, Poisson, bec de plongeon,
Verra la queüe: Porte sera serrée.

There shall be a change at Beaume, Nuis, Chalons, Dijon,
The Duke going about to raise Taxes,
The Merchant near the River shall see the tail
Of a Fish, having the Bill of a Cormorant : the door shall
be shut.

Les plus Lettrez dessus les faits Cælestes, 18
Seront par Princes ignorans reprouvez,
Punis d'Edict, chassez, comme scelestes,
Et mis à mort là où seront trouvez.

The most Learned in the Celestial Sciences,
Shall be found fault with, by ignorant Princes.
Punished by proclamation, chased away as wicked,
And put to death where they shall be found.

Devant Roüan d'Insubres mis le Siege, 19
Par Terre & Mer enfermez les passages,
D'Hainaut, de Flândres de Gând & ceux de Liege,
Par leurs levées raviront les Rivages.

Before Rouan a Siege shall be laid by the Insubrians.
By Sea and Land the passages shall be shut up,
Those of Hainaut, Flanders, Ghent, and Liege,
With their Troops shall plunder the Sea-shore.

Paix uberté long temps on ne loüera, 20
Par tout son Regne desert la fleur de Lis,
Corps morts d'Eau, Terre on apportera,
Sperans vain heur d'estre là ensevelis.

Peace and plenty shall not be long praised,
All the time of his Reign the Flower de Luce shall be
deserted,
Bodies shall die by water, Earth shall be brought,
Hoping vainly to be there Buried.

Le changement sera fort difficile, 21
Cité Province au change gain fera,
Cœur haut, prudent mis, chassé l'Inhabile,
Mer, Terre, Peuple, son estat changera.

The change shall be very hard,
The City and Countrey shall gain by the change,
A high prudent heart shall be put in, the unworthy
expelled,
Sea, Land, People shall change its conditions.

La grand Copie qui sera deschassee, 22
Dans un moment fera besoing au Roy,
La Foy promise de loing sera faucée,
Nud se verra en piteux desarroy.

The great Army that shall be rejected,
In a moment shall be wanted by the King.
The faith promised a far off shall be broken,
So that he shall be left naked in a pitiful case.

La Legion dans la Marine classe, 23
Calcine, Magnes, Souphre & Poix bruslera,
Le long repos de l'asseurée place,
Port Selyn, chercher, feu les consumera.

The Legion in the Maritine Fleet,
Calcineth Magnes, shall burn Brimstone and Pitch,
The long rest of the secure place,
They shall seek Port Selyn, but fire shall consume them.

Ouy soubs Terre Sainte Dame voix feinte,	24
Humaine flamme pour Divine voir luire,	
Fera des sœurs de leur sang Terre tainte,	
Et les Saints Temples par les impurs destruire.	

24 Under ground shall be heard the fainted voice of a Holy Dame,
An humane flame to see a Divine one
Shall cause the ground to be died with the sisters blood,
And the Holy Temples to be destroyed by the wicked.

Corps sublimes sans fin à l'œil visibles,
Obnubiler viendront par ces raisons,
Corps, front compris, sens & chefs invisibles,
Diminuant les Sacrées Oraisons.

25 The Celestial bodies that are always visible to the eye,
Shall be darkened for these reasons,
The body with the forehead sense and head invincible.
Diminishing the Sacred Prayers.

Lou grand Cyssame se levera d'abelhos,
Que non lauran don te siegen venguddos,
Denuech lênbousq, lun gach dessous las treilhos,
Ciutad trahido per cinq lengos non nudos.

26 The great swarm of Bees shall rise,
And it shall not be known whence they come,
Towards the Ambush the Jay shall be under a Vine,
A City shall be betray'd by five tongues not naked.

Salon, Mansol, Tarascon, de Sex, Larc,
Où est debout encor la Pyramide,
Viendront livrer le Prince Denemarçk,
Rachat honny au Temple d'Artemide.

27 Salon, Mansol, Tarascon, Desex, and arche,
Where to this day standeth the Pyramis,
Shall come to deliver the Prince of Denmark,
A shameful ransom shall be paid in the Temple of Artemis,

Lors que Venus du Sol sera couvert,
Soubs la splendeur sera la forme occulte,
Mercure au feu les aura descouvert,
Par bruit Bellique sera mis à l'Insulte.

28 When Venus shall be covered by the Sun,
Under the Splendor of it shall be an occult form,
Mercury in the fire shall discover them,
And by a Warlike rumor shall be provoked.

Le Sol caché, eclipse par Mercure,
Ne sera mis que pour le Ciel second,
De Vulcan Hermes sera faicte Pasture,
Sol sera veu pur, rutilant & blond.

29 The Sun shall be hid and eclipsed by Mercury,
And shall not be set but for the second Heaven,
Hermes shall be made a prey to Vulcan,
And after that the Sun shall be seen pure, shining and yellow.

Plus d'unze fois Luna Sol ne voudra,
Tous augmentes & baissez de degre,
Et si bas mis que peu d'Or on coudra,
Qu'apres faim, peste, descouvert le secret.

30 The Moon will not have the Sun above eleven times,
Then both shall be encreased and lessened in degree,
And put so low, that a little Gold shall be sowed up,
So that after hunger and plague, the secret shall be discovered.

La Lune au plain de nuit sur le haut Mont,
Le nouveau Sophe d'un seul cerueau la veu,
Par ses Disciples estre immortel semond,
Yeux au Midy, enfin, mains corps au feu.

31 The Moon at full by night upon the high Mount,
The new Sophe with one onely Brian hath seen it,
Invited by his Disciples to become immortal,
His eyes to the South, conclusion, his hands and body to the fire.

Es lieux & temps chair au poisson donra lieu,	32	In places and times, flesh shall give place to fish,
La loy commune sera faite au contraire,		The common Law shall be made against it,
Vieux tiendra fort puis osté du milieu,		The old man shall stand fast, then being taken away
Le Panta, Chiona Philon mis fort arriere.		The Panta, Choina, Philon, shall be set aside.
Jupiter joint plus Venus qu'a la Lune,	33	Jupiter being more joyned to Venus then to the Moon,
Apparoissant de plenitude blanche,		Appearing in a full whiteness,
Venus cachée soubs la blancheur Neptune,		Venus being hid under the whiteness of Neptune,
De Mars frappée par la gravée blanche.		Stricken by Mars through the ingraved branch.
Le grand mené captif d'estrange Terre,	34	The great one brought Prisoner from a far Countrey,
Dor enchainé au Roy Chyren offert,		And chained with Gold, shall be presented to the King Chyren,
Qui dans Ausone, Milan perdra la Guerre,		Back then at Ausone. Milan shall loose the War.
Et tout son Oft mis a Feu & a fer.		And all its Host shall be put to fire and sword.
Le feu esteint, les vierges trahiront,	35	The fire being put out, the Virgins shall betray,
La plus grand part de la bande nouvelle,		The greatest part of the new troup,
Ponldre à feu les feuls Rois garderont,		Gunpowder, Lance, shall keep only the Kings,
Hetrusque & Corse, de nuit gorge alumelle.		In Hetruria and Corsica by night throats shall be cut.
Les jeux nouveaux en Gaule redressez,	36	The new plays shall be set up again in France,
Apres Victoire de l'Insubre Campaigne,		After the Victory obtained in Piemont,
Monts d'Esperie, les grands liez troussez,		Mountains of Spain, the great ones tied, carried away,
De peur trembler la Romagne & l'Espagne.		Romania and Spain shall quake for fear.
Gaulois par saults Monts viendra penetrer,	37	The French by leaping shall go over the Mountains,
Occupera le grand Mont de l'Insubre,		And shall seize upon the great Mount of the Savoyard,
Au plus profond son Ost fera entrer,		He shall cause his Army to go to the furthermost,
Genes, Monech pousseront classe rubre.		Genoa, and Monaco shall set out their red Fleet.
Pendant que Duc, Roy, Roine occupera,	38	While the Duke shall busie the King and the Queen,
Chef Bizantim captif en Samothrace,		A great man of Constantinople shall be prisoner in Samothracia,
Avant lassault l'un l'autre mangera,		Before the assault on shall eat up the other,
Rebours ferré suivra du sang la trace.		Rebours shod shall trace one by the blood.
Les Rhodiens demanderont secours,	39	The Rhodiens shall ask for succours,
Par le neglect de ses hoirs delaissée.		Being forsaken by the neglect of her Heirs,
L'Empire Arabe revalera son cours,		The Arrabian Empire shall slack his course,
Par Hesperie la cause redressée.		By the means of Spain the case shall be mended.

Les forteresses des Assiegez serrez,	40	The strong places of the Besieged shall be straightned,
Par poudre à feu profondez en abysme,		By Gunpowder they shall be plunged into a pit,
Les proditeurs seront tous vifs serrez,		The Traytors shall be shut up alive,
Onc aux Sacristes navint si piteux schisme.		Never did happen so pitiful a schisme to the Sacristes.
Gynique Sexe captive par Hostage,	41	Gynical sexe being captive by Hostage,
Viendra de nuit custodes decevoir,		Shall come by night to deceive her keepers,
Le Chef du Camp deçeu par son langage,		The Chief of the Camp being deceived by her Language,
Lairra la gente, fera piteux à voir.		Shall leave her folks, a thing pitiful to behold.
Geneve & Lâgres par ceux de Chartre & Dole,	42	Geneve and Langres by those of Chartres and Dole,
Et par Grenoble captif au Montlimar,		Aud by one of Grenoble captive at Montlimar,
Seysset, Lausane, par fraudulente dole,		Seisset, Lozanne by a fraudulent deceit,
Les trahiront pour Or soixante mark.		Shall betray them for thirty pounds weight of Gold.
Seont ouis au Ciel les Armes batre,	43	There shall be heard in the Air noise of Weapons,
Celuy an mesme les Divins ennemis,		And in that same year the Divines shall be enemies,
Voudront Loix Sainctes injustement debatre,		They shall unjustly put down the Holy Laws,
Par Foudre & guerre bien croians à mort mis.		And by the Thunder and the War true believers shall die.
Deux gros de Mende, de Rhodéz & Milland,	44	Two great ones of Mende, of Rhodez and Milliaud,
Cahors, Limoges, Castres, malo sepmano,		Cahors, Limoges, Castres and evil week,
De nuech l'intrado, de Bourdeaux an cailhau,		By night the entry shall be from Bourdeaux one cailhan,
Par Perigort au toc de la Campano,		Through Perigort at the ringing of the Bell.
Par conflict, Roy Regne abandonera,	45	By a Battle of King shall forsake his Kingdom,
Le plus grand Chef faillira au besoing,		The greatest Commander, shall fail in time of need,
Morts profligez peu en rechapera,		They shall be killed and routed, few shall escape,
Tous destranchéz, un en sera tesmoin.		They shall be cut off, one only shall be left for a witness.
Bien defendu le fait par excellence,	46	The fact shall be defended excellently well
Garde toy Tours de ta proche ruine,		Tours beware of thy approaching ruine,
Londres & Nantes par Rheims fera defense,		London and Nantes by Rhemes shall stand upon their defence,
Ne passe outre au temps de la bruine.		Do not go further in foggy weather.
Le noir farouche quand aura essayé,	47	The wild black one, after he shall have tryed,
Sa main sanguine par feu, fer, arcs tendus,		His bloody hand by fire, Sword, bended Bows,
Trestout le peuple sera tant effrayé,		All the people shall be so frightened,
Voir les plus grands par col & pieds pendus.		To see the greatest hanged by the neck and feet.

Planure Ausone fertile spacieuse,	48	The Plain about Bourdeaux fruitful and spacious,
Produira taons, & tant de sauterelles,		Shall produce so many Hornets and so many Grashopers,
Clarté solaire deviendra nubilense,		That the light of the Sun shall be darkened,
Ronger le rout, grand peste venir delles.		They shall crap all, a great plague shall come from them.

Devant le peuple sang sera respandu,
Qui du haut Ciel ne viendra esloigner,
Mais d'un long temps ne sera entendu,
L'Esprit d'un seul le viendra tesmoigner.

49 Before the people blood shall be spilt,
Who Shall not come far from the high Heaven,
But it shall not be heard of for a great while,
The Spirit of one shall come to witness it.

Libra verra regner les Hesperies,
De Ciel & Terre tenir la Monarchie,
D'Asie forces nul ne verra peries,
Que sept ne tiennent par rang la Hierarchie.

50 Libra shall see Spain to Reign,
And have the Monarchy of Heaven and Earth,
No body shall see the forces of Asia to parish,
Till seven have kept the Hirearchy successively,

Un Duccupide son ennemy poursuivre,
Dans entrera empeschant la Phalange,
Hastez à pied si pres viendront poursuivre,
Que la journée conflite aupres du Gauge.

51 A Duke being earnest in the pursute of his enemy
Shall come in, hindering the Phalange,
Hastened on foot shall follow them so close,
That the day of the Battle shall be near Ganges.

En Cité obsesse aux murs hommes & femmes,
Enemis hors, le chef prest à soy rendre,
Vent sera fort encontre les gens darmes,
Chassez seront par chaux, poussiere & cendre.

52 In a besieged City, men and women being upon the walls,
The enemies without, the Governour ready to surrender,
The Wind shall be strong against the Souldiers,
They shall be driven away by lime, dust, and ashes.

Les fugitifs & bannis revoques,
Peres & Fils garnissant les hauts puits,
Le cruel pere & les siens suftoquez,
Son Fils plus pire submergé dans le puits.

53 The runnaways and banished men being recalled,
Fathers and Sons garnished the high wells,
The cruel father and his retinue shall be suffocated,
His Son being worse, shall be drowned in the Well.

Du nom qui onc ne fut au Roy Gaulois,
Jamais ne fut un Foudre si craintif,
Tremblant l'Italie, l'Espagne, & les Anglois,
De femmes estrangers grandement attentif.

54 Of the name that a French king never was,
There was never a Lightning so much feared,
Italy shall tremble, Spain and the English,
He shall be much taken with women strangers,

Quand la Corneille sur Tour de Brique jointe,
Durant sept heures ne fera que crier,
Mort presag'e de sang Statue teinte,
Tyran meudry, aux Dieux peuple prier.

55 When the Crow upon a Tower made of Brick,
For seven hours shall do nothing but cry,
Death shall be foretold, and the Statue died with blood,
Tyrant shall be murdered, and the people pray to the Gods.

Apres Victoire de rabieuse Langue,	
L'Esprit tempté, en tranquil & repos,	
Victeur sauguin par conflict, fait Harangue,	
Roustir la Langue, & la Chair & les Os.	

56 After the Victory got over a raging tongue,
The mind that was tempted, shall be in tranquility and rest,
The bloody Conqueror by Battle shall make a Speech,
And roast the tongue, the flesh, and the bones.

Ignare envie au grand Roy supportée,
Tiendra propos deffendre les escripts,
Sa femme non femme par un autre tentée,
Plus double deux ira au fort de cris.

57 Ignorant envy being supported by the great King,
Shall talk of prohibiting the writtings,
His wife no wife, being tempted by another,
Shall more then they two prevail by crying.

Soleil ardent dans la grosier couler,
De sang humain arrouser Terre Etrusque,
Chef seille d'eau, mener son fils filer,
Captive Dame conduite Terre Turque.

58 Burning Sun shall be poured into the throat,
This human blood shall wet the Hetrurian ground,
The chief pale of water, shall lead his son to Spin,
A captive Lady shall be carried into the Turkish Countrey.

Deux assiegez en ardente ferveur,
Ce soif estaints pour deux plaines Tasses,
Le fort limé & un vieillard resueur,
Au Genois, de Nizza monstrera trace.

59 Two besieged, being in a burning heat,
Shall die for thirst, want of two Bowls full,
The Fort being filled, in old doting man,
Shall show to the Genoese the way to Nizza.

Les sept enfans en Hostage laissez,
Le tiers viendra son enfant trucider,
Deux par son fils seront d'estoc percez,
Genes, Florence, les viendra senconder.

60 The seven Children being left in Hostage,
The third shall come to kill his child,
Two by their sons shall be run through,
Genoa and Florence shall second them.

Le vieux mocqué privé de sa place,
Par l'Estranger qui le subornera,
Mais de son filz mangé devant sa face,
Le Frere a Chartres, Orl. Roüan trahira.

61 The old man shall be baffled and deprived of his place,
By the stranger that shall suborn him.
But of his son shall be eaten before his face,
The Brother at Chartres. Orl. shall betray Rouen.

Un Coronel machine ambition,
Se saisira de la grande Armée,
Contre son Prince feinte invention,
Et descouvert sera soubs sa ramée.

62 A Colonel deviseth a plot by his ambition,
He shall seize upon the best part of the Army,
Against his Prince he shall have a fained invention,
And shall be discovered under the Harbour of the Vine.

L'Armée Celtique contre les Montaignars,
Qui seront sus & prins a la pipée,
Paisants irez polseront rost faugnars,
Precipitez tous au fils de l'Espee.

63 The Celtique Army shall go against the Highlanders,
Who shall stand upon their guard, and be taken with Bird-lime twigs,
The Peasant being angry, shall roll down the stones,
They shall be all put to the edge of the sword.

Le'defaillant en habit de Bourgeois,	
Viendra le Roy tenter de son offense,	
Quinze Soldats la pluspart Villageois,	
Vie derniere & chef de sa chevance.	

64 The guilty, in a Citizens habit,
Shall come to tempt the King concerning his offence,
Fifteen Soldiers the most part Countrey men,
The last shall be his life, and the best part of his Estate.

Au deserteur de la grande Fortresse,
Apres qu'aura son lieu abandonné,
Son adversaite fera grand provesse,
L'Empereur tost mort sera condamné.

65 After that the desertor of the great Fort,
Shall have forsaken his place,
His adversary shall do so great feats,
That the Emperor, shall soon be condemned to death.

Sous couleur fainte de sept testes rasces,
Seront sormez divers explorateurs,
Puits & Fontains de poison arrousées,
Au Fort de Genes humains devorateurs.

66 Under the fained colour of seven shaven heads,
Shall divers spies be framed,
Wells and Fountains shall be sprinkled with poison,
In the Fort of Genoa shall be humane devourers.

L'An que Saturne & Mars esgaux combust,
L'Air fort seiché, longue trajection,
Par feux secrets d'ardeur grands lieux adust,
Peu pluye, Vent chauds, Guerres, Incursions.

67 In the year that Saturn and Mars shall be fiery,
The Air shall be very dry, in many Countreys,
By secret fires, many places shall be burnt with heat,
There shall be scarcity of Rain, hot Winds, Wars, in-roads.

En l'an bien proche non esloigné de Venus.
Les deux plus grands de l'Asie & d'Aphrique,
Du Rhine & Ister qu'on dira sont venus,
Cris pleurs à Malthe, & costé Ligustique.

68 In a year that is to come shortly, and not far from Venus,
The two greatest ones of Asia and Affrica,
Shall be said to come from the Rhine and Ifter,
Crying and tears shall be at Maltha and in the Ligurian
shore.

La Cité grande les exilez tiendront,
Les Citadins morts, meurtris & chassez,
Ceux d'Aquilée à Parme promettront,
Monstrer l'entrée par les lieux non tracez.

69 The banished shall keep the great City,
The Citizens being dead, murdered and expelled,
Those of Aquileia shall promise to Parma,
To shew the entrance by unknown paths,

Bien contigu des grands Monts Pyrenées,
Un contre l'Aigle grand copie, adresser,
Ouvertes veines, forces exterminées,
Que jusqu'au Pau le chief viendra chasser.

70 Near the great Pyrenean Mountains.
One shall raise a great Army against the Eagle,
Veins shall be opened, forces driven out.
So that the chief shall be driven as far as the Pau.

En lieu d'Espouse les Filles trucidées,
Meurtre à grand faute, ne fera superstile,
Dedans le puis vestu inondées,
L'Espouse estainte par haut d'Aconite.

71 Instead of the Bride, the Maid shall be killed,
The murder shall be a great fault, none shall be surviving,
In the Well they shall be drowned with their Cloaths,
The Bride shall be extinguished by an high Aconite.

Les Artomiques par Agen & Lectoure,	72	The Artomiques through Agen and Lectoure,
A saint Felix feront leur Parliament,		Shall keep their Parliament at Saint Fœlix,
Ceux de Bazas viendront à la malhoure,		These of Bazas shall come in an unhappy hour,
Saisir Condon & Marsan promptement.		To seize upon Condoa and Marsan speedily.

Le neveu grand par force prouvera,	73	The great nephew by force shall provoke,
Le peche fait de Cœur pusillanime,		The fin committed by the pusillanimous heart,
Ferrare & Ast le Duc esprouvera,		Ferrara and Ast shall make tryal of the Duke,
Par lors qu'au soir sera le Pantomime		When the Pantomime shall be in the evening.

Du lac Leman & ceux des Brannonices,	74	From lake Leman, and from the Brannonues,
Tous assemblez contre ceux d'Aquitaine,		They shall be gathered against those of Aquitania,
Germans beaucoup encores plus Sovisses,		Great many Germans, and many more Switzers,
Seronts des faits avec ceux du Maine.		Shall be routed together with those of Maine.

Prest à combattre fera defection,	75	One being ready to fight, shall faint,
Chef adversaire obtiendra la victoire,		The chief of the adverse party shall obtain the victory,
Larriere garde fera defension,		The rearegard, shall withstand it out,
Les defaillans mort au blanc territoire.		Those that fall away shall die in the white Terretory,

Les Nictobriges par ceux de Perigort,	76	The Nictobriges by those of Perigort,
Seront vexez tenant jusques au Rhosne,		Shall be vexed as far as the Rhosne,
L'Associé de Gascons & Bigorre,		The associate of the Gascons and Bigorre,
Trahir le Temple le prestre estant au Prosne.		Shall betray the Church while the Priest is in his Pulpit.

Selyn Monarque, l'Italie pacifique,	77	Selyn being Monarch, Italy shall be in peace,
Regnes unis, Roy Chrestien du monde,		Kingdoms shall be united, a Christian King of the world,
Mourant voudra coucher en Terre Blesique,		Dying, shall desire to be buried in the Countrey of Blois,
Apres Pyrates avoir chassé de l'onde.		After he shall have driven the Pyrates from the Sea.

La grand Armée de la pugne civile,	78	The great Army belonging to the Civil War,
Pour de nuit Parme à l'Estranger trouvée,		Having found by night Parma possessed by Strangers,
Septante neuf meurtris dedans la Ville,		Shall kill seventy nine in the Town,
Les estrangers passez tous à l'Espée.		And put all the Strangers to the Sword,

Sang Royal fuis, Monheurt, Mars. Aiguillon,	79	Royal blood run away from Monheurt, Marsan, Aiguillon,
Remplis seront de Bourdelois les Landes,		The Landes shall be full of Bourdeloir,
Navarre, Bigorre, pointes & Aiguillons,		Navarre, Bigorre, shall have points and Pricks.
Profonds de faim, vorer de Liege, Glandes,		Being deep in hunger, they shall devour the Cork and Akorns.

Pres du grand Fleuve, grand fosse, terre egeste,
En quinze parts l'eau sera divisée,
La Cité prinse, feu, sang, cris conflict mettre,
Et la plus part concerne au collisée.

80 | Near the great River, a great pit, Earth digged out,
In fifteen parts the Water shall be divided,
The City taken, fire, blood, cries, fighting,
And the greatest part concerneth the Collisee.

Pont on fera promptement de nacelles,
Passer l'Armée du grand Prince Belgique,
Dans profondes, & non loing de Bruxelles,
Outrepassez detrenchez sept à picque.

81 | A Bridge of Boats shall suddenly be made,
To pass over the Army of the great Belgick Prince,
In deep places, and not far from Bruxelles,
Being gone over, there shall be seven cut with a Pike.

Amas s'approche venant d'Esclauonie,
L'Olestant vieux cité ruynera,
Fort desolée verra sa Romanie,
Puis la grande flamme esteindre ne sçaura.

82 | A great troop gathered, shall come from Sclavonia,
The old Olestant shall ruine a City,
He shall see his Romania very desolate,
And after that, shall not be able to quench that great flame.

Combat nocturne le vaillant Capitaine,
Vaincu fuira peu de gens profligé,
Son peuple esmeu, sedition non vain,
Son propre fils le tiendra assiegé.

83 | In a fight by night, the valliant Captain,
Being vanquished shall run away, overcome by few,
His people being moved, shall make no small mutiny,
His own son shall besiege him.

Vn grand d'Auxerre mourra bien miserable,
Chassé de ceux qui sous luy ont esté,
Serré de chaines, apres d'vn rude cable,
En l'an que Mars, Venus & Sol mis en esté.

84 | A great man of Auxerre shall die very miserably,
Being expelled by those that have been under him,
Bound with Chains, and after that with a strong Cable,
In the year that Mars, Venus and Sol shall be in a conjunction in the Summer.

Le Charbon blanc du noir sera chassé,
Prisonier fait, mené au Tombereau,
More Chameau sus pieds entrelassez,
Lors le puisné sillera l'Aubereau.

85 | The white Coal shall be expelled by the black one,
He shall be made Prisoner, carried in a Dung-cart,
His feet twisted upon a black Camel,
Then the youngest, shall suffer the Hobby to have more thread.

L'An que Saturne en eau sera conjoint,
Avecques Sol le Roy fort puissant,
A Rheims & Aix sera receu & oingt,
Apres Conquestes meurtrira innocens.

86 | In the year that Saturn in Aquarius shall be in conjunction
With Sol, the King being strong and powerful,
Shall be received and Anointed at Rheines and Aix,
After Conquest he shall murder innocent persons.

Un fils de Roy tant de Langues apprins,
A son Aisné au Regne different,
Son Pere beau au plus grand fils comprins,
Fera perir principal adherant.

87 | A son of a King having learned divers Languages,
Shall fall out with his elder Brother for the Kingdom,
His father in Law being more concerned with his elder son,
Shall cause the principal adherent to perish.

Le grand Antoine de nom de fait sordide,	88
De Phtyriaise à son dernier rongé,	
Un qui de plomb voudra este cupide,	
Passant le port d'Esleu sera plongé,	

The great Antony by name, but in effect sordid,
Of Phtyriasis shall at last be eaten up,
One that shall be covetous of Lead,
Going upon Port d'Esleu shall fall into the Water.

Trente de Londres secret conjureront,	89
Contre Leur Roy, sur le pont l'Entreprise,	
Les, Satallites là mort desgouteront,	
Un Roy esleu blond, natif de Frize.	

Thirty of London shall secretly conspire
Against their King, upon the Bridge the Plot shall be
made,
These Satellites shall taste of death,
A King shall be elected, fair, and born in Friezeland.

Les deux copies au murs ne pourrônt joindre,	90
Dans cet instant trembler Misan, Thesin,	
Faim soif, doutance si fort les viendront prendre,	
Chair, pain, ne vivres nauront un seul boucin.	

The two Armies shall not be able to joyn by the Walls,
At that instant Milan and Thesin shall tremble,
Hunger, thirst, and fear shall so seize upon them,
They shall not have a bit of meat, bread, nor victuals,

Au Duc Gaulois contraint battre au Duelle,	91
La nef de Mole, Monech naprochera,	
Tort accusé, prison perpetuelle,	
Son Fils regner avant mort taschera.	

A French Duke compelled to fight a Duel,
The Ship of Mole shall not come near Monaco,
Wrongfully accused shall have a perpetual Prison,
His son shall endeavour to Reign before his death,

Teste tranchée du vaillant Capitaine,	92
Sera jettée devant son adversaire,	
Son corps pendu de la Classea l'Ancienne,	
Confus fuira par rames avent contraire.	

The head cut off the valliant Captain
Shall be thrown down before his adversary,
His body hanged at the Sails Yard,
Confused, they shall fly with Oars against the Wind.

Un serpent veu proche du lict Royal,	93
Sera par Dame nuict chien n'abageronts,	
Lors nastre en France un Prince tant Royal,	
Du Ciel venu tous les Princes verront.	

A Serpent shall be seen near the Royal bed,
By a Lady in the night, the Dogs shall not bark,
Then shall be born in France a Prince so Royal,
Come from Heaven all the Princes shall see it,

Deux grand, freres seront chassez d'Espaigne,	94
L'aisne vaincu soubs les Monts Pyrænæes,	
Rougis Mer, Rhosne, sang Leman, d'Alemagne,	
Narbon, Blyterre, d'Agath contaminées.	

Two great Brothers shall be driven from Spain,
The elder of them shall be overcome under the Pyrenean
Mountains
Bloody Sea, Rhosne, Blood Leman of Germany,
Narbon, Bliterre of Agath polluted.

Le Regne a deux laissé bien peu tiendront,	95
Trois ans sept mois passez feront la guere,	
Les deux vestales contre rebelleront,	
Victor puisnay en Armorique Terre.	

The Kingdom being left to two, they shall keep it but a
little while,
Three years and seven months being past, they shall make
War,
The two Vestals shall rebel against them,
The youngest shall be Conquerour in the Armorick
Countrey.

La sœur aisnée de l'Isle Britannique,	**96** The eldest Sister of the Brittain Island,
Quinze ans devant le frere aura naissance,	Shall be born fifteen years before her Brother,
Par son promis moyenant verifique,	By what is promised her, and help of the truth,
Succedera au Regne de Balance.	She shall succeed in the Kingdom of Libra.

L'An que Mercure, Mars, Venus retrograde, **97** When Mercury, Mars and Venus shall retrograde,
Du grand Monarque la ligne ne faillit, The Line of the great Monarch shall be wanting,
Esleu du peuple Lusitant pres de Pactole. He shall be elected by the Lusitanians near Pactole,
Qu'en Paix & Regne viendra fort envieillir. And shall Reign in Peace a good while.

Les Albanois passeront dedans Rome, **98** The Albanians shall pass through Rome,
Moyennant Langres demipler affubles, By the means of Langres covered with half Helmets,
Marquis & Due ne pardonnes à l'homme, Marquess and Duke shall spare no man,
Feu, sang, morbilles point d'eau faillir les bles. Fire, blood, small Pox, Water shall fail us, also Corn.

L'Aisné vaillant de la fille du Roy, **99** The valliant eldest son of the daughter of the King,
Respoussera si profond les Celtiques, Shall beat back so far those of Flanders,
Qu'il mettra Foudres, combien en tel arroy, That he will cast Lightnings, O how many in such orders
Peu & loing puis profond és Hesperiques. Little and far, after shall go so deep in Spain.

Du feu Celeste au Royal edifice. **100** Fire shall fall from the skies on the Kings Palace,
Quand la lumiere de Mars defaillira, When Mars's light shall be Ecclipsed,
Sept mois grand Guerre, mort gent de malefice A great War shall be for seven months, people shall die by
Roüan, Eureux au Roy ne faillira. witchcraft.
Rouen, and Eureux shall not be wanting to the King.

Century V

Vant venuë de ruine Celtique,
Dedans le Têmple d'eux parlementerônt,
Poignard cœur d'un monté au coursier & picque,
Sans faire bruit le grand enterreront.

1 Before the coming of the ruine of Flanders,
Two shall discourse together in the Church,
Dagger in the heart by one, on Horse-back and Spurring,
Without noise they shall bury the great one.

Sept conjurez au Banquet feront luire,
Contre les trois le Fer hors de Navire :
L'un les deux classes au grand fera couduire,
Quand par le mail dernier au front luy tire.

2 Seven Conspirators at a Banquet shall make their Iron glister
Against three, out of a Ship :
One shall carry the two Fleets to the great one,
When in the Palle-malle the last shall shoot him in the forehead.

Le Successeur de la Duché viendra.
Beaucoup plus outre que la Mer de Toscane,
Gauloise branche la Florence tiendra,
Dans son Giron d'accord nautique Rane.

3 The Successor to the Dukedom shall come,
Far beyond the Tuscane Sea,
A French branch shall hold Florence
In its Lap, to which the Sea-frog shall agree.

Le gros Mastin de Cité dechassé,
Sera fasché de l'estrange Alliance,
Apres aux Champs avoir le Cerf chassé,
Le Loup & l'Ours se donront defiance.

4 The great Mastis being driven from the City,
Shall be angry at the strange Alliance,
After he shall have hunted the Hart in the Fields,
The Wolf, and the Bear shall defie one another.

Sous ombre faincte d'oster de servitude,
Peuple & Cité l'usurpera luy-mesmes,
Pire fera par fraus de jeune pute,
Livré au Champ lisant le faux poësme.

5 Under the fained shadow of freeing people from slavery,
He shall usurpe the people and City for himself;
He shall do worse by the deceit of a young Whore,
For he shall be betrayed in the field reading a false proem.

Au Roy l'Augur sur le chef la main mettre,
Viendra prier pour la Paix Italique,
A la main gauche viendra changer le Sceptre,
Du Roy viendra Empereur pacifique.

6 The Augur shall come to put his hand upon the Kings head,
And pray for the Peace of Italy,
In the left hand he shall change the Scepter,
Of a King he shall become a peaceful Emperour.

Du Triumuir seront trouvez les os,
Cherchant profond Thresor ænigmatique,
Ceux d'alentour ne seront en repos,
Ce concaver Marbre & plomb Metallique.

7 The bones of the Triumuir shall be found out,
When they shall seek for a deep and ænigmatical Treasure,
Those there about shall not be in rest,
This concavity shall be Marble and Metallick Lead.

Sera laissé feu vif, mort caché,
Dedans les Globes horrible espouvantable,
De nuict a classe Cité en poudre lasché,
La Cité à feu, l'ennemy favourable.

8 The fire shall be left burning, the dead man shall be hid,
Within the Globes terrible and fearful,
By night the Fleet shall shoot against the City,
The City shall be on fire, the enemy shall be favourable unto it.

Jusques au fond la grand Arche Molüe,
Par chef Captif l'amy anticipé,
Naistra de Dame front, face cheveluë,
Lors par astuce Duc à mort attrapé.

9 To the bottom of the great Arch Malüe,
By a Captain that is a Prisoner, the friend shall be anticipated,
One shall be born of a Lady with a hoary face and forehead,
Then by craft shall a Duke be put to death.

Un chef Celtique dans le conflict blessé,
Aupres de Cave, voiant, siens mort abattre,
De sang & playes & d'ennemis pressé,
Est se couru par incogneus de quattre.

10 A General of Flanders wounded in Battle,
Near a Cellar, seeing death to overthrow his people,
Being much oppressed with blood, wounds and enemies,
Is succoured by four unknown.

Mer par solaires seure passera,
Ceux de Venus tiendronr toute l'Affrique,
Leur Regne plus Saturne n'occupera,
Et changera la part Asiatique.

11 By solaries she shall pass secure,
Those of Venus shall hold all Africa,
Saturn shall hold their Kingdom no longer,
And shall change the Asiatick part,

Au pres du lac Leman sera conduite,
Par garse estrange Cité voulant trahir,
Avant son meurtre à Ausbourg la grand suite,
Et ceux du Rhin la viendront envahir.

12 Near the Leman lake shall be a Plot,
By a strange Whore to betray a City,
Before she be kill'd her great retinue will come to Ausbourg,
And those of the Rhine shalt come to invade her.

Par grand fureur le Roy Romain Belgique,
Veexer voudra par phalange Barbare,
Furent grinssent chassera gent Lybique,
Depuis Pannons jusque Hercules la bare.

13 Through great anger the Roman Belgick King,
Shall come to vex with Barbarian Troops,
Gnashing with fury, he shall draw away the Lybian people,
From the Pannons as far as Hercules.

Saturne & Mars en Leo Espagne-captisue,
Par chef Lybique au conflict attrapé,
Proche de Malte, Herode Prinse vive,
Et Romain Sceptre sera par Coq frappé.

14 Saturn and Mars being in Leo, Spain shall be captive,
By a Lybian General taken in the Battle,
Near Malta, an Heirse shall be taken alive,
And the Roman Scepter shall be strucken by the Cock.

En navigant Captif prins grand pontife,
Grand apres faillir les clercs tumultuez,
Second esleu absent son bien debife,
Son favory Bastard à mort tué.

15 In Sailing a Pope shall be taken Captive;
After which, shall be a great uproar amongst the Clergy,
A second absent elected, consumeth his goods,
His favourite Bastard shall be killed.

A son haut prix plus la larme Sabæe,
D'humaine chair par mort en cendre mettre,
L'Isle Pharos par Croisars pertubée,
Alors qua Rhodes paroistra dur espectre.

16 The Sabæan Tear shall be no more at its high price,
To turn humane flesh by death into ashes,
The Island Pharos shall be troubled by Croisars,
When at Rhodes shall a hard Phantasm appear.

De nuit passant le Roy pres d'une Andronne,
Celuy de Cipres & principal querre,
Le Roy failly la main fuit long du Rhosne,
Les conjurez liront la à mort mettre.

17 | The King going along by night near an Andronne,
He of Cyprus and chief of the War,
The King having missed the hand, runneth away along by the Rhosne,
The Conspirators shall put him to death there.

De duel mourra l'infelix profligé,
Celebrera son vitrix l'hecatombe,
Pristine loy, franc edict redigé,
Le mur & Prince septiesme ira au tombe.

18 | The unhappy being overcome, shall die for grief,
His Victrix shall celebrate the Hecatomb,
The fromer Law and free Edict shall be brougt again,
The wall and seventh Prince shall go to the Grave.

Le grand Royal d'Or, d'Airain augmenté,
Rompu la pache par jeune ouverte querre,
Peuple affligé par un chef lamenté,
De sang barbare sera couverte Terre.

19 | The great Golden Royal, being increased with Copper,
The agreement being broken by a young man, there shall be open War,
People afflicted by the loss of a General lamented,
The ground shall be covered with barbarous blood.

De là les Alpes grande Armée passera,
Un peu devant naistre monstre vapin,
Prodigieux, & subit tournera,
Le grand Toscan à son lieu plus propin.

20 | Beyond the Alpes shall a great Army go, and
A little before shall be born a Vapin Monster,
Prodigious and suddenly the great Toscan
Shall return to his nearest place.

Par le trespas du Monarque Latin,
Ceux quil aura par Regne secourus,
Le feu livra divisé le butin,
La mort publique aux hardis accourus.

21 | By the death of the Latine Monarque,
Those that he shall have succourned in his Reign.
The fire shall shine, the booty shall be divided,
The stout comers in shall be put to publick death.

Avant, qu'a Rome grand aye rendu l'Ame,
Effrayeur grande à l'Armée estrangere,
Par escadrons l'embusche pres de Parme,
Puis les deux rouges ensemble feront chere.

22 | Before that a great man yeildeth up his Soul at Rome,
The Army of strangers shall be put into a great fright,
By Squadrons the ambush shall be nearr Parma.
After that, the two red ones shall make good cheer together.

Les deux contens seront unis ensemble,
Quand la pluspart à Mars seront conjoints,
Le grand d'Affrique en effrayeur & tremble,
Duumuirat par la classe desjoint.

23 | The two contended shall be united together,
When the most part shall be joyned to Mars,
The great one of Africa shall be in fear and terrour,
Duumuirat shall by the pursuit be disjointed.

Le Regne & Roy soubs Venus eslevé,
Saturne aura sus Jupiter Empire,
La Loy & Regne par Jupiter levé,
Par Saturnins endurera le pire.

24 | The Kingdom and King being raised under Venus,
Saturn shall have power over Jupiter,
The Law and Reign raised by Jupiter,
Shall be put to the worse by the Saturnins.

Le Prince Arabe, Mars, Sol, Venus, Lion,	25
Regne d'Eglise par Mer succombera,	
Devers la Perse bien pres d'un Million,	
Bizance, Ægypte, Ver. Serp. invadera.	

25
The Arabian Prince, Mars, Sol. Venus, Leo,
The Kingdom of the Church shall be overcome by Sea
Towards Persia very near a Million,
Byzance, Ægypt, Ver. Serp. shall invade.

La gent esclave par un heur Martial,
Viendra en haut degré tant eslevée,
Changeront Prince, naistra un Provincial,
Passer la Mer copie aux Monts levée.

26
The Slavish Nation shall by a Martial luck
Be raised to so high a degree,
That they shall change their Prince, and elect one among themselves,
They shall cross the Sea with an Army raised in the Mountains.

Par feu & armes non loin de la Mar negro,
Viendra de Perse occuper Trebisonde,
Trembler Pharos, Metelin, Sol alegro,
De sang Arabe d'Adrie couvert l'Onde.

27
By Fire and Sword not far from the black Sea,
They shall come from Persia to seize upon Trebisonde,
Pharos and Methelin shall quake, Sun be merry,
The Sea of Adria shall be covered with Arabian blood.

Le bras pendu & la jambe liée,
Visage pasle, au sein poignard caché,
Trois qui seront jurez de la meslée,
Au grand de Genes sera le Fer lasché.

28
The arm hanging, and the leg bound,
With a pale face, a Dagger in the bosom,
Three that shall be sworn to the fray,
To the great one of Genoa the Iron shall be darted.

La liberté ne sera recouvrée,
L'Occupera noir, fier, vilain, inique;
Quand la matiere du Pont sera ouvrée,
D'Hister, Venise faschée la Republique.

29
The liberty shall not be recovered,
It shall be occupied, by a black, fierce, and wicked villain ;
When the work of the Hister-Bridge shall be ended,
The Venetian Common-wealth shall be vexed.

Tout a l'entour de la grande Cité,
Seront soldats logez par Champs & Villes,
Donner l'assaut Paris, Rome incité,
Sur le Pont sera faite grand pille.

30
Round about the great City,
Soldiers shall lye in the Fields and Towns,
Paris shall give the Assault, Rome shall be attached;
Then upon the Bridge shall be great plundering.

Par Terre Attique chef de la sapience,
Qui de present est la Rose du Monde,
Pour ruiné, & sa grand preeminence,
Sera subdite & naufrage des Ondes.

31
In the Countrey of Attica which is the head of wisdom,
And now is the Rose of the World,
A Bridge shall be ruinated with its great preeminence,
It shall be subdned, and made a wrack by the Waves.

Ou tout bon est, tout bien Soleil & Lune,
Est abondant, sa ruine s'approche,
Le Ciel s'advance a changer ta fortune,
En mesme estat que la septiesme Roche.

32
Where all well is, all good O Sun and Moon,
Is existent, his ruine draweth near,
The Heaven is making hast to change thy fortune,
Into the same case as the seventh Rock is.

Des principaux de Cité rebellée,	33	Of the chief men in a rebelled City,
Qui tiendront fort pour liberté r'avoir,		Who shall stand out to recover their liberty,
Detrencher masles, infælice meslée,		The Males shall be cut in pieces, O unhappy quarrel !
Cris, hurlemens à Nantes piteux voir.		Cries and houlings, it shall be pity to see at Nantes.
Du plus profond de l'occident Anglois,	34	From the deepest Westerly part of England,
Où est le chef de l'Isle Britanique,		Where the chief of the Britain Island is,
Entrera classe ens Garonne par Blois,		A fleet shall come into the Garonne by Blaye,
Par Vin & Sel faux cachez aux barriques.		By Wine and Salt fire shall be hidden in Barrels,
Par Cité franche de la grand Mer Seline,	35	By a free City of the Selyne Sea,
Qui porte encor l'estomach la pierre,		Which carrieth yet the stone in the Stomach,
Angloise classe viendra soubs la bruine,		An English Fleet shall cometh under a fog,
Prendre un rameau de grand ouverte querre.		To taketh a branch of a great open War.
De sœur le frere par simulte feintise,	36	The Brother of the Sister, with a fained dissimulation,
Viendra mesler rosee en Mineral,		Shall mix Dew with Mineral,
Sur la placente donne à vieille tardive,		In a Cake given to a slow old woman,
Meurt le goustant, sera simple rural.		She dieth tasting of, the deed shall be simple, and Countrey like.
Trois cens seront d'un vouloir & accord,	37	Three hundred shall be of one mind and agreement,
Qui pour venir au bout de leur attainte,		That they may compass their ends,
Vingt mois apres tous eux & leurs record,		Twenty months after by all them and their partners,
Leur Roy trahy simulant haine, feinte.		Their King shall be betrayed, by dissembling a fained hatred.
Ce grand Monarque qu'au mort succedera,	38	The great Monarch that shall succeed to the great one,
Donnera vie illicite & lubrique,		Shall lead a Life unlawfull, and lecherous,
Par nonchalance à tous concedera,		By carelessness he shall give to all,
Qua la parfin faudra la loy Salique,		So that in Conclusion the Salique Law shall fail.
Du vray rameau de fleur de Lis issu,	39	Issued out of the true branch of the City,
Mis & logé heritier d'Hetrurie,		He shall be set for Heir of Hetruruia,
Son sang antique de longue main tissu,		His ancient blood waved by a long while,
Fera Florence florir en l'Armoirie.		Shall cause Florence to flourish in the Scutcheon.
Le sang Roial sera si tres meslé,	40	The Royal blood shall be so much mixed,
Contraints seront Gaulois de l'Hesperie,		The French shall be constrained by the Spaniards,
On attendra que terme soit coulé,		They shall stay till the term be past,
Et que memoire de la voix soit perie.		And the remembrance of the voice be over.

Nay soubs les ombres & journée nocturne,	41	Being born in the shadows and nocturnal time,
Sera en Regne & bonté Souveraine,		He shall be a Soveraign in Kingdom and bounty,
Fera renaistre son sang de l'antique Urne,		He shall cause his blood to come again from the ancient Urn,
Renouvelant siecle d'Or pour l'airain,		Renewing a golden Age instead of a brazen one.

Mars eslevé en son plus haut befroy,
Fera retraire les Allobrox de France,
La gent Lombarde fera si grand effroy,
A ceux de l'Aigle comprins soubs la Balance.

42   Mars being elevated in its higher Steepte,
Shall cause the Allobrox to retreat from France,
The people of Lombardy shall be in so great fear
Of those of the Eagle comprehended under Libra.

La grand ruine des sacrez ne sesloigne,
Provence, Naples, Scicile, Seez & Ponce,
En Germanie, au Rhin & la Cologne,
Vexez à mort par tous ceux de Magonce.

43   The great ruine of the sacred things is not far off,
Provence, Naples, Sicily, Sez and Ponce,
In Germany towards the Rhyne and Colen,
They shall be vexed to death by those of Moguntia.

Par Mer le rouge sera prins the Pyrates,
La paix sera par son moyen troublée,
L'une & l'auare commettra par fainct acte,
Au grand Pontife sera l'Armée doublée.

44   By Sea the red one shall be taken by Pyrates,
The peace by that means shall be troubled,
He shall commit anger and coveteousness by a feigned action,
The High Priest shall have a double Army.

Le grand Empire sera tost desolé,
Et translaté pres d'Arduenne silve,
Les deux batards par l'aisné decollé,
Et Regnera Ænodarbnez de milve.

45   The great Empire shall soon be made desolate,
And shall be translated near the Forrest of Arden,
The two Bastards shall have their heads cut off by the eldest son,
And he that shall reign, shall be Bronzebeard.

Par Chapeaux rouges querelles & nouveaux scismes,
Quand on aura esleu le Sabinois,
On produira contre luy grands sophismes,
Et sera Rome leslée par Albanois.

46   By red Hats, quarrels and new schismes,
When the Sabin shall be Elected,
Great sophismes shall be produced against him,
And Rome shall be endamaged by the Albanois.

Le grand Arabe marchera bien avant,
Trahy sora par le Bisantinois :
L'Antique Rhodes luy viendra au devant,
Et plus grand malpar Austre Pannonois.

47   The great Arabian shall proceed a great way,
He shall be betrayed by the Bisantines,
The ancient Rhodes shall come to meet him ;
And a greater evil by a South wind from Hungary.

Apres la grande affliction du sceptre,
Deux ennemis par eux seront defaicts :
Classe d'Affrique aux Pannons viendra naistre,
Par Mer & Terre seront horribles faicts.

48   After the great afflictions of the Scepter,
Two enemies shall be overcome by themselves,
A Fleet of Affrica shall be born to the Hungarians.
By Sea and Land shall be horrid facts.

Nul de l'Espagne, mais de l'antique France, *Sera esleu pour le tremblant nacelle,* *A l'ennemy sera faicte fiance,* *Qui dans son Regne sera peste cruelle.*	49	None out of Spain, but of the ancient France, Shall be Elected to govern the tottering Ship. The enemy shall be trusted, Who to his Kingdom shall be a cruel plague.
L'An que les Freres du Lys seront en Aage, *L'Un d'euz tiendra la grand Romanie :* *Trembler les Monts, ouvert Latin passage,* *Bache macher contre Fort d'Armenie.*	50	In the year that the Brethern of the Lillies shall be at Age, One of them shall hold the great Romanie : The Mountains shall tremble, the Latine Passage shall be opened, A Bassha shall march against the Fort of Armenia.
La gent de Dace, d'Angleterre, Polone, *Et de Boësme feront nouvelle ligue,* *Pour passer outre d'Hercules la Colonne,* *Barcins, Tyrrans dresser cruelle brigue.*	51	The people of Dacia, England, and Poland, And of Bohemia shall make a new League, To go beyond Hercules Pillars, Barcins and Thyrrens shall make a cruel plot.
Un Roy sera qui donra l'opposite. *Les exilz esleuez sur le Regne,* *De sang nager la gent caste hypolite,* *Et florira long-temps sous telle enseigne.*	52	A King shall be, who shall be opponent To the banished persons raised upon the Kingdom, The chast Hippolite Nation shall swim in blood, And shall flourish a great under such an Ensign:
La Loy du Sol, & Venus contendans, *Appropriant l'Esprit de Prophetie :* *Ne l'un ne l'autre ne seront entendus,* *Par Sol tiendra la Loy du grand Messie.*	53	The Law of the Sun and Venus contending, Appropriating the spirit of Prophecy, Neither one nor the other shall be heard, By Sol the Law of the great Messias shall subsist.
Du pont Exine, & la grand Tartarie, *Un Roy sera qui viendra voir la Gaule,* *Transpercera Alane & l'Armenie,* *Et dans Bisance Lairra sanglante Gaule.*	54	From the Euxin Sea, and Great Tartaria, A King shall come to see France, He shall go through Alanea and Armenia, And shall leave a bloody rod in Constantinople.
De la felice Arabie contrade, *Maistra puissant de la loy Mahometique,* *Vexer l'Espagne, conquester la Grenade,* *Et plus par Mer la gent Ligustique.*	55	Out of the Countery of Arabia the happy, Shall be born a powerful man of the Mahometan Law, Who shall vex Spain and conquer Grenada; And by Sea shall come to the Ligurian-Nation.
Par le traspas du tres-vieillard Pontife, *Sera esleu Romain de bon aage,* *Qui sera dit que le siege debiffe,* *Et long tiendra & de picquant courage.*	56	By the death of the very old high Priest, Shall be a Roman elected of good age, Of whom shall be said, that he dishonoureth the Seat, And shall live long, and be of a fierce courage.

Istra du Mont Gaulfier & Aventine,	57	One shall go out of the Mountains Gaulsier and Aventine,
Qui par le trou advertira l'Armée,		Who through a hole shall give notice to the Army,
Entre deux Rocs sera prins le butin,		Between two Rocks the booty shall be taken,
De Sext. Mansol faillir la renommée.		Of Sext. Monsol shall loose his renown.

De l'Aque duct d'Vticense, Gardoing,
Par la Forest & Mort inacessible,
Emmy du pont sera taché ou poing,
Le chef Nemans qui tant sera terrible.

58 From the Conduit of Uticense and Gardoing,
Through the Forrest and unacessible Mountain,
In the middle of the Bridge shall be tyed by the Wrist,
The chief Nemans, that shall be so terrible.

Au chef Anglois à Nismes trop sejour,
Devers l'Espagne au secours Ænobarbe,
Plusieurs mourront par Mars ouvert ce jour,
Quand en Artois faillir estoile en Barbe.

59 The chief English shall stay too long at Nismes,
A red haird man shall go to the succours of Spain,
Many shall die by open War that day,
When in Artois the Star shall fail in the Beard.

Par teste rase viendra bien mal eslire,
Plus que sa charge ne porte passera,
Si grand fureur & rage fera dire,
Qua feu & sang tout Sexe trenchera.

60 By a shaven head shall be made an ill choice,
That shall go beyond his commission,
He shall proceed with so great fury and rage,
That he shall put both Sexes to fire and Sword.

L'Enfant du grand nestant à sa naissance,
Subjuguera les hauts Monts Apennis,
Fera trembler tous ceux de la balance,
Depuis Monts Feurs jusques à Mont Senis.

61 The Child of the great man that was not at his birth,
Shall subdue the high Apennine Mountains,
Shall make all those under Libra to quake,
From Mount Feurs, as far as Mount Senis.

Sur les Rochers sang on verra pleuvoir,
Sol Orient, Saturne Occidental,
Pres d'Orgon Guerre, à Rome grand mal voir,
Nefs parfondrées, & prins Tridental.

62 It shall rain blood upon the Rocks,
The sun being in the East, and Saturn in the West,
War shall be near Oigon, and great evil at Rome,
Ships shall be cast away, and the Trident be taken.

De vaine emprise l'honneur indue plainte,
Galliots errants par Latins froid, faim vagues,
Non loin du Tybre de sang la Terre teinte,
Et sur humaine seront diverses plagues.

63 Honour bringeth a complaint against a vain undertaking,
Galleys shall wander through the Latin Seas, cold, hunger,
Waves,
Not far from Tyber the Earth shall be died with blood,
And upon Mankind shall be several plagues.

Les assembles par repos du grand nombre,
Par Terre & Mer conseil contremandé,
Pres de l'Antonne, Genes, Nue, de lombre,
Par Champs & Villes le Chef contrebandé.

64 The gathered by the rest of the great numbers,
By Land and Sea shall recall their Councel,
Near Autonne, Genes, and Nue of the shadow,
In Fields and Towns the Chief shall be one against another.

Subit venu l'effrayeur sera grande,
Des principaux de l'affaire cachés :
Et Dame Embraise plus ne sera en veüe,
Et peu à peu seront le grands fachés.

Sous les antiques edifices Vestaux,
Non esloignez d'Aqueduct ruiné,
De Sol & Lune sont les luissans metaux,
Ardente Lampe Trajan d'or buriné.

Quand Chef Perouse n'osera sa Tunique,
Sens au counvert tout nud s'expolier :
Seront prins sept faict Aristocratique,
Le Pere & Fils morts par pointe au collier.

Dans le Danube & le Rhine viendra boire,
Le grand Chameau, ne sen repentira :
Trembler le Rhosne & plus fort ceux de Loire,
Et pres des Alpes Coq le ruinera.

Plus ne sera le grand en faux sommeil,
L'Inquietude viendra prendre repos,
Dresser Phalange, d'Or, Azur, & vermeil,
Subjuguer Affrique & ronger jusqu'aux os.

Les Regions subietes à la Balance,
Feront trembler les Monts par grande Guerre,
Captifs tout sexe, avec toute Bizance,
Qu'on criera à l'Aube Terre à Terre.

Par la fureur d'un qui attendra l'eau,
Par la grand rage tout l'exercite esmeu,
Charge des Nobles a dixsept Barreaux,
Au long du Rhosne tard Messager venud.

Pour le plaisir d'Edict voluptueux,
On meslera la poison dans la Loy,
Venus sera en cours si vertueux,
Qu'obfusquera du Soleil tout alloy.

65 | One coming upon a suddain shall cause a great fear,
To the Chief men that were hidden and concerned in the business,
And the Lady Ambraise shall be seen no more,
And by little and little the great one shall be angry.

66 | Under the ancient edifices of the Vestals,
Not far from an Aqueduct ruinated,
Are the bright metals of Sun and Moon,
A burning Lamp of Trajan of ingraven gold.

67 | When the Chief of Perouse shall not dare without a Tunick,
To expose himself naked in the dark,
Seven shall be taken for setting up Aristocracy,
The Father and the Son shall die by pricks in the Collar.

68 | In Danubius and the Rhine shall come to drink,
The great Camel, and shall not repent,
The Rhosne shall tremble and more of Loire,
And near the Alpes the Cock shall ruine him.

69 | The great one shall be no more in a false sleep,
The restlessness shall take rest,
He shall raise an Army of Gold and Azure,
He shall conquer Affrica and gnaw it to the bones.

70 | The Regions under the sign of Libra,
Shall make the Mountains quake with great War,
Slaves of all sexes, with all Bizance,
So that in the dawning of the day, they shall cry to Land to Land.

71 | By the fury of one staying for the Water,
By his great rage the whole Army shall be troubled,
There shall be seventeen Boats full of Nobleman,
Along the Rhosne, the Messenger shall come too late.

72 | By the pleasure of a voluptuous proclamation,
The poison shall be mixed in the Law,
Venus shall be in so great request,
That it shall darken all the allay of the sun.

Persecutée sera de dieu l'Eglise,	**73** The Church of God shall be persecuted,
Et les Saints Temples seront expoliez,	And the holy Temples shall be spoiled,
L'Enfant la mere mettra nud en chemise,	The Child shall turn out his Mother in her Smock,
Seront Arabes au Polons ralliez.	Arrabians shall agree with Polonians.

De sang Trojen naistra cœur Germanique,　**74** Of Trojan blood shall be born a German heart.
Qui deviendra en si haute puissance,　Who shall attain to so high a power,
Hors chassera gent estrange Arabique,　That he shall drive away the strange Arrabian Nation,
Tournant l'Eglise en pristine préeminence.　Restoring the Church to her former splendor.

Montera haut sur le bien plus à dextre,　**75** He shall go up upon the good more on the right hand,
Demourra assis sur la pierre carrée,　He shall stay fitting upon the square stone,
Vers le midy posé a la senestre,　Towards the South ; being ser, on the left hand,
Baston tortu en main, bouche serrée.　A crooked stick in his hand, and his mouth shut.

En lieu libere tendra son Pavillon,　**76** He shall pitch his Tent in the open air,
Et ne voudra en Citez prendre place,　Refusing to lodge in the City,
Aix, Carpentras, Lisle, Volce, Mont Cavaillon,　Aix, Carpentras, Lisle Voice, Mont Cavaillon,
Par tous ces lieux abolira sa trace.　In all those places, he shall abolish his trace.

Tous les degres d'honneur Ecclesiastique,　**77** All the degrees of Ecclesiastical honour,
Seront changez en Dial Quirinal,　Shall be changed into a Dial Quirinal,
En Martial, quirinal, Flaminique,　Into Martial, Quirinal, Flaminick;
Puis un Roy de France le rendra Vulcanal.　After that, a King of France shall make it Vulcanal.

Les deux unis ne tiendront longuement,　**78** The two united shall not hold long,
Et dans treize ans au Barbare Satrape,　Within thirteen years to the Barbarian Satrape,
Aux deux costez feront tel perdement,　They shall cause such loss on both sides,
Qu'un benira le Barque & sa cappe.　That one shall bless the Boat and its covering.

La sacrée Pompe viendra baisser les aisles,　**79** The sacred Pomp shall bow down her wings,
Par la venue de grand Legislateur,　At the coming of the great Lawgiver,
Humble haussera, vexera les rebelles,　He shall raise the humble and vex the rebellious,
Naistra sur Terre aucun Æmulateur.　No Emulator of his shall be born.

L'Ogmion grande Bizance approchera,　**80** The Ogmion shall come near great Bizance,
Chassée sera la Barbarique ligue,　And shall expel the Barbarian League,
Des deux Loix l'une unique lachera,　Of the two Laws, the wicked one shall yeild,
Barbare & Franche en perpetuelle brigue.　The Barbarian, and the French shall be in perpetual jar.

L'Oyseau Royal sur la Cité solaire,
Sept mois devant fera nocturne augure :
Mur d'Orient cherra Tonnerre esclaire,
Sept jours aux Portes les ennemies à l'heure.

81 | The Royal Bird upon the solar City,
Seven Months together shall make a nocturn augury,
The Eastern Wall shall fall, the Lightning shall shine,
Then the enemies shall be at the Gate for seven days.

Au conclud pache hors la Forteresse,
Ne sortira celuy en desespoir mis:
Quand ceux d'Arbois, de Langres, contre Bresse,
Auront mis Dolle bouscade d'ennemis,

82 | Upon the agreement made, out of the Fort,
Shall not come he that was in despair,
When those of Arbois of Langres, against Bresse,
Shall have put in Dolle an Ambuscado of foes.

Ceux qui auront entreprins subvertir,
Nompareil Regne, puissant & invincible,
Feront par fraude, nuicts trois advertir,
Quand le plus grand à Table lira Bible.

83 | Those that shall have undertaken to subvert
The Kingdom that hath no equal in power and victories,
Shall cause by fraud, notice to be given for three nights together,
When the greatest shall be reading a Bible at the Table.

Naistra du Gouphre & Cité immesurée,
Nay de parens obscurs & tenebreux :
Qui la puissance du grand Roy reverée,
Voudra destruire par Roüen & Eureux.

84 | One shall be born out of the Gulf and the unmeasurable City,
Born of Parents obscure and dark,
Who by the means of Rouen and Eureux,
Will go about to destroy the power of the great King.

Par les Sueves & lieux circonvoisins,
Seront en guerre pour cause des nuées :
Gammmares, locustes & cousins,
Du Leman fautes seront bien desnuées.

85 | Through Swedeland and the Neighbouring places,
By reason of the Clouds shall fall to War,
The Lobstars, Grass-hoppers and Gnats,
The faults of Leman shall appear very naked.

Par les deux testes, & trois bras separéz,
La grande cité sera par eaux vexée :
Des Grands d'entre eux par esgaréz,
Par teste Perse Byzance fort pressée.

86 | Divided in two heads and parted into three arms,
The great City shall be troubled with Waters,
Some great ones among them scattered by banishment,
By a Persian head Byzanee shall be sore oppressed.

L'An que Saturne hors de servage,
Au franc terroir sera d'eau inondé,
De sang Troien sera son mariage,
Et sera seur d'Espagnols circundé.

87 | In the year that Saturn out of slavery,
In the free Countrey shall be drowned by water,
With Troian blood his marriage shall be,
And for certain he shall be hedged about with Spaniards.

Sur le Sablon par un hideux Deluge,
Des autres Mers trouvé Monstre Marin,
Proche du lieu sera fait un refuge,
Tenant Savone esclave de Turin.

88 | Upon the sand through an hideous Deluge,
Of other Seas, shall be found a Sea Monster,
Near to that place shall be made a Sanctuary,
Which shall make Savone a slave to Turin.

Dedans Hongrie par Boheme, Navarre,
Et par Banieres seintes seditions,
Par fleurs de Lis paix portant la barre,
Contre Orleans fera esmotions.

89 In Hungaria, through Bohemia and Navarre,
And by banners fained seditions,
Through flower de Luce the Countrey that wears the Bar,
Against Orleans shall make commotions.

Dans le Cyclades, en Corinthe, & Larisse,
Dedans Sparte tout le Peloponese,
Si grand famine, peste far faux conisse,
Neuf mois tiendra & tout le Cherronese.

90 In the Cyclades, in Corinthe, and Larisse,
In Sparta, and all Peloponesus,
There shall be so great a famine and plague by false arts,
That shall last nine months in Chersonesus.

Au grand marché qu'on dit des mensongiers,
Du tout Torrent & Champ Athenien,
Seront surpris par les Chevaux legers,
Par Albanois, Mars, Leo, Sat. au Versien.

91 In the great Market called of the Liars,
Which is all Torrent and Athenian Field,
They shall be surprised by the light Horse,
Of the Albanese, Mars in Leo, Saturn in Aquarius.

Apres le siege tenu dixsept ans,
Cinq changeront en tel revolu terme,
Puis sera l'un esleu de mesme temps,
Qui des Romains ne sera trop conforme.

92 After the seat possessed seventeen years,
Five shall change in such a space of time;
After that, one shall be elected at the same time,
Who shall not be very conformable to the Romans.

Soubs le terroir du rond Globe Lunaire,
Lors que sera dominateur Mercure,
L'Isle d'Escosse fera un Lumenaire,
Que les Anglois mettra à deconfiture.

93 Under the Territory of the round Lunary Globe,
When Mercury shall be Lord of the ascendant,
The Island of Scotland shall make a Luminary,
That shall put the English to an overthrow.

Translatera en la grand Germanie,
Brabant & Flandres, Gand, Bruges & Bolongne,
La trefue fainte le grand Duc d'Armenie,
Assaillira Vienne & la Coloigne.

94 He shall translate into the great Germany,
Brabant, Flanders, Gand, Bruges, and Bullee;
The truce fained, the great Duke of Armania,
Shall assult Vienna and Colen.

Nautique rame invitera les umbres,
Du grand Empire lors viendra conciter,
La mer Ægée des lignes des Encombres,
Empeschant londe Tirrhene de flotter.

95 The Sea Oare shall invite the shades,
Of the great Empire, then shall it come to stir,
The Ægean Sea, with lines of Encumbers,
Hindering the Tirrhene Sea to roll.

Sur le milieu du grand monde la Rose,
Pour nouveaux faits sang public espandu,
A dire uray on aura bouche close,
Lors au besoing viendra tard lattendu.

96 The Rose shall be in the middle fo the great world,
Blood shall be publicly spilt for new deeds;
To say the truth, everyone shall stop his mouth,
Then at the time of need shall come long looked for.

Le na difforme par horreur suffoqué,
Dans la Cité du grand Roy habitable,
L'edit severy des captifs revoqué,
Gresle & Tonnerre, Condon inestimable.

97 | The deformed born shall suffocate,
In the habitable City of the great King,
The severe, edict of the captives revoked,
Hail and thunder, Condom inestimable.

A quarante huit degré Climacterique,
A fin de Cancer si grande secheresse,
Poisson en Mer, Fleuve, Lac cuit hectique,
Bearn, Bigorre, par feu Ciel en detresse.

98 | At the Climacterical degree of eight and forty,
At the end of Cancer, shall be such a drought,
That Fish in the Sea, River, and Lake shall be boiled to a consumption,
Bearn and Bigorre by Heavenly fire shall be in distress.

Milan, Ferrare, Turin & Aquilee,
Capue, Brundis vexez par geut Celtique,
Par le Lion & Phalange Aquilée,
Quand Rome aura le chef vieux Britannique.

99 | Milan, Ferrara, Turin, and Aquileia,
Capne, Brundis, Shall be vexed by the French,
By the Lion and troop of Aquileia,
When Rome shall have an old Brittanick Head.

Le boutefeu par son feu attrapé,
Du feu du Ciel à Tartas & Gomminge,
Foix, Aux, Mazere, haut vieillard escapé,
Par ceux de Hass, de Saxe & de Turinge.

100 | The incendiary shall be overtaken by his own fire,
Heavenly fire shall at Tartas and Cominge,
Foix, Auch, Mazerre, a tall old man shall escape,
By the means of those of Hessia, Saxony, and Turinge.

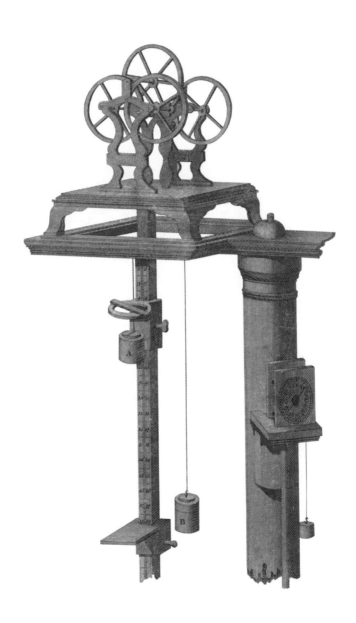

Century VI

Utour des Monts Pyrenees grand amas,
De gent estrange secourir Roy nouveau,
Pres de Garonne du grand Temple du Mas,
Un Romain Chef le craindra dedans
l'Eau.

1 About the Pyrenean Mountains there shall be a great gathering
Of strange Nations to succour a new King,
Near Garonne and the great Temple of Mas,
A Roman Captain shall fear him in the Water.

En la cens octante plus ç moins,
On attendra le siecle bien estrange,
En l'an sept cens ç trois cieux en tesmoins,
Regnes plusieurs un à cinq feront change.

2 In the year five hundred four score more or less,
There shall be a strange Age,
In the year seven hundred and three witness Heaven,
Many Kingdoms, one to five shall be changed.

Fleuve qu'esproune le nouveau hay Celtique
Sera en grande de l'Empire discorde :
Le jeune Prince par gent Ecclesiastique,
Le Sceptre osté Corone de concorde,

3 The River that makes tryal of the new born Celtick,
Shall be at great variance with the Empire,
The young Prince shall be an Ecclesiastical person,
And have his Scepter taken off, and the Crown of concord.

Fleuve Celtique changera de Rivage,
Plus ne tiendra la Cité d'Agripine,
Tout transmué horsmis le viel Langage,
Saturn, Leo, Mars, Cancer en rapine.

4 The River of the Low-Countreys shall change her Shoare,
It shall touch no more the City of Agrippiana,
All shall be transformed, except the old Language,
Saturn, Leo, Mars, Cancer in Rapine.

Si grand famine par une pestifere.
Par pluye longue le long du Pole Artique.
Samarobryn cent lieux de l'Hemisphere,
Vivront sans loy exempt de politique.

5 So great a famine with a plague,
Through a long Rain shall come along the Artick Pole,
Somarobryn a hundred Leagues from the Hemisphere,
Shall live without Law, exempt from policy.

Apparoistra vers le septentrion,
Non loing de Cancer l'estoille cheveluë,
Suze, Sienne, Boëce, Eretrion,
Mourra de Rome grand, la nuict disperuë.

6 Twards the North shall appear,
Not far from Cancer a blazing Star,
Suza, Sienna, Boëce, Eretrion,
There shall die at Rome a great man, the night being past.

Norvege ç Dace, ç l'Isle Britanique,
Par les unis freres seront vexées,
Le chef Romain issu de sang Gallique,
Et les copies aux forests repousees.

7 Norvegia, and Dacia, and the Brittish Island,
Shall be vexed by the Brothers united.
The Roman Captain issued from French-blood,
His Forces shall be beaten back to the Forrest,

Ceux qui estoient en regne pour scavoir,
Au Royal change deviendront a pouvris,
Uns exilez sans appuy, Or navoir,
Lettréz ç lettres ne seront a grand pris.

8 Those that were in esteem for their learning,
Upon the change of a King shall become poor,
Some banished, without help, having no Gold,
Learned and leaning shall not be much valued.

Aus Temples Saints feront faits grans scandales,	9
Comptez seront par honneurs & loüanges,	
D'un que lon grave d'Argent, d'Or les Medals,	
La fin sera en tourmens bien estranges.	

To the holy Temples shall be done great scandals,
That shall be accounted for honours and praises,
By one, whole medals are graven in Gold and Silver,
The end of it shall be in very strange torments.

Un peu de temps les Temples des Couleurs,	10
De blanc & noir des deux entremessée,	
Rouges & jaunes leur embleront les leurs,	
Sang, terre, peste, faim, feu, eau affol ée.	

Within a little while the Temples of the Colours,
White and Black shall be intermixt,
Red and Yellow shall take away their Colours,
Blood, earth, plague, famine, fire, water shall destroy them.

Les sept rameaux a trois seront reduits,	11
Les plus aisnez seront surpins par mort,	
Fratricider les deux seront seduits,	
Les Conjures en dormans seront morts.	

The seven branches shall be reduced to three,
The oldest shall be surprised by death,
Two shall be said to kill Brothers,
The Conspirators shall be killed, being asleep.

Dresser Copie pour monter a l'Empire,	12
Du Vatican le sang Royal tiendra:	
Flamens, Anglois, Espagne aspire,	
Contre l'Italie & France contendra.	

To raise an Army, for so ascend unto the Empire,
Of the Vatican, the Royal blood shall endeavour,
Flemings, English, Spain shall aspire,
And shall contend against Italy and France.

Un dubieux ne viendra loing du regne,	13
La plus grand part le voudra soustenir,	
Un Capitole ne voudra point quil regne,	
Sa grande Chaire ne pourra maintenir.	

A doubtful man shall not come far from the Reign,
The greatest part will uphold him,
A Capitol will not consent that he should Reign,
His great Chair he shall not be able to maintain.

Loing de sa Terre Roy perdra la Bataille,	14
Prompt, eschapé poursuivy, suiuant pris,	
Ignare pris soubs la dorée maille,	
Soubs feint habit, & l'Ennemy surpris.	

Far from his Countrey the King shall loose a Battle,
Nimble, escaped, followed, following, taken.
Ignorantly taken under the gilded Coat of Mail,
Under a feigned habit the enemy taken.

Dessous la Tombe sera trouvé le Prince,	15
Qu'aura le pris par dessus Nuremberg :	
L'Espagnol Roy en Capricorne mince,	
Feinct & trahy par le grand Uutitemberg,	

Under the Tomb shall be found the Prince,
That shall have a price above Nuremberg,
That Spanish King in Capricorn shall be thine,
Deceived and betrayed by the great Vutitemberg.

Ce que ravy sera de jeune Milve,	16
Par les Normans de France & Picardy,	
Les noirs du Temple du lieu de Negrisilve,	
Feront aux Berge & feu de Lombardie.	

That which shall be taken from the young Kite,
By the Normans of France and Picardie,
The black ones of the Temple of the place called black Forrest.
Shall make Rendezvouz and a fire in Lombardie.

Apres les livres bruslez les Asiniers,
Contrains seront changer d'habits divers:
Les Saturnins bruslez par les meusniers,
Hors la pluspart qui ne sera convers.

Par les Physiques le grand Roy delaissé,
Par sort non art de l'Ebrieu est en vie,
Luy & son Genre au Regne haut pousé,
Grace donnée à gent qui Christ envie.

La vraye flamme engloutira la Dame,
Qui voudra mettre les Innocens a feu,
Pres de l'assaut l'exercite s'enflamme,
Quand dans Seville monstre en Bœuf sera veu.

L'vnion feinte sera peu de durée,
Des un changez reformez la plus part :
Dans les Vaisseaux sera gent endurée,
Lors aura Rome un nouveau Leopart.

Quant ceux du Polle Artique unis ensemble,
Et Orient grand effrayeur & crainte,
Esleu nouveau soustenu le grand tremble,
Rodes, Bisance de sang Barbare taincte.

Dedans la Terre du grand Temple Celique,
Neveu a Londres par paix feinte meurtry,
La Barque alors deviendra Schismatique,
Liberté feincte sera au corne & cry.

Despir de Roy, numismes descriez,
Peuples seront esmeus contre leur Roy,
Paix sait nouveau, Saintes Loix empirées,
Rapis onc fut en si piteux arroy.

Mars & le Sceptre se trouuera conjoint,
Dessoubs Cancer calamiteuse guerre,
Un peu apres sera nouveau Roy oingt,
Qui par long temps pacifiera la Terre.

17 | After the Books shall be burnt, the Asses,
Shall be compelled several times to change their Cloaths,
The Saturnins shall be burnt by the Millers,
Except the greater part, that shall not be discovered.

18 | The great King being forsaken by the Physicians,
Shall be kept alive by the Magick and not by the art of a Jew,
He, and his kindred shall be set at the top of the Kingdom,
Grace shall be given to a Nation that envieth Christ.

19 | The true flame shall swallow up the Lady,
That went about to burn the guiltless,
Before the Assault the Army shall be incouraged,
When in Seville, a Monster like an Ox shall be seen.

20 | The feigned union shall not last long,
Some shall be changed, others for the most part reformed,
In the Ships people shall be pen'd up,
Then shall Rome have a new Leopard.

21 | When those of the Artick Pole shall be united together,
There shall be in the East a great fear and trembling,
One shall be newly Elected, that shall bear the brunt,
Rhodes, Bisance, shall be dy'd with Barbarian blood.

22 | Within the ground of the great Cœlestial Temple,
A Nephew at London by a fained pace shall be murdered,
The Boat at the time shall become Schismatical,
A fained liberty shall be with Hue and Cry.

23 | The delight of a King, and Coin being brought lower
People shall rise against their King,
Pace newly made, Holy Laws being made worse,
Rapis was never in such a great disorder.

24 | Mars and the Scepter, being conjoined together,
Under Caneer shall be a calamitous War,
A little while after a new King shall be anointed,
Who for a long time shall pacifie the Earth.

Par Mars contraire sera la Monarchie,	25 By Mars contrary shall the Monarchy
Du grand Pescheur en trouble ruineux,	Of the great Fisherman be brought into ruinous trouble,
Jeune, noir, rouge prendra la Hierarchie,	A young, black, red shall possess himself of the Hierarchy,
Les proditeurs iront jour bruineux.	The Traitors shall undertake it on a misty day.

Quattre ans le siege quelque peu bien tiendra,   26   Four years he shall keep the Papal feel pretty well,
Un surviendra libidineux de vie,   Then shall succeed one of the libidinous life,
Ravenne & Pyse, Verone soustiendront,   Ravenna, Pisa, shall take Verona's part,
Pour eslever la Croix de Pape envie.   To raise up the Popes Cross to Life.

Dedans les Isles de cinq fleuves a un,   27   In the Islands from five Rivers to one,
Par le croissant du grand Chyren Selin,   By the increase of great Chyren Selin,
Par les bruynes de l'air fureur de l'un,   By the Frost of the Air one shall under furious,
Six eschapez, cachez fardeaux de lin.   Six shall escape, hidden within bundles of Flax.

Le grand Celtique entrera dedans Rome,   28   The great Celtique shall enter into Rome,
Menant amas d'exilez & bannis,   Leading with him a great number of banished men,
Le grand Pasteur mettra a mort tout homme,   The great Shepheard shall put to death every man,
Qui pour le Coq estoient aux Alpes unis.   This was united for the Cock near the Alpes.

La Veufve Sainte entendant les nouvelles,   29   The holy Widow hearing the News
De ses rameaux mis en perplex & trouble,   Of her Branches put in perplexity or trouble,
Qui sera duit appaiser les querelles,   That shall be skilfull in appeasing of quarrels,
Par son pourchas de Razes fera comble.   By his purchase shall make a heap of shaven heads.

Par l'apparence de feinte Saincteté,   30   By the appearance of a feigned holiness,
Sera trahy aux ennemis le siege.   The siege shall be betrayed to the enemies,
Nuict qu'on croioid dormir en seureté,   In a night that every one thought to be secure,
Pres de Brabant marcheront ceux du Liege.   Near Brabant shall march those of Liege.

Roy trouvera ce quil desiroit tant,   31   A King shall find what be so much longed for,
Quand le Prelat sera repris a tort,   When a Prelate shall be censured wrongfully,
Responce au Duc le rendra mal content,   An answer to the Duke will make him discontented,
Qui dans Milan mettra plusieurs a mort.   Who in Milan shall put many to death.

Par trahison de verges a mort battu,   32   By Treason one shall be beaten with rods to death,
Prins surmonté sera par son desordre,   Then the Traitor shall be overcome by his disorder,
Conseil frivole au grand captif sentu,   The great Prisoner shall try a frivolous Counsel,
Nez par fureur quand Berich viendra mordre.   When Berich shall bite anothers nose through anger.

Sa main derniere par Alus sanguinaire,
Ne se pourra par la Mer garentir,
Entre deux fleuves craindre main militaire,
Le noir l'Ireux le fera repentir.

33 | His last hand bloody through Alus,
Shall not save him by Sea,
Between two Rivers he shall fear the military hand,
The black and Cholerick one shall make him repent.

De feu volant la machination,
Viendra troubler le Chef des Assiegez,
Dedans sera telle sedition,
Qu'en desespoir seront les profligez.

34 | The device of flying fire
Shall trouble so much the Captain of the Besieged,
And within shall be such mutiny,
That the Besieged shall be in despair.

Pres de Rion & proche Blanchelaine,
Aries, Taurus, Cancer, Leo, La Vierge,
Mars, Jupiter, le Sol ardra grand plaine,
Bois & Citez, Lettres cachez au Cierge.

35 | Near Rion going to Blancheline,
Aries, Taurus, Cancer, Leo, Virgo,
Mars, Jupiter, Sol shall burn a great Plain,
Woods and Cities, Letters hidden in a wax Candle.

Ne bien ne mal par bataille terrestre,
Ne parviendra au confins de perouse,
Rebeller pise, Florence voir mal estre,
Roy nuit blessé sur mulet a noire house.

36 | Neither good nor evil by a Land-fight,
Shall extend to the Borders of Perusa,
Pisa shall rebel, Florence shall be in an ill case,
A King being upon his Mule shall be wounded in the night time.

L'œuvre ancienne se parachevera,
Du toit cherra sur le grand mal ruine,
Innocent fait, mort on accusera,
Nocene caché, taillis a bruine.

37 | The ancient work shall be finished,
From the tiling shall fall upon the great one an evil ruine,
The innocent declared to be so; shall be accused after his death,
The guilty shall be hidden in a wood in a misty weather.

Aux profligez de Paix les ennemis,
Apres avoir l'Italie superée,
Noir sanguinaire, rouge sera commis,
Feu, sang verser, eau de sang colorée.

38 | To the vanquished the enemies of peace,
After they shall have overcome Italy,
A bloody black one shall be committed,
Fire and blood shall be powerd, and water coloured with blood.

L'Enfant du Regne par Paternelle prinse,
Expolier sera pour delivrer:
Aupres du Lac Trasym en la Tour prinse,
La troupe hostage pour trop fort s'enyvrer.

39 | The Child of the Kingdom, through his Fathers imprisonment,
Shall be deprived of his Kingdom for delivering of his father,
Near the Lake Trasymene shall be taken in a Tower,
The troop that was in Hostage, being drunk.

Grand de Mogonce pour grande soif esteindre,
Sera privé de sa grand dignité,
Ceux de Cologne si fort le viendront plaindre,
Que la grand Groppe au Rhin sera jetté.

40 | The great one of Ments for to quench a great thirst,
Shall be deprived of his high dignity,
Those of Colen shall bemoan him so much,
That the great Groppe shall be thrown into the Rhine.

Le second Chef du Regne Dannemark,	41	The second head of the Kingdom of Dannemark,
Par ceux de Frize & l'Isle Britannique,		By those of Friezeland, and the Brittish Island,
Fera despendre plus de cent mille mark,		Shall cause to be spent above 100000 Mark,
Vain exploiter voiage en Italique.		Vainly endeavouring a journey into Italy.
A l'Ogmion sera laissé le Regne,	42	Unto I'Ogmion shall be left the Kingdom,
Du grand Selin, qui plus fera de fait,		Of great Selyn, who shall do more then rest,
Par l'Italie estendra son enseigne,		Through Italy he shall spread his Ensigns,
Regira par prudent contrefait.		He shall govern by a prudent dissimulation.
Long temps sera sans estre habitée,	43	A great while shall be unhabited,
Ou Siene & Marne autour vient arrouser,		Where Seine, and Marne comes to water about,
De la Tamise & Martiaux tentée,		Being attempted by the Thames and Martial people,
Deceus les gardes en evidant repousser.		The Guards deceived in thinking to resist.
De nuict par Nantes l'Iris apparoistra,	44	By night in Nantes the Rain-bow shall appear,
Des Arcs Marins susciteront la pluye:		Sea Rain-bows shall cause Rain ;
Arabique Goulsre grand classe parfondra,		The Arabian Gulf shall drownd a great Fleet,
Un Monstre en Saxe naistra d'Ours & Truye.		A Monster shall be in Saxony from a Bear and a Sow.
Le Governeur du Regne bien scavent,	45	The Governour of the Kingdom being learned,
Ne consentir voulant au faict Royal :		Shall not confess to the Kings will :
Medite classe par le contraire vent,		He shall intend to set out a Fleet by a contrary Wind,
Le remettra a son plus desloyal.		Which he shall put into the hands of the most disloyal,
Unjuste sera en exil Anyoyé,	46	A just person shall be banished,
Par pestilence aux confins de non seggle,		By plague to the Borders of Non seggle,
Response au rouge le fera desvoye,		The answer to the red one shall make him deviate,
Roy retirant a la Rane & a l'Aigle.		Retiring himself to the Frog and the Eagle,
Entre deux Monts les deux grands Assemblez,	47	Between two Mountains the two great ones shall meet,
De laisseront leur simulte secrete,		They shall forsake their secret enemity.
Bruxelle & Dolle par Langres accablez,		Brusselle and Dolle shalt be crushed by Langres,
Pour a Maline executer leur peste.		To put their plague in Execution at Maline.
La saincteté trop feinte & seductive,	48	The fainted and seducing holiness,
Accompagne d'une langue diserte,		Accompanied with a fluent tongue,
La Cité vieille, & Parme trop nastive,		Shall cause the old City, and too hastly Parma,
Florence & Sienne rendront plus desertes.		Florence and Sienna to be more desert.

De la partie de Mammer grand Pontife,
Subjuguera les confins du Danube,
Chasser la croix, par fer raffe ne riffe,
Captifs, Or, bagues, plus de cent mille Rubles.

49

From the party of Mammer high Priest,
They shall subdue the borders of Danubius,
They shall expel crosses, by Sword topse-turvy,
Slaves, Gold, Jewels, more then 100000. Rubles.

Dedans le puis seront trouvez les os,
Se l'inceste commis par la Marastre,
L'estat changé, en sera bruit des os,
Et aura Mars ascendant pour son astre.

50

In the Well shall be found be bones,
Incest shall be committed by the Stepmother,
The case being altered, there shall be great stir about the bones.
And she shall have Mars for her ascending Planet.

Peuple assemble voir nouveau spectacle,
Princes & Roys par plusieurs assistans,
Pilliers faillir, murs, mais comme miracle,
Le Roy sauve & trente des instans.

51

People assembled to see a new show,
Princes and Kings, with many assistants,
Pillars shall fail, walls also, but as a miracle,
The King saved, and thirty of the standers by.

En lieu du grand qui sera condamné,
De prison hors, son amy en sa place,
L'espoir Troyen en six mois joins, mort né,
Le Sol a l'Urne seront prins fleuves en glace.

52

Instead of the great one that shall be condemned
And put out of Prison, his friend being in his place,
The Trojan hope in six months joyn, still born,
The Sun in Aquarius, then Rivers shall be frozen.

Le grand Prelat Celtique a Roy suspect,
De nuict par cours sortira hors du Regne,
Par Duc fertile a son grand Roy Bretagne,
Bisance a Cypres, & Tunis insuspect.

53

The great Celtique Prelate suspected by his King,
Shall in hast by night go out of the Kingdom
By the means of a Duke the fruitful Britanie,
Bisance by Cyprus, and Tunis shall be unsuspected.

Au point du jours au second chant du Coq,
Ceux de Tunes, de Fez, & de Bugie,
Par les Arabes captif le Roy Maroq,
L'an mil six cens & sept, de Liturgie,

54

At the break of the day, at the second crowing of the Cock,
Those of Tunis, and Fez, and Bugia,
By means of the Arabians, shall take Prisoner the King of Morocco
In the year *1607* by Liturgie.

Au Chelme Duke, in pulling a spunge,
Voile Arabesque voir, subit descouverte:
Tripolis, Chio, & ceux de Trapesonce,
Duc prins, Marnegro & la Cité deserte.

55

The Chelme Duke, in pulling a spunge,
Shall see Arabian Sails suddenly discovered:
Tripolis, Chios, and those of Trapesan,
The Duke shall be taken, Marnegro and the City shall be desert.

La crainte Armée de l'ennemy Narbon,
Effroyera si fort les Hesperiques,
Parpignan vuide par l'aveugle d'Arbon,
Lors Barcelon par Mer donra les piques.

56

The feared Army of the enemy Narbon,
Shall so much terrifie the Spaniards,
That Parpignan shall be left empty by the blind d'Arbon,
Then Barcelon by Sea shall give the Chase.

Celuy qu'estoit bien avant dans le Regne,	57	He that was a great way in the Kingdom,

Celuy qu'estoit bien avant dans le Regne,
Ayant Chef rouge proche a la Hierarchie,
Aspre & cruel, & se fera tant craindre,
Succedera a sacrée Monarchie.

57 He that was a great way in the Kingdom,
Having a red head and near the Hierarchy,
Harsh and cruel, shall make himself so dreadful,
That he shall succeed to the Sacred Monarchy.

Entre les deux Monarques esloignez,
Lors que le Sol par Selin clair perdue:
Simulté grande entre deux indignez,
Qu'aux Isles & Sienne la liberté rendue.

58 Between the two Monarchs that live far one from the other,
When the Sun shall be Ecclipsed by Selene,
Great enmity shall be between them two,
So that liberty shall be restored to the Isles and Sienne.

Dame en fureur par rage d'adultere,
Viendra a son Prince conjurer non dire,
Mais bref cogneu sera la vitupere,
Que seront mis dixsept a Martyre.

59 A Lady in fury by rage of an Adultery,
Shall come to her Prince and conjure him to say nothing,
But shortly shall the shameful thing be known,
So that seventeen shall be put to death.

Le Prince hors de son Terroir Celtique,
Sera trahy, deceu par interprete:
Rouen, Rochelle, par ceux de l'Armorique,
Au Port de Blavet deceux par Moin & Prestre.

60 The Prince being out of his Celtick Countrey,
Shall be betrayed and deceived by an Interpreter,
Rouen, Rochel, by those of Gascony,
At the Port of Blavet shall be deceived by Monk and Priest.

Le grand Tapis plié ne monstrera,
Fors qu'a demy la pluspart de l'Histoire,
Chassé du Regne aspre loin paroistra,
Au fait Bellique chacun le viendra croire.

61 The great Carpet folded shall not shew,
But by half the greatest part of the History,
The driven out of the Kingdom shall appear sharp afar off,
In Warlike matters every one shall believe him.

Trop tard tous deux les fleurs seront perdües,
Contre lay loy Serpent ne voudra faire,
Des liqueurs forces par gallops confondü s,
Savone, Albingue, par Monech grand martyre.

62 Both the flowers shall be lost too late,
Against the Law the Serpent will do nothing,
The forces of the Leaguers by gallops shall be confounded,
Savone, Albingue, by Monech shall suffer great pain.

La Dame seule au Regne demurée.
L'uniqe esteint premier au lict d'honneur,
Sept ans sera de douleur eplevrée,
Puis longue vie au regne par bonheur.

63 The Lady shall be left to reign alone,
The only one being extinguished, first in the Bed of
Honour.
Seven years she shall weep for grief,
After that she shall live long in the Reign by good luck.

On ne tiendra pache aucune arresté,
Tous recevants iront par tromperie,
De trefue & paix, Terre & Mer protesté,
Par Barcelone classe prins d'industrie.

64 No agreement shall be kept,
All those that shall admit of it deal falsly,
There shall be protestations made by Land and Sea,
Barcelone shall take a Fleet by craft,

Gris & bureau demy ouverte querre,
De nuit seront assaillis & pillez,
Le bureau prins passera par la serre,
Son Temple ouvert, deux au plastre grillez.

65 | Between the Gray and sad Gray shall be half open War,
By night they shall be assaulted and plundered,
The sad Gray being taken, shall be put in Custody,
His Temple shall be open, two shall be put in the Grate.

Au fondement de nouvelle secte,
Seront les os du grand Romain trouvez,
Sepulchre en Marbre, apparoistra converte,
Terre trembler en Auril mal enfeüvez.

66 | At the foundation of a new sect,
The Bones of the great Roman shall be fond,
The Sepulchre shall appear covered with Marble,
The Earth shall quake in April, they shall be ill buried.

Au grand Empire par viendra tout un autres,
Bonté distant plees de felicité,
Regi par un issu non loing du peautre,
Corruer Regnes grande infelicité

67 | To the great Empire quite another shall come,
Being farther from goodness and happiness,
Governed by one of base parentage,
The Kingdom shall fall, a great unhappiness.

Lors que soldats fureur seditieuse.
Contre leur chef feront de nuict fer luire:
Ennemy d'Albe soit par main furieuse,
Lors vexer, Rome, & principaux seduire.

68 | When the seditions fury of the Souldiers,
Against their Chief shall make the Iron shine by night,
The enemy d'Albe shall by a furious hand
Then vex Rome, and seduce the principal one.

La grand pitie sera sans long tarder,
Ceux qui donnoient seront contraints de prendre
Nuds affamez, de froid, soif, soy bander,
Passer les Monts en saisant grand esclandre.

69 | What a great pitty will it be be e're-long,
Those that did give shall be constrained to receive,
Naked, famished with cold, thirst, to mutiny,
To go over the Mountains making great disorders.

Un Chef du Monde le grand Cheirea sera,
Plus outre, apres aime, craint, redouté,
Son bruit & los les Cieux surpassera,
Et du seul titre victeur fort contente.

70 | A Chief of the World the great Cheiren shall be,
Moreover, beloved afterwards, feared, dreaded,
His fame and praise shall go beyond the Heavens.
And shall be contended with the only title Victor.

Quand on viendra le grand Roy parenter,
Avant quil ait du tout l'Ame rendue,
On le verra bien tost apparenter,
D'Aigles, Lions, Croix, Courone de Rüe.

71 | When they shall come to the celebrate the obsequies of the great King,
A day before he be quite dead,
He shall be seen presently to be allyed
With Eagles, Lions, Crosses, Crowns of Rüe

Par fureur feinte devotion Divine,
Sera la femme du grand fort violée,
Judges voulants damner telle Doctrine,
Victime au peuple ignorant immolée.

72 | By a feigned fury of Divine inspiration,
The wife of the great one shall be ravished,
Judges willing to condemn such a Doctrine,
A Victimo shall be sacrifised to the ignorant people.

En Cité grande en moyne & artisan,	**73** In a great City a Monk and an Artificer,
Pres de la porte logez & aux murailles,	Dwelling near the Gate, and the Walls,
Contre modene secret, Cave disant,	Near an old woman, 'tis a secret saying Cave,
Trahis pour faire sous couleur d'espousailles.	A Treason shall be plotted under pretence of a Marriage.

La dechassee au regne tournera,
Ses ennemis trouvez des conjurez,
Plus que jamais son temps triomphera,
Trois & septante a mort trop asseurez.

74 The expelled shall come again to the Kingdom,
Her enemies shall be found to be the Conspirators,
More then ever his time shall triumph,
Three and seventy appointed for death.

Le grand Pilot sera par Roy mandé,
Laisser la classe pour plus haut lieu atteindre,
Sept ans apres sera contrebandé,
Barbare Armée viendra Venise craindre.

75 The great Pilot shall be sent for by the King,
To leave the Fleet, and be preferred to a higher place,
Seven years after he shall be countermanded,
A Barbarian Army shall put Venice to a fright.

La Cité antique d'Antenorée forge,
Plus ne pouuant le tyran supporter
Le manche feint au Temple couper gorge,
Les siens le peuple à mort viendra bouter.

76 The ancient City founded by Antenor,
Being not able to bear the Tyrant any longer,
With a fainted haft, in the Church cut a throat,
The people will come to put his servants to death.

Par la victoire du deceu fraudulente,
Deux classes une, la revolte Germaine,
Le Chef meurtry & son fils dans la Tente,
Florence, Imole pourchassez dans Romaine.

77 By the deceitful victory of the deceived,
One of the two Fleets shall revolt to the Germans,
The Chief and his Son murdered in their Tent,
Florence, Imole persecuted in Romania.

Crier victoire du grand Selin croissant,
Par les Romains sera l'Aigle clamé,
Ticin, Millan et Gennesny consent,
Puis par eux mesmes Basil grand reclamé.

78 They shall cry up the victory of the great Selins half Moon,
By the Romans the Eagle shall be claimed,
Ticin, Milan and Genoa, consent not,
Then by themselves the great Bafil shall be claimed.

Pres de Tesin les habitants de Logre,
Garonne & Saone, Seine, Tar, & Gironde:
Outre les Monts dresseront promonitoire,
Conflict donné, Pau sranci, submerge onde.

79 Near the Tesin the Inhabitants of Logre,
Garonne and Soane, Seine, Tar and Gironde,
Shall erect a promontory beyond the Mountains,
A Battle shall be fought, the Po shall be passed over; some
shall be drowned in it.

De Fez le Regne parviendra a ceux d'Europe,
Feu leur Cité, & Lame tranchera,
Le grand d'Asie terre & Mer a grand troupe,
Que bleux, pars, Croix a mort dechassera.

80 The Kingdom of Fez shall come to those of Europe,
Fire and Sword shall destroy their City,
The great one of Asia by Land and Sea with a great troop,
So that blews, greens, Crosses to death he shall drive.

Pleurs, cris & plaincts, heurlemen, effrayeur,
Cœur inhumain, cruel, noir & transy :
Leman, les Isles de Gennes les majeurs,
Sang espancher, tochsain, a nul mercy.

81 | Tears, cryes and complaints, howlings, fear,
An inhumane heart, cruel, black, astonished,
Leman, the Islands the great ones of Genoa,
Shall spill blood, the Bell shall ring out, no mercy shall be given.

Par les Deserts de lieu libre & farouche,
Viendra errer Neveu du grand Pontife,
Assomme a sept avec lourde souche,
Par ceux qu apres occuperont le Scyphe.

82 | Through the Deserts of a free and ragged place,
The Nephew of the Pope shall come to wonder,
Knockt in the head by seven with heavy Club,
By those who after shall obtain the Scyphe.

Celuy qu'aura tant d'honneur & caresses.
A son entrée en la Gaule Belgique.
Un temps apres sera tant de rudesses,
Et sera contre a la fleur tant bellique.

83 | He that shall have had so many honours and welcomes,
At his going into Flanders,
A while after shall commit so many rudenesses,
And shall be against the warlike flower.

Celuy qu'en Sparte Claude ne veut regner,
Il fera tant par voye seductive,
Que du court, long, le fera araigner,
Que contre Roy fera sa perspective.

84 | He that Claudius will not have to reign in Sparta,
The fame shall do so much by deceitful way,
That he shall cause him to be arranged short and long,
As if he made his prospect upon the King.

La grand'Cité de Tharse par Gaulois,
Sera d'estriute captifs tous a Turban,
Secours par Mer du grand Portugalois,
Premier d'esté le jour du sacre Urban.

85 | The great City of Tharsis shall be taken by the French,
All those that were at Turban shall be made slaves,
Succours by Sea from the great Portugals,
The first day of the Summer, and of the installation of Urban.

Le grand Prelat un jour apres son songe,
Interprete au rebours de son sens,
De la Gascogne luy surviendra un Monge,
Qui fera eslire le grand Prelat de Sens.

86 | The great Prelate the next day after his dream,
Interpreted contrary to his sense,
From Gascony shall come to him Monge,
That shall cause the great Prelate of Sens to be elected.

L'election faicte dans Francfort,
N'aura nul lieu, Milan s'opposera,
Le sien plus proche semblera si grand fort,
Qu'oute le Rhin Marais les chassera.

87 | The election made at Francord,
Shall be void, Milan shall oppose it,
He of the Milan party shall be so strong,
As to drive the other beyond the Marshes of the Rhine.

Un Regne grand demourra desolé,
Aupres de l'Hebro se feront assemblées,
Monts Pyrenees le rendront consolé,
Lors que dans May seront Terres tremblées.

88 | A great Kingdom shall be left desolate,
Near the River Hebrus an assembly shall be made,
The Pyrenean Mountains shall comfort him,
When in May shall be an Earth-quake.

Entre deux cymbes pieds & mains attachez,	89	Between two Boats one shall be tyed hand and foot,
De miel face oingt, & de laict substante,		His face annointed with Honey, and he nourished with
Guespes & mouches feront amour fachez,		Milk,
Poccilateurs faucer, Scyphe tente.		Wasps and Bees shall make much of him in anger,
		For being treacherous Cup-bearers, and poisoning the Cup.

L'honnessement puant abominable
Apres le faict sera felicité,
Grand excuse, pour n'estre favorable,
Qu'a paix Neptune ne sera incité.

90 The stinking and abominable defiling
After the secret shall succeed well,
The great one shall be excused for not being favourable,
That Neptune might be perswaded to pace.

Lu conducteur de la guerre Navale,
Rouge effrené, severe, horrable grippe,
Captif eschapé de l'aisné dans la baste,
Quand il naistra du grand un Fils Agrippe.

91 The leader of the naval forces,
Red, rash, severe, horrible extortioner,
Being slave, shall escape, hidden amongst the Harnesses,
When a Son named Agrippa, shall be born to the great one.

Princesse de beauté tant venuste,
Au chef menée, le second faict trahy,
La Cité au Glaive de poudre face aduste,
Par trop grand meurtre le chef du Roy hay.

92 A Princess of an exquisite beauty,
Shall be brought to the General, the second time the fact
shall be betrayed,
The City shall be given to the Sword and fire,
By two great a murder the chief Person about the King
shall be hated.

Prelat avare, d'ambition trompé,
Rien ne sera que trop cuider viendra,
Ses Messagers, & luy bien attrapé,
Tout au rebours voit qui les bois fendra.

93 A covetous Prelate, deceived by ambition,
Shall do nothing but covet too much,
His messengers and he shall be trapt,
When they shall see one cleave the Wood the contrary way.

Un Roy iré sera aux sedifragues,
Quand interdicts feront harnois de guerre,
La poison taincte au succre par les fragues,
Par eaux meurtris, morts, disant, serre, serre.

94 A King shall be angry against the Covenant-breakers,
When the Warlike Armour shall be forbidden,
The Poison with Sugar shall be put in the Strawberries,
They shall be murdered and die, saying, close, close.

Par detracteur calomnie puis nay,
Quand istront faicts enormes & martiaux,
La moindre part dubieuse a l'aisné,
Et tost au Regne seront faicts partiaux.

95 The youngest Son shall be calumniated by a slanderer,
When enormous and Martial deeds shall be done,
The least part shall be left doubtfull to the
Eldest and soon after they shall be both equal in the
Kingdom.

Grand Cité à Soldats abandonnée,
One ny eut mortel tumult si proche,
O quelle hideuse calamités approche,
Fors vne offence n'y sera pardonnée.

96 A great City shall be given up to the Souldiers,
There was never a mortal tumult so near,
Oh ! what a hideous calamity draws near,
Except one offence nothing shall be spared.

Century VI - 120

Cinq & quarante degrez ciel bruslera, *Feu approcher de la grand Cité neuve,* *Instant grand flamme esparse sautera,* *Quand on voudra des Normans faire preuve.*	97 The Heavens shall burn at five and forty degrees, The fire shall come near the great new City, In an instant a great flame dispensed shall burst out, When they shall make a trial of the Normans.
Ruyne aux Volsques de peur si fort terribles, *Leur grand Cité taincte, faict pestilent :* *Piller Sol, Lune & violer leur Temples:* *Et les deux Fleuves rougir de sang coulant.*	98 A ruine shall happen to the Volsques that are so terrible, Their great City shall be dyed, a pestilent deed : They shall plunder Sun and Moon, and violate their Temples, And the two Rivers shall be red with running blood.
L'Ennemy docte se tournera confus, *Grand Camp malade, & de faict par embusches,* *Monts Pyrenees luy seront faicts refus.* *Roche du Fleuve descouvrant antique ruches.*	99 The learned enemy shall go back confounded, A great Camp shall be sick, and in effect through ambush, The Pyrenean Mountains shall refuse him. Near the River discovering the ancient Hives.
Fill de Laure, asyle du mal sain, *Ou jusqu'au Ciel se void l'Amphitheatre :* *Prodige veu, ton mal est fort prochain,* *Seras captive, & des fois plus de quatre.*	100 Daughter of Laura, Sanctuary of the sick, Where to the Heavens is seen the Amphitheatre, A prodigy being seen, the danger is near, Thou shalt be taken captive above four times.

LEGIS CAUTIO CONTRA INEPTOS CRITICOS

Qui legent hos versus, maturè censunto,
Prophanum vulgus & inscium ne attrectato :
Omnesque, Astrologi, Blenni, Barbari procul sunto,
Qui aliter faxit, is rite sacer esto.

Century VII

'Arc du Thresor par Achilles deceu,
Aux procées sceu le Quadrângulaire,
Au fait Roial le cômmênt sera sceu,
Corps veu pêndu au Sceu du
populaire.

1 | The bow of the Treasure by Achilles deceived,
Shall shew to posterity the Quadrangulary,
In the Royal deed the Comment shall be known,
The body shall be seen hanged in the knowledge of the people.

Par Mars ouvert Arles ne donra guerre,
De nuit seront les Soldats estonnez,
Noir, blanc, à l'Inde dissimulez en terre.
Soubs la feinte ombre traistre verrez sonnez.

2 | Arles shall not proceed by open War,
By night the Souldiers shall be astonished,
Black, white, and blew, dissembled upon the ground.
Under the fained shadow you shall see them proclaimed Traitors.

Apres de France la victoire Navale,
Les Barchinons, Sailimons, les Phocens,
Lierre d'or, l'Enclume serré dans balle,
Ceux de Toulon au fraud seront consents.

3 | After the Naval victory of the French,
Upon those of Tunis, Sally, and the Phocens,
A golden Juy the Anvil shut up in a pack,
Those of Toulon to the fraud shall consent.

Le Duc de Langres assiegé dedans Dole,
Accompagné d'Anthun & Lionnois,
Geneve, Ausbourg, ceux de la Mirandole,
Passer les Monts contre les Anconois.

4 | The Duke of Langres shall be besieged in Dole,
Being in company with those of Autun and Lion,
Geneva, Auspourg, those of Mirandola,
Shall go over the Mountains against those of Ancona.

Vin sur la Table en sera respandu,
Le tiers naura celle quil pretendoit,
Deux fois du noir de Parme descendu,
Perouse & Pise fera ce qu'il cuidoit.

5 | Wine shall be spilt upon the Table,
By reason that a third man shall not have her whom he intended,
Twice black one descended from Parma,
Shall do to Perusa and Pisa what he intended.

Naples, Palerme, & toute la Sicile,
Par main Barbare sera inhabitée,
Corsique, Salerne & de Sardaigne l'Isle,
Faim, peste, guerre, fin de maux intemptée.

6 | Naples, Palermo, and all Sicily,
By barbarous hands shall be depopulated,
Corsica, Salerno, and the Island of Sardinia.
In them shall be famine, plague, war, and endless evils.

Sur le combat des grands chevaux legers,
On criera le grand croissant confond,
De nuit tuer Moutons, Brebis, Bergers,
Abysmes rouges dans le fossé profond.

7 | At the fight of the great light Horsmen,
They shall cry out confound the great half Moon,
By night they shall kill Sheep, Emes, and Shepherds,
Red pits shall be in the deep ditch.

Flora fuis, fuis le plus proche Romain,
Au Fesulan sera conflict donné,
Sang espandu les plus grands pris en main,
Temple ne Sexe ne sera pardonné.

8 | Flora fly, fly from the next Roman,
In the Fesulan shall be the fight,
Blood shall be spilt, the greatest shall be taken,
Temple nor Sex shall be spared.

Dame en l'abscence de son grand Capitaine,	9
Sera priée d'amour du Viceroy,	
Feinte promesse & malheureuse estreine,	
Entre les mains du grand Prince Barroy.	

A Lady in the absence of her great Captain,
Shall be intreated of love by the Viceroy,
Afained promise, and unhappy new years gift,
In the hand of the great Prince of Bar.

Par le grand Prince limitrophe du Mans, **10**
Preux & vaillant chef de grand exercite,
Par Mer & Terre de Galois & Normans,
Cap passer Barcelonne pillé l'Isle.

The great Prince dwelling near the Mans,
Stout and valiant, General of a great Army
Of Welchmen and Normans by Sea and Land,
Shall pass the Cape Barcelone, and plunder the Island

L'Enfant Roial contemnera la Mere, **11**
Oeil, pieds blessez, rude inobeissant,
Nouvelle à Dame estrange & bien amere,
Seront tuez des siens plus de cinq cens.

The Royal Child shall despise his Mother,
Eye, feet wounded, rude disobedient,
News to a Lady very strange and bitter,
There shall be killed of hers above five hundred.

Le grand puisnay fera fin de la guerre, **12**
En Deux assemble les excusez,
Cahors, Moissac, iront loing de la serre,
Refuc, Lectoure, les Agenois rasez.

The great younger Brother shall make an end of the War,
In two places he shall gather the excused,
Cahors, Moissac, shall go out of his clutches,
Ruffec, Lectoure, and those of Agen shall be cut off.

De la Cité Marine & tributaire, **13**
La teste rase prendra la Satrapie,
Chasser sordide qui puis sera contraire,
Par quatorze and tiendra la Tyrannie.

Of the City Maritine and tributary,
The shaven head shall take the Government,
He shall turn out a base man who shall be against him,
During fourteen years he will keep the tyranny.

Faux exposer viendra Topographie, **14**
Seront les Urnes des Monumens ouvertes,
Pulluler Sectre, saincte Philosophie,
Pour blanches noires, & pour antiques vertes.

They shall expound Topography falsly,
The Urnes of the Monuments shall be open,
Sects shall multiply, and holy Philosophy
Shall give black for white, and green for old.

Devant Cité de l'Insubre Contrée, **15**
Sept ans sera le Siege devant mis,
Le tres-grand Roy fera son entrée,
Cité puis libre hors de ses ennemis.

Before a City of Piemont,
Seven years the Siege shall be laid,
The most great King shall make his entry into it,
Then the City shall be free being out of the enemies hand.

Entrée profonde par la grand Roine faite, **16**
Rendra le lieu puissant inaccessible,
L'Armée des trois Lions sera defaite,
Faisant dedans cas hideux & terrible.

The deep entry made by the Queen,
Shall make the place powerful, and inaccessible,
The Army of the three Lions shall be routed,
Doing within an hideous and terrible thing.

Le Prince rare en pitié & clemence,	
Apres avoir la paix aux siens baillé,	
Viendra chânger par mort grand cognoissance,	
Par grand repos le regne travaillié.	

17

The Prince rare in pity and Clemency,
After he shall have given peace to his Subjects,
Shall by death change his great knowledge,
After great rest he Kingdom shall be troubled.

Les Assiegez couloureront leur paches,
Sept jours apres feront cruelle issüe,
Dans reponlsez, feu, sang, sept mis à l'hache,
Dame captive qu'avoit la paix issüe.

18

The Besieged shall dawn their Articles,
Seven days after they shall make a cruel event,
The shall be beaten back, fire, blood, seven put to death,
The Lady shall be Prisoner who endeavoured make peace.

Le Fort Nicene ne sera combatu,
Vaincu sera par rutilant metal,
Son fait sera un long temps debatu,
Aux Citadins estrange espouvental.

19

The Fort Nicene shall not be fought against,
By shining metal it shall be overcome,
The doing of it shall be long and debating,
It shall be a strange fearful thing to the Citizens.

Ambassadeurs de la Toscane langue,
Avril & May Alpes & Mer passer,
Celuy de Veau exposera l'harangue,
Vie Gauloise ne voulant effacer.

20

The Embassadors of the Tuscan tongue,
In April and May, shall go over the Alpes and the Sea,
One like a Caif shall make a speech:
Attempting to defame the French customes.

Par pestilente inimitié Volsicque,
Dissimulée chassera le Tyran,
Au Pont de Sorgues se fera la trafique,
De mettre à mort luy & son adherant.

21

By a pestilent Italian enmity,
The dissembler shall expel the Tyrant,
The bargain shall be made at Sorgues Brige,
To put him and his adherent to death.

Les Citoiens de Mesopotamie,
Irez encontre amis de Tarragone,
Jeux, Ris, Banquets toute gent endormie,
Vicaire au Prone, pris Cité, ceux d'Ausone.

22

The Citizens of Mesopotamia.
Being angry with the friends of Tarragone,
Playes, laughter, feasts, every body being asleep,
The Vicar being in the Pulpit, City taken by those of
Ausone.

Le Roial Sceptre sera contraint de prendre,
Ce que ses Predecesseurs voient engagé,
Puis a Laigneau on fera mal entendre,
Lors qu'on viendra le Palais saccager.

23

The Royal Scepter shall be constrained to take
What his Predecessors bad mortgaged,
After that, they shall mis-inform the Lamb,
When they shall come plunder to Palace.

L'Ensevely sortira du tombeau,
Fera de chaisnes lier le fort du pont,
Empoisoné avec œufs de Barbeau,
Grand de Lorraine par le Marquis du pont.

24

The buried shall come out of his Grave,
He shall cause the fort of the Bridge to be tied with Chains,
Poisoned with Barbels hard Row,
Shall a great one of Lorrain be by the Marqes du pont.

Par guerre longue tout l'exercite espuiser,	25

Par guerre longue tout l'exercite espuiser,
Que pour Soldats ne trouveront pecune,
Lieu d'Or, d'Argent, cair on viendra cuser,
Gaulois Ærain, signe croissant de Lune.

25 By a long War, all the Army drained dry,
So that a raise Souldiers they shall find no Money,
Instead of Gold and Silver, they shall stamp Leather,
The French Copper, the mark of the stamp the new Moon.

Fustes Galées autour de sept Navires,
Sera livrée une mortelle guerre,
Chef de Madrid recevra coups de vires,
Deux eschapées & cinq menez à Terre.

26 Fly-boats and Galleys round about seven Ships,
A mortal War there shall be,
The chief of Madrid shall receive blows of Oars,
Two shall escape, and five carried to Land.

Au coin de Vast la grand Cavalerie,
Proche à Ferrare empeschée au Bagage,
Pompe à Turin front telle volerie,
Que dans le fort raviront leur hostage.

27 In the corner of Vast the great Troop of Horse,
Near Ferrara, shall be busied about the baggage,
Pompe at Turin, they shall make such a robbery,
That in the Fort they shall ravish their hostage.

Le Capitaine conduira grande proye,
Sur la Montagne des ennemis plus proche,
Environné par feu fera telle voye,
Tous eschapez, or trente mis en broche.

28 The Captain shall lead a great Prey
Upon the Mountain, that shall be nearest to the Enemies,
Being encompassed with fire, he shall make such a way,
That all shall escape, but thirty that shall be spitted.

Le grand Duc d'Albe se viendra rebeller,
A ses grands peres fera le tradiment,
Le grand de Guise le viendra debeller,
Captif mené & dressé monument.

29 The great Duke of Alba shall rebel,
To his Grandfathers be shall make the Plot,
The great Guise shall vanquish him,
Led Prisoner, and a Mountain erected.

Le sac sapproche, feu, grand sang espandu,
Pau grand Fleuves, aux Bouviers l'entreprise,
De Genes, Nice apres long temps attendu,
Foussan, Thurin, à Savillan la prise.

30 The plundering draws near, fire, abundance of blood spilt,
Pau a great River, an enterprise Herdsman,
Of Genes, Nice after they shall have staid long,
Fossan, Thurin, the prize shall be at Savillan.

De Languedoc, & Guienna plus de dix
Mille, voudront les Alpes repasser.
Grans Allobroges marcher contre Brundis,
Aquin & Bresse les viendront recasser.

31 From Languedoc and Guienna more then 10000.
Would be glad to come back over the Alpes.
Great Allobroges shall march against Brundis,
Aquin and Bressle shall beat them back.

Du Mont Royal naistra d'une Casane,
Qui Duc, & Compte viendra tyranniser,
Dresser Copie de la marche Millane,
Favence, Florence d'or & gens espuiser.

32 Out of the Royal Mount shall be born in a Cottage,
One that shall tyranise over Duke and Earl,
He shall raise an Army in the Land of Millan,
He shall exhaust Favence and Florence of their gold.

Par fraude Regne, forces expolier,
La classe, obsesse, passages à l'espie,
Deux faincts amis se viendront r'allier,
Esueillier haine de long temps assoupie.

33 By fraud a Kingdom and an Army shall be spoilt,
The Fleet shall be put to a strait, passages shall be made to the spies,
Two feigned friends shall agree together,
They shall raise up a hatred that had been long dormant.

En grand regret sera la gent Gauloise,
Cœur vain, leger croira temerité,
Pain, sel, ne vin eau venin ne ceruoise,
Plus grand captif, faim, froid, necessité.

34 In great regret shall the French Nation be:
Their vein and light heart shall believe rashly,
They shall have niether Bread, Salt, Wine, nor Beer,
Moreover they shall be Prisoners, and shall suffer hunger, cold and need.

La grande poche viendra plaindre pleurer,
D'avoir esleu, trompez seront en l'Aage,
Guiere avec eux ne voudra demeurer,
Deceu sera par ceux de son langage.

35 The great Pocket shall bewaile and bemoan,
For having Elected one, they shall be deceived in his Age;
He shall not stay long with them,
He shall be deceived by those of his own language.

Dieu, le Ciel tout le Diuin Verbe a l'Onde,
Porté par rouges sept razes à Bizance,
Contre les oingts trois cens de Trebisconde,
Deux Loix mettront, & horreur, puis credence.

36 God, Heaven, all the Divine Word in water,
Carryed by red ones, seven shaved heads at Bisantium,
Against the anointed three hundred of Trebisond,
They shall put two Laws, and horror, and afterwards believe.

Dix envoyez, chef de nef mettre à mort,
D'un adverty, en classe guerre ouverte,
Confusion chef, l'un se picque & mord,
Leryn, Stecades nefs, cap dedans la nerte.

37 Ten shall travel to put the Captain of the Ship to death,
He shall have notice by one, the Fleet shall be in open War.
A confusion shall be among the Chief, one pricks and bites,
Leryn, Stecades nefs, caps dedans la nerte.

L'Aisné Roial sur coursier voltigeant,
Picquer viendra si rudement courir,
Gueule, lipée, pied dans l'Estrein pleignant,
Traine, tiré, horriblement mourir.

38 The eldest Royal prancing upon a Horse,
Shall spur, and run very fiercely
Open mouth the foot in the Stirrup, complaining,
Drawn, pulled, die horribly.

Le conducteur de l'Armée Françoise,
Cuidant perdre le principal Phalange,
Par sus pavé de l'Avaigne & Ardoise,
Soy parfondra par Gennes gent estrange.

39 The leader of the French Army,
Thinking to rout the chiefest Phalange,
Upon the Pavement of Avaigne, and Slate,
Shall sink in the ground by Gennes, a strange Nation.

Dedans tonneaux hors oingts d'huile & graisse,
Seront vingt un devant le port fermez,
Au second guet seront par mort proüesse,
Gaigner les portes & du guet assommez.

40 With Pipes annointed without with Oyl and Grease,
Before the harbour, one aud twenty shall be shut,
At the second Watch, by death, they shall do great feats of Arms,
To win the Gates, and be killed by the Watch.

Les os des pieds & des mains enserrez,
Par bruit maison long temps inhabitée,
Seront par songes concavant deterrez,
Maison salubre & sans bruit habitée.

41 The bones of the feet and of the hands in shackles,
By a noise a house shall be a long time deserted,
By a dream the buried shall be taken out of the ground,
The house shall be beautiful, and inhabited without noise.

Quand Innocent tiendra le lieu de Pierre,
Le Nizaram Sicilian se verra,
En grands honneurs, mais apres il cherra,
Dans le bourbier d'une Civile querre.

42 When Innocent shall hold the place of Peter,
The Sicilian Nizaram shall see himself
In great honors, but after that he shall fall
Into the dirt of a Civil war.

Lutece en Mars, Senateurs en credit,
Par une nuict Gaule sera troublée,
Du grand Cræsus l'Horoscope predit,
Par Saturnus, sa puissance exillée.

43 Lutecia in Mars, Senators shall be in credit.
In a night France shall be troubled,
The Horoscope of the great Cræsus fortelleth,
That by Saturn his power shall be put down.

Deux de poison faisis nouveaux Venus
Dans la cuisine du grand Prince verser,
Par le souillard tous deux au fait cogheus,
Prins qui cuidoit de mort l'aisné vexer.

44 Two newly come being provided with poison,
To pour in the Kitchen of the great Prince,
By the scullion let it all be known,
And he taken, that thought by death to vex the elder.

AUTRES QUATRAINS

tirez de 12. soubz la Centurie septiesme:
dont en ont esté rejectez 8. qui se sont
trouuez és Centuries prudentes.

OTHER STANZAS

taken out of twelve, under the seventh Century, out
of which eight have been rejected because they were
found in the foregoing Centuries.

Renfort de Sieges manubis & maniples,
Changez le sacre & passe sur le prosne,
Prins & captifs n'arreste les prez triples,
Plus par fonds mis, eslevé, mis au trosne.

73 Recruit of Sieges, spoils and prizes,
Corpus Christi day shall be changed, and the pronsne slighted,
They shall be taken and made Prisoners, do not stay in the threefold Field.
Moreover, one put in the bottom shall be raised to the Throne.

L'Occident libre les Isles Britanniques,
Le recogneu passer le bas, puis haut,
Ne content triste Rebel corss. Escotiques,
Puis rebeller par plur & par nuict chaut.

80 The West shall be free, and the Brittish Islands,
The discovered shall pass low, then high,
Scottish Pirates shall be, who shall rebel,
In a rainy and hot night.

La stratageme simulte sera rare,
La Mort en voye rebelle par contrée,
Par le retour du voyage Barbare,
Exalteront la potestante entrée.

82 The stratagem and grudge shall be scarce,
Death shall be in a rebellious way through the Countrey,
By the return from a Barbarian travel,
They shall exalt the Protestant entrance.

Vent chaut, conseil pleurs, timidité,
De nuict au lict assailly sans les Armes :
D'oppression grande calamité,
L'Epithalame converty pleurs & larmes.

83 Hot wind, councel, tears, fearfulness,
He shall be assaulted in his bed by night without Arms,
From that oppression shall he be raised a great calamity,
The Epithalamium shall be converted into tears.

Century VIII

1

Au, Nay, Loron, plus feu qu'à sang sera,
Laude nager, fuir grands aux Surrez,
Les Agassas entrée refusera,
Pampon, Durance les tiendra enserez.

Pau, Nay, Loron, more in fire then blood shall be,
Lauda to swim, great ones run to the Surrez,
The Agassas shall refuse the entry,
Pampon, Durance shall keep them enchifed.

2

Condon & Aux, & autour de Mirande,
Je voy du Ciel feu qui les enuironne,
Sol, Mars, conjoint au Lion, puis Marmande,
Foudre, grand guerre, mur tomber dans Garônne.

Condon and Aux, and about Mirande,
I see a fire from Heaven that encompasseth them,
Sol, Mars, in conjunction with the Lion, and then Marmande;
Lightning, great War, Wall falls into the Garonne.

3

Au fort Chasteau de Vigilanne & Resviers,
Sera serré le puisnay de Nancy,
Dedans Turin seront ards les premiers,
Lors que de dueil Lyon sera transy.

In the strong Castle of Vigilanne and Resviers,
Shall be kept close the youngest son of Nancy,
Within Turin the fist shall be burnt up,
When Lyon shall be overwhelmed with sorrow.

4

Dedans Monech le Coq sera receu,
Le Cardinal de France apparoistra,
Par Logation Romain sera deceu,
Foiblesse à l'Aigle, & force au Coq croistra.

Within Monech the Cock shall be admitted,
The Cardinal of France shall appear,
By Logarion, Roman shall be deceived,
Weakness to the Eagle, and strength to the Cock shall grow.

5

Apparoistra Temple luisant orné,
La Lampe & Cierge à Borne & Bretueil,
Pour la Lucerne le Canton destourné,
Quand on verra le grand Coq au Cercueil.

A shining adorned Temple shall appear,
The Lamp and wax Candle at Borne and Brctueil,
For Lucerne the Canton turned of,
When the great Cock shall he scan in his Coffin.

6

Clarté fulgure à Lyon apparante,
Luysant, print Malte, subit sera esteinte,
Sardon, Mauris traitera decevante,
Geneve à Londes à Coq trahison fainte.

A thundering light at Lyons appearing,
Bright, took Maltha, instantly shall be put out,
Sardon shall treat Mauris deceitfully,
To Geneva, London, and the Cock a fained treason.

7

Verceil, Milan donra intelligence,
Dedans Tycin sera faicte la playe,
Courir par Seine eau, sang, feu par Florence,
Unique choir d'hault en bas faisant maye.

Verceil, Milan shall give intelligence,
In the Tycin shall the Peace be made,
Run through Seine water, blood, fire through Florence,
The only one shall fall from top to bottom making maye.

8

Pres de Linterne dans des tonnes fermez,
Chivas fera pour l'Aigle la menée,
L'Esleu chassé, luy ses ges enfermez,
Dedans Turin rapt epouse emmenée.

Near Linterne, enclosed within Tuns,
Chivas shall drive the plot for the Eagle,
The Elect cashiered, he and his men shut up,
Within Turin, arape, and Bride carried away.

Pendant que l'Aigle & le Coq à Sauone,	Whilst the Eagle and the Cock at Savona,
Seront unis, Mer, Leuant & Hongrie,	Shall be united, Sea, Levant, and Hungary,
L'Armée à Naples, Palerne, Marque d'Ancone,	Army at Naples, Palermo, Mark of Ancona,
Rome, Venise, par barbe horrible crie.	Rome, Venice, cry because of a horrid beard.

9

Puanteur grande sortira de Lausane,
Qu'on ne sçaura l'origine du fait,
L'on mettra hors toute la gent lointaine,
Feu veu au Ciel peuple estranger deffait.

10

A great stink shall come forth out of Lausane,
So that no body shall know the ofspirng of it,
They shall put out all the Forreiners,
Fire seen in Heaven, a strange people defeated.

Peuple infiny paroistre à Vicence,
Sans force feu brusler la Basilique,
Pres de Lunage des fait grand de Valence,
Lors que Venise par morte prendre pique.

11

Infinite deal of people shall appear at Vicence,
Without force, fire shall burn in the Basilick,
Near Lunage the great one of Valence shall be defeated,
When Venice by death shall rake the pique.

Apparoistra aupres de Bufalore,
L'haut & procere entré dedans Milan,
L'Abbé de Foix avec ceux de Sainct Maure,
Feront la fourbe habillez en vilan.

12

Near the Busalore shall appear,
The high and tall, come into Milan,
The Abbot of Foix with those of Saint Maure,
Shall make the trumpery being cloathed like rogues.

Le croisé Fere par amour effrenée,
Fera par Praytus Bellerophon mourir,
Classe à mil ans, la femme forcenée,
Beu le breueage, tous deux apres perir.

13

The crossed Brother through unbridled love,
Shall cause Bellerophon to be killed by Praytus,
Fleet to thousand years, the woman out of her wit,
The drink being drunk, both after that, perish.

Le grand credit, d'or, d'argent l'abondance,
Aveuglera par Libide l'honneur,
Cogneu sera d'adultere l'offence,
Qui parviendra à son grand deshonneur.

14

The great credit, the abundance of Gold and Silver,
Shall blind honour by lust,
The offence of the Adulterer shall be known,
Which shall come to his great dishonour.

Vers Aquilon grands efforts par hommasse,
Presque l'Europe, l'Univers vexer,
Les deux Eclipses mettra en telle chassé,
Et aux Pannons vie & mort renforcer.

15

Towards the North great endeavours by a manly woman,
To trouble Europe, and almost all the world,
She Shall be put to flight the two Eclipses,
And shall re-inforce life and death to the Pannons.

Au lieu que Hieson fit sa nef fabriquer,
Si grand Deluge sera & si subite,
Qu'on n'aura lieu ne Terre s'attaquer,
L'onde monter Fesulan Olympique.

16

In the place where Jason caused his Ship to be built,
So great a Flood shall be, and so sudden,
That there shall be neither place nor Land to save themselves,
The Waves shall climb upon the Olympick Fesulan.

Les bien aisez subit seront desmis,	17	Those that were at ease shall be put down,
Le monde mis par les trois freres trouble,		The world shall be put in trouble by three Brothers,
Cité Marine saisiront ennemis,		The Maritine City shall be seized by its enemies,
Fain, feu, sang, peste, & de tous maux le double.		Hunger, fire, blood, plague, and the double of all evils.
De Flore issue de sa mort sera cause,	18	Issued from Flora shall be in the cause of her own death,
Un temps devant par jeusne & vieille bueyre,		One time before, through fasting and old drink,
Car les trois lis luy feront telle pause,		For the three Lillies shall make her such a pause,
Par son fruit sauve comme chair crue mueyre.		Saved by her fruit, as raw flesh dead.
A soustenir la grande cappe troublee,	19	To maintain up the great troubled Cloak,
Pour l'esclaireir les rouges marcheront,		The red ones shall march for to clear it,
De mort famille sera presque accablée,		A family shall be almost crushed to death,
Les rouges reouges, le rouge assommeront.		The red, the red, shall knock down the red one.
Le faux message par election feinte,	20	The contract broken, stoppeth the message,
Courir par Urbem rompue pache arreste,		From going about the Town, by it fained election,
Voix acheptées de sang chappelle teinte,		Voices shall be bought, and a Chappel died with blood,
Et à un autre l'Empire conteste.		By another, who chalengeth the Empire.
Au port de Agde trois fustes entreront,	21	Three Galleys shall come into the port of Agde,
Pourtant l'infection avec foy, pestilence,		Carrying with them infection and Pestilence,
Passant le pont mil milles embleront,		Going beyond the Bridge, they shall carry away thousands;
Et le pont rompre à tierce resistance.		At the third resistance the Bridge shall be broken.
Gorsan, Narbonne, par le Sel advertir,	22	Gorsan, Narbonne, by the Salt shall give notice,
Tucham, la Grace Parpignan trahie,		To Tucham, the Grace Perpignan betrayed,
La ville rouge n'y voudra consentir,		The rek Town will not give consent to it,
Par haute Voldrap, Gris vie faillie.		By high Woldrap, Gray, life ended.
Lettres trouvées de la Royne les Coffres,	23	Letters found in the Queens Coffers,
Point de subscrit, sans aucun nom d'Autheur,		No superscription, no name of the Author,
Par la police seront cachez les offres,		By policy shall be concealed the offers,
Qu'on ne sçaura qui sera l'amateur.		So that no body shall know who shall be the lover.
Le lieutenant à l'entrée l'huys,	24	The Lieutenant shall at the doors entry,
Assommera le grand de Parpignan,		Knock down the great one of Perpignan:
En se cuidant sauver à Montpertuis,		And the Bastard of Lusignan shall be decived,
Sera deçeu Bastard de Lusignan.		Thinking to save himself at Montpertuis.
Cœur de l'Amant ouvert d'amour fortive,	25	The Lovers heart being by a stoln love,
Dans le ruisseau fera ravir la Dame,		Shall cause the Dame to be ravished in the Brook,
Le demy mal contrefaira laseive,		The lascivious shall counterfeit half a discontent,
Le Pere à deux privera corps de l'Ame.		The Father shall deprive the bodies of both of their souls.

De Caronés trouves en Barcelonne,
Mys desouvers, lieu terrouers & ruine,
Le grand qui tient ne voudra Pampelone,
Par l'Abbaye de Monferrat bruine.

26 | The Carones fond in Barcelona,
Put discovered, place soil and ruine,
The great that hold will not Pampelona,
By the Abbeye of Montserrat, mist.

La voye Auxelle l'un sur l'autre fornix,
Du muy de ser hor mis brave & genest,
L'Escript d'Empereur la Phœnix,
Veu en celuy ce qu'à nul autre n'est.

27 | The way Auxelle, one Arch upon another,
Being brave and gallant put out of the Iron vessel,
The writing of the Emperour the Phœnix,
In it shall be seen, what no where else is.

Les Simulachres d'or & d'argent enflez,
Qu'apres le rapt, Lac au feu furent jettez,
Au descouvert estaints tous & troublez,
Au Marbre escripts, prescrips interjettez.

28 | The Images sweld with Gold and Silver,
Which after the rape were thrown into the Lake and fire,
Being discovered after the putting out of the fire,
Shall be written in Marble, prescripts being intermixed.

Au quart pilier ou l'on sacre à Saturne,
Par tremblant Terre & Deluge fendu,
Soubs l'edifice Saturnin trouuée urne,
D'or Capion, ravy puis tost rendu.

29 | At the fourth Pillar where they sacrifice to Saturn,
Cloven by an Earth-quake and a Flood,
An Urne shall be found under that Saturnian building,
Full of Capion gold stoln, and then restored.

Dedans Tholouse non loin de Beluzer,
Faisanr un puis loing, Palais d'espectacle,
Thresor trouvé vn chacun ira vexer,
Et en deux locs tour aupres des Vesacle.

30 | Within Tholose not far from Beluzer,
Digging a Well, for the Pallace of spectacle,
A treasure found that shall vex every one,
In two parcels, in, and near the Basacle.

Premier grand fruit le Prince de Pesquiere,
Mais puis viendra bien & cruel malin,
Dedans Venise perdra sa gloire fiere,
Et mis à mal par plus joyve Celin.

31 | The first great fruit the Prince of Pesquiere,
But he shall become very cruel and malicious,
He shall loose his fierce priced in Venice,
And shall be put to evil by the younger Celin.

Garde toy Roy Gaulois de ton Nepveu,
Qui fera tant que ton unique filz,
Sera meurtry à Venus faisant vœu,
Accompagné de nuit que trois & six.

32 | Take heed O French King of thy Nephew,
Who shall cause that thine only Son,
Shall be murdred making a vow to Venus,
Accompanied with three and six.

Le grand naistra de Verone & Vicence,
Qui portera un surnom bien indigne,
Qui à Venise voudra faire vengeance,
Luy mesme prins homme du guet & signe.

33 | The great one Verona and Vicenza shall be born,
Who shall bear a very unworthy surname,
Who shall endeavour at Venice to avenge himself,
But he shall be taken by a Watch-man.

Apres Victoire du Lion au Lion,
Sus la Montagne de Jura Secatombe,
Delues, & Brodes septiesme milion,
Lyon ulme à Mansol mort & tombe.

34 | After the Victory of the Lion against the Lion,
Upon the Mountain Jura Secatomb,
Delues, and Brodes the seventh Million,
Lyons, Ulme fall dead at Mausol.

Dedans l'entree de Garonne & Blaye,
Et la Forest non loing de Damazan,
Du Marsaves gelées, puis gresle & Bize,
Dordonnois gelé par erreur de Mezans.

35 | Within the entrance of Garonne and Blaye,
And the Forrest nor far from Damazan,
Of Marsaves frosts, then Hail and North wind,
Dordonois frozen by the error of Mezan.

Sera commis contre Oinde a Duché
De Saulne, & Saint Aubin, & Belœuvre,
Paver de Marbre, de tours loing pluché,
Non Bleteram resister & chef d'œuvre.

36 | A Dukedom shall be committed against Oinde,
Of Saulne, and Saint Aubin, and Belœuvre,
To pave with Marble, and of Towers well pickt,
Not Bleteran to resist, and master-piece.

La forteresse aupres de la Tamise,
Cherra par lors, le Roy dedans serré,
Aupres du pont sera veu en chemise,
Un devant mort, puis dans le fort barré.

37 | The stong Fort near the Thames
Shall fall then, the King that was kept within,
Shall be seen near the Bridge in his Shirt,
One dead before, then in the Fort kept close.

Le Roy de Blois dans Avignon regner,
Un autrefois le peuple emonopole,
Dedans le Rhosne par murs fera baigner,
Jusques à cinq, le dernier pers de Nole.

38 | The King of Blois in Avignon shall Reign
Another time the people do murmur,
He shall bathe in the Rhofne to be bathed through the Walls,
As many as five, the last shall be near Nole.

Qu'aura esté par Prince Bizantin,
Sera tollu par Prince de Tholose,
La foy de Foix, par le chef Tholentin,
Luy faillira ne refusant l'espouse.

39 | What shall have been by a Bizantin Prince,
Shall be taken away by the Prince of Tholose,
The faith of Foix by the chief Tholentin,
Shall fail him not refusing the Sponse.

Le sang du Juste par Taur & la Dorade,
Pour se vanger contre les Saturnins,
Au nouveau Lac plongeront la Mainade,
Puis marcheront contre les Albanins.

40 | The blood of the just by Taur and Dorade,
To avenge themselves against the Saturnins,
In the new Lake shall sink the Mainade,
Then shall go forth against the Albanins.

Esleu sera Renard ne sonnant mot,
Faisant le Saint public, vivant pain d'orge,
Tyranniser apres tant à un cop,
Mettant le pied des plus grands sur la gorge.

41 | A Fox shall be elected that said nothing.
Making a publick Saint, living with Barley bread,
Shall tyrannise after upon a sudden,
And put his foot upon the Throat of the greatest.

Par avarice, par force & violence,
Viendra vexer les siens chef d'Orleans,
Prez Saint Memire assaut & resistance,
Mort dans sa Tente, diront qu'il dort leans.

42 | By avarice, by force and violence,
Shall come to vex his own chief of Orleans,
Near Saint Memire assult and resistance,
Dead in his Tent, they'l say he sleepeth there.

Par le decide de deux choses Bastards,	43	By the decision of two things, Bastards,
Nepveu du sang occupera le Regne,		Nephew of the Blood shall occupy the Kingdom,
Dedans Lectoure seront les coups de dards,		Within Lectoure shall be strokes of Darts,
Nepveu par peur pliera l'Enseigne.		Nephew through fear shall fold up his Ensign.
Le procrée nature d'Ogmion,	44	The natural begotten of Ogmyon,
De sept à neuf du chemin destorner:		From seven to nine shall put out the way,
A Roy de longue & amy au my hom.		To King of long, and friend to the half man,
Doit à Navarre fort de Pau prosterner.		Ought to Navarre prostrate the fort of Pau.
La main escharpe & la jambe bandée,	45	The hand on a Scarf, and the leg swadled,
Louis puisnée de Calais partira,		The younger Lewis shall go from Palais,
Au mot du guet la mort sera tardée,		At the Watch word his death shall be protracted,
Puis dans le Temple à Pasque saignera.		Then afterwards at Easter he shall bleed in the Temple.
Pol Mensolée mourra trois lieües du Rhosne,	46	Paul Mensolée Shall die three Leagues from Rhosne,
Fuis les deux prochains Tarare destrois,		Avoid the Two straights near the Tarare;
Car Mars fera le plus horrible Throsne,		For Mars shall keep such a horrible Throsne,
De Coq & d'Aigle, de France freres trois.		Of Cock and Eagle, of France three Brothers.
Lac Trasmenien portera tesmoignage,	47	Trasmenian Lake shall bear witness
Des conjurez serrez dedans Perouse,		Of the Conspirators shut up in Perugia,
Un Despolle contrefera le sage,		A Despolle shall counterfeit the wife,
Tuant Tedesque de Sterne & Minuse.		Killing Tedesque of Sterne and Minuse.
Saturne en Cancer, Jupiter avec Mars,	48	Saturn in Cancer, Jupiter with Mars,
Dedans Fevrier Caldondon, Saluterre,		In February Caldondon, Salvaterre,
Sault, Castallon, assailly de trois pars,		Sault, Casralon, assaulted on thee sides,
Pres de Verbiesque, conflict mortelle querre.		Near Verbiesque, fight and mortal War.
Satur au Bœuf, Jove en l'Eau, Mars en fleche,	49	Satur in Ox, Jupiter in water, Mars in arrow,
Six de Fevrier mortalité donra,		The sixth of February shall give mortality,
Ceux de Tardaigne à Bruges si grand breche		Those of Tardaigne shall make in Bruges so great a breach.
Qu'à Ponterose chef Barbarin mourra.		That the chief Barbarin shall die at Pontrose.
La Pestilence l'entour de Capadille,	50	The Plague shall be round about Capadille,
Un autre faim pres de Sagunt s'apreste,		Another famine cometh near to that of Sagunce,
Le Chevalier Bastard de bon senille,		The Knight Bastard of the good old man,
Au grand de Thunes fera trancher la teste.		Shall cause the great one of Tunis to be beheaded.
Le Bizantin faisant oblation,	51	The Bizantin, making an offering,
Apres avoir Cordube à soy reprinse,		After he hath taken Cordua to himself again,
Son chemin long, repos, pamplation,		His way long, rest, contemplation,
Mer passant proye par la Cologne a prinse.		Crossing the Sea hath taken a pray by Cologne.

Le Roy de Blois dans Avignon Regner,
D'Amboise & Seme viendra le long de Lindre.
Ongle à Poitiers Saintes aisles ruiner,
Devant Bony:

52 | The King of Blois shall Reign in Avignon,
He shall come from Amboise and Seme, along the Linder,
A Nail at Poitiers shall ruine the Holy Wings,
Before Bony.

Dedans Bolongne voudra laver ses fautes,
Il ne poura au Temple du Soleil,
Il volera faisant choses si hautes,
En Hierarchie n'en fut onc pareil.

53 | He shall desire to wash his misdeeds in Bullion,
In the Church of the Sun, but he shall not be able,
He shall fly doing so high things,
That the like equal in Hierarchy.

Soubs la couleur du traité mariage,
Fait magnanime par grand Chiren Selin,
Quintin, Arras, recouvrez au voiage,
D'Espagnols fait second banc Macelin.

54 | Under pretence of Treaty of Merriage,
A Magnanimous act shall be done by the great Cheiren Selin,
Quintin, Arras recovered in the journey,
Of Spaniards shall be made a second Macelin Bench.

Entre deux Fleuves se verra enserré,
Tonneaux & caques unis à passer outre,
Huit Pont rompus chef à tant enferré,
Enfans parfaits sont jugulez en coultre.

55 | Between two Rivers he shall find himself shut up,
Tuns and Barrels put together to pass over,
Eight Bridges broken, the chief at last in Prison,
Compleat children shall have their throat cut.

La bande foible la Terre occupera,
Ceux du haut lieu feront horribles cris,
Le gros troupeau d'estre coin troublera,
Tombe pres Dinebro discouvert les escrits.

56 | The weak party shall occupy the ground,
Those of the high places shall make fearfull cries,
It shall trouble the great flock in the right corner,
He falleth near D. nebro discovereth the writings.

De soldat simple parviendra en Empire,
De Robe courte parviendra à la longue,
Vaillant aux Armes en Eglise ou plus pire,
Vexer les Prestres comme l'eau fait l'esponge.

57 | From a simple Souldier he shall come to have the supreme command,
From a short Gown he shall come to the long one,
Vaillant in Arms, no worse man in the Church,
He shall vex the Priests, as water doth a Spunge.

Regne en querelle aux freres divisé,
Prendre les Armes & les nom Britannique,
Tiltre Anglican sera tard advisé,
Surprins de nuit, mener à l'air Gallique.

58 | A Kingdom in dispute, and divided between the Brothers,
To take the Arms and the Britannick name,
And the English title, he shall advise himself late,
Surprised in the night and carried into the French air.

Par deux fois haut, par deux fois mis à bas,
L'Orient aussi l'Occident foiblira,
Son adversaire apres plusieurs combats,
Par Mer chassé au besoing faillira.

59 | Twice set up high, and twice brought down,
The East also the West shall weaken,
His adversary after many fights,
Expelled by Sea, shall fail in need.

Premier en Gaule, premier en Romaine,
Par Mer & Terre aux Anglois & Paris,
Merveilleux faits par cette grand mesqme,
Violant, Terax perdra le NORLARIS.

60 The first in France, the fist in Romania
By Sea and Land to the English and Paris,
Wonderful deeds by that great company,
By ravishing, Terax shall spoil the Norlaris.

Jamais par le decouvrement du jourd,
Ne parviendra au signe Sceptifere,
Que tous Sieges ne soient en seiour,
Portant au Coq don du TAG a mifere.

61 Never by the discovering of the day,
He shall attain to the Sceptriferous sign,
Till all his feats be settled.
Carrying to the Cock a gift from the Tag to misery.

Lors qu'on verra expiler le Saint Temple,
Plus grand du Rhosne, & sacres prophaner:
Par eux naistra pestilence si grande,
Roy fait injuste ne fera condamner.

62 When one shall see spoiled the Holy Temple,
The greatest of the Rhosne and sacred things prophesied.
From them shall come so great a pestilence,
That the King being unjust shall not condemn them.

Quand l'adultere blessé sans coup aura,
Meurdry la femme & le fils par depit,
Femme assommée l'Enfant estranglera,
Huit captifs prins, s'estoufer sans respit.

63 When the Adulterer wounded without a blow,
Shall have murdered the wife and son by spight,
The woman knocked down, shall strangle the child,
Eight taken prisoners, and stifled without tarrying.

Dedans les Isles les enfans transportez,
Les deux de sept seront en desespoir:
Ceux du terroüer en seront supportez,
Nompelle prins, des ligues fuy l'espoir.

64 In the Islands the Children shall be transported,
The two of seven shall be in despair,
Those of the Countrey shall be supported by,
Nompelle taken, avoid the hope of the League.

Le vieux frustré du principal espoir,
Il parviendra au chef de son Empire,
Vingt mois tiendra le Regne à grand pouvoir,
Tyran, cruel en delaissant un pire.

65 The old man frustrated of his chief hope,
He shall attain to the head of his Empire,
Twenty months be shall keep the Kingdom with great
power,
Tyrant, cruel, and leaving a worse one.

Quand l'Escriture D.M. trouvée,
Et Cave antique à Lampe descouverte,
Loy, Roy, & Prince Ulpian esprouvée,
Pavillon Royne & Duc soubs la couverte.

66 When the writing D. M. shall be found,
And an ancient Cave discovered with a Lamp,
Law, King, and Prince Ulpian tried,
Tent, Queen and Duke under the rugge.

Par. Car. Nersaf, à ruine grand discorde,
Ne l'un ne l'autre n'aura election,
Nersaf du peuple aura amour & concorde,
Ferrare, Collonne grande protection.

67 Par. Car. Nersaf, to ruine great discord,
Neither one nor the other shall be Elected,
Nersaf, shall have of the people love and concord,
Ferrare, Colonna, great protection.

Vieux Cardinal par le jeune deceu,
Hors de sa charge se verra desarmé,
Arles ne monstres double fort apperceu,
Et l'Aqueduct & le Prince embaumé.

68 | An old Cardinal shall be cheated by a young one,
And shall see himself out of his imployment,
Arles do not shon, a double fort perceived,
And the Aqueduct, and the embalmed Prince.

Aupres du jeune se vieux Ange baiser,
Et le viendra surmonter à la fin,
Dix ans esgaux aux plus vieux rabaisser,
De trois deux l'un huictiesme Seraphin.

69 | Near the young one the old Angel shall bowe,
And shall at last overcome him,
Ten years equal, to make the old one stoop,
Of three, two, one the eight a Seraphin.

Il entrera vilain, meschant, infame,
Tyrannisant la Mesopotamie,
Tous amis fait d'Adulterine Dame,
Terre horrible noir de Physiognomie.

70 | He shall come in villaen, wicked, infamous,
To tyranise Mesopotamia,
He maketh all friends byi an adulteress Lady,
Foul, horrid, black in his Physiognomie.

Croistra le nombres si grand des Astronomes,
Chassez, bannis & livres censureq̲
L'An mil six cens & sept par sacrez glomes,
Que nul au sacres ne seront asseurez.

71 | The number of Astronomers shall grow so great,
Driven away, banished, Brooks censured,
The year one thousand and six hundred and seven by
sacred glomes,
That none shall be secure in the sacred places.

Champ Perusin 0 l'Enorme deffaite,
Et le conflict tout aupres de Ravenne,
Passage sacra lors qu'on fera la feste.
Vainqueur vaincu, Cheval mange L'avenne.

72 | Perugian Field, O the excessive rout,
And the fight about Ravenna,
Sacred passage when the Feast shall be celebrated,
The victorious vanquished, the Horse to eat up his Oats.

Soldat Barbare le grand Roy frapera,
Injustement non esloigré de mort,
L'Avare Mere du fait cause sera,
Conjurateur & Regne en grand remort.

73 | A Barbarous Souldier shall strike the King,
Unjustly, not far from death,
The covetous Mother shall be the cause of it,
The Conspirator and Kingdom in great remorse.

En Terre neuve bien avant Roy entré,
Pendant subiets luy viendront faire accueil,
Sa perfidie aura tel rencontré,
Qu'aux Citadins lieu de feste & recueil.

74 | A King being entered far into a new Countrey,
Whilst his Subjects shall come to welcome him,
His persidiousness shall find such an encounter,
That to the Citizens it shall be instead of feast and welcom.

Le Pere & fils seront meurtris ensemble,
Le Prefecteur dedans son Pavillon,
La Mere à Tours du fils ventre aura enfle,
Cache verdure de fueilles papillon.

75 | The Father and Son shall be murdered together,
The Governour shall be so in his Tent,
At Tours the Mother shall be got with child by her son,
Hide the greenness with leaves Butter-flye.

Plus Macelin que Roy en Angleterre,
Lieu obscur ne ay par force aura l'Empire,
Lasche, sans foy, sans loy, seignera Terre,
Son temps s'aproche si presque ie souspire.

76 More Macelin then King in England,
Born in obscure place, by force shall reign,
Of loose disposition, without faith, without Law, the
ground shall bleed,
His time is drawing so near that I fight for it.

L'Antechrist bien tost rrois annichilez,
Vingt & sept ans durera sa guerre,
Les Heretiques morts; captifs exilez,
Sang corps humain eau rogie, gresler Terre.

77 By Antichrist three shall shortly be brought to nothing,
His War shall last seven and twenty years,
The Hereticks dead, Prisoners banished.
Blood, humane body, water mad: red, Earth hailed.

Un Bragamas avec la langue torte,
Viendra des dieux rompre le Sanctuaire,
Aux Heretiques il ouvrira la porte,
En suscitant l'Eglise Militaire.

78 A Bragmas with his crooked Tounge,
Shall come and break the Gods Sanctuary,
He shall open the Gates unto Hereticks,
By raising the Militant Church.

Qui par fer pere perdra, n'ay de Nonnaire,
De Gorgon sur la fin sera sang perfetant,
En Terre estrange fera si tout de taire,
Qu'il bruslera luy mesme & son entant.

79 He that by Iron shall destroy his Father, born in Nonnaire,
Shall in the end carry the blood of Gorgon,
Shall in a strange Countrey make all so silent,
That he shall burn himself and his intent.

Des innocens le sang de vesue & vierge,
Tant de maux faits par moien ce grand Roge,
Saints simulachres trempez en ardant cierge,
De frayeur crainte ne verra nul que boge.

80 The blood of the innocent Widow and Virgin,
So many evils committed by the means of that great Rogue,
Holy Images, dipt in burning wax Candles,
For fear no body shall be seen to stir.

Le neuf Empire en desolation,
Sera changé du Pole Aquilonaire,
De la Sicile viendra l'emotion,
Troubler l'Emprise à Philip tributaire.

81 The new Empire in desolation,
Shall be changed from the Northern Pole,
The commotion shall come from Sicily,
To trouble the undertaking, tributary to Philip.

Ronge long, sec, faisant du bon valet,
A la par fin n'aura que son congie,
Poignant poison & Lettres au colet.
Sera saisy, eschapé, en dangié.

82 Long gnawer, dry, cringing and fawning,
In conclusion shall have noting but leave to be gone,
Piercing poison and Letters in his Collar,
Shall be seised, escape, and in danger.

Le plus grand voile hors du port de Zara,
Pres de Bizance fera son entreprise,
D'Ennemy perte & l'amy ne sera,
Le tiers à deux fera grand pille & prise.

83 The greatest Sail out of the Port of Zara,
Near Bizance shall make his undertaking,
There shall be no loss of foes or friends,
The third shall make a great pillage upon the two.

Paterne aura de la Sicile crie,
Tous les aprests du Gouphre de Trieste,
Qui s'entendra jusques à la Trinacrie,
De tant de voiles, fuy, fuy, l'horrible peste.

Entre Bayonne & a Saint Jean de Lux,
Sera posé de Mars la promottoire,
Aux Hanix d'Aquilon, Nanar hostera Lux,
Puis suffoqué au lit sans adjoutoire.

Par Arnani, Tholose, & Villefranque,
Bande infinie par le Mont Adrian,
Passe Riviere, hutin par pont la planque,
Bayonne entrer tous Bichoro criant.

Mort conspirée viendra en plein effet,
Charge donnée & voyage de mort,
Esleu, crée, receu, par siens desfait,
Sang d'innocence devant soy par remort.

Dans la Sardaigne un noble Roy viendra,
Qui ne tiendra que trois ans le Royaume,
Plusieurs couleurs avec soy conjoindra,
Luy mesme apres soin sommeil Matrirscome.

Pour ne tomber entre mains de son oncle,
Qui ses enfants par regner trucidez,
Orant au peuple mettant pied sur Peloncle,
Mort & traisné entre Chevaux bardez.

Quand des croisez un trouvé de sens trouble,
En lieu du sacre verra un Bœuf cornu,
Par vierge porc son lieu lors sera double,
Par Roy plus ordre ne sera soustenu.

Parmy les Champs des Rhodanes entrées,
Où les croisez seront presques unis,
Les deux Brassiers en Pisces rencontrées
Et un grand nombre par Deluge punis.

84 | Paterne shall have out of Sicily a cry,
All the preparations of the Gulph of Trieste,
That shall be heard as far as Trinacry,
Of so many Sails, fly, fly, the horrid plague.

85 | Between Bayonne and Saint John de Lux,
Shall be put down the promoting of Mars,
From the Hunix of the North, Nanar shall take away Lux,
Then shall be suffocated in his bed without help.

86 | By Arnani, Tholose, and Villefranche,
An infinite deal of people by the Aprian,
Cross Rivers, noise upon the Bridge and plank,
Come all into Bayonne crying Bichoro.

87 | A conspired death shall come to an effect,
Charge given, and a journey of death.
Elected, created, received, by his own defeated,
Blood of Innocency before him by remorse.

88 | A noble King shall come into Sardinia
Who shall hold the Kingdom only three years,
He shall joyn many Colours to his own,
Himself afterwards, care, sleep matrirscome.

89 | That he might not fall into the hands of his Uncle,
That had murdered his Children for to rule,
Taking away from the people, and putting his foot upon Peloncle,
Dead and drawn among armed Horses.

90 | When of the crossed, one of a troubled mind,
In a sacred place shall see a horny Oxe,
By Virgin Pork then shall his place be double,
By King no henceforth, order shall be maintained.

91 | Through the Fields of the Rhodanes comings in,
Where the crossed shall be almost united,
The two Brassiers met in Pisces,
And a great number punished by a Flood.

Loin hors du Regne mis en hazard voiage,	92	Far from the Kingdom a hazardous journey undertaken,

Loin hors du Regne mis en hazard voiage,
Grand Ost duyra, pour soy l'occupera,
Le Roy tiendra les siens captif, ostage,
A son retour tout Pais pillera.

92 Far from the Kingdom a hazardous journey undertaken,
He shall lead a great Army, which he shall make his own,
The King shall keep his prisoners, and pledges,
At his return he shall plunder all the Countrey.

Sept mois sans plus obtiendra prelature,
Par son decez grand scisme fera naistre,
Sept mois tiendra un autre la Preture,
Pres de Venise paix union renaistre.

93 Seaven months and no more, he shall obtain the Prelacy,
By his decease he shall cause a great Schime,
Another shall be seven months chief Justice,
Near Venice peace and union shall grow again.

Devant le Lac ou plus cher fut getté,
De sopt mois & son Ost desconfit,
Seront Hispans par Albanois gastez,
Par delay perte en donnant le conflict.

94 Before the Lake wherein most dear was thrown,
Of seven months, and his Army overthrown,
Spaniards shall be spoiled by Albaneses,
By delaying ; loss in giving the Battle.

Le Seducteur sera mis dans la Fosse,
Et estaché jusques à quelque temps,
Le Clerc uny, le Chef avec sa Crosse,
Pycante droite attraira les contems.

95 The Deceiver shall be put into the Dungeon,
And bound fast for a while,
The Clerk united, the head with his Crosierstaf,
Pricking upright, shall draw in the contended.

La Synagogue sterile sans nul fruit,
Sera receue entre les Infideles,
De Babylon la fille du poursuit,
Misere & triste luy trenchera les Aisles.

96 The Synagogue barren, without fruit,
Shall be received among the Infidels,
In Babylon, the daughter of the persecuted,
Miserable and sad shall cut her wings.

Au fins du Var changer le Pompotans,
Pres du Rivage, les trois beaux enfans naistre,
Ruine au peuple par Aage competans,
Regne au Pais changer plus voir croistre.

97 At the ends of the Var to change the Pompotans,
Near the Shore shall three fair Children be born,
Ruine to the people, by competent Age,
To change that Countreys Kingdom, and see it grow no
more.

Des gens d'Eglise sang sera espanché,
Comme de l'eau en si grande abondance,
Et de long temps ne sera rerranché,
Veüe au Clerc ruine & doleance.

98 The blood of Churchmen shall be spilt,
As water in such abundance,
And for a good while shall not be stayed,
Ruine and grievance shall be seen to the Clerk.

Par la puissance des trois Rois temporels,
En autre lieu sera mis le Saint Siege,
Où la substance de l'Esprit corporel,
Sera remis & receu pour vray Siege.

99 By the power of the Temoral Kings,
The Holy See shall be put in another place,
Where the substance of the Corporeal Spirit,
Shall be restored, admitted for a true seat.

Century VIII - 146

Pour l'abondance de l'Armé respandue,
Du haut en bas, par le bas au plus haut,
Trop grande foy par jeu vie perdue,
De soif mourir par abondant defaut.

100 | Through the abundance of the Army scattered,
High and low, low and high,
Too great a belief a life lost in jesting,
To die by thirst, through abundance of want.

AUTRES QUATRAINS
Cy devant imprimez soubz la Centurie huietiesme

OTHER STANZAS
heretofore Printed, under the VIII Century.

Seront confus plusieurs de leurs attente,
Aux habitans ne sera pardonné,
Qui bien pensoient perseverer l'attente,
Mais grand loisir ne leur sera donné.

1 | Many shall be confounded in their expectation,
The Citizens shall not be forgiven,
Who thought to persevere in their resolution,
But there shall not be given them a great leisure for it.

Plusieurs viendront, & parleront de Paix,
Entre Monarques & Seigneurs bien puissans,
Mais ne sera accordé de si prés,
Que ne se rendent plus qu'autres obeissans.

2 | Many shall come and shall talk of Peace,
Between Monarchs and Lords very powerful,
But it shall not be agreed to it so soon,
If they do not shew themselves more obedient then others.

Las quelle fureur, helas quelle pitié,
Il y aura entre beaucoup de gens !
On ne vit onc une telle amitié,
Qu'auront les loups à courir diligens.

3 | Ha ! what fury, alas what pitty,
There shall be betwixt many people,
There was never seen such a friendship,
As the Wolfs shall have in being diligent to run.

Beaucoup de gens voudront perlementer,
Aux grands Seigneurs qui leur feront la guerre,
On ne voudra en rien les escouter,
Helas! si Dieu n'envoye paix en terre.

4 | Many folks shall come to speak,
To great Lords that shall make War against them,
They shall not be admitted to a hearing,
Alas ! if God doth not send Peace upon Earth.

Plusieurs secours viendront de tous costez,
De gens loingtains qui voudront resister,
Ils seront tout à coup bien hastez,
Mais ne pourront pour ceste heure assister.

5 | Many helps shall come on all sides,
Of people far off, that would fain to resist,
They shall be upon a sudden all very hasty,
But for the present they shall not be able to assist.

Las quel desir ont Princes estrangers!
Garde toy bien qu'en ton pays ne vienne,
Il y auroit de terribles dangers
En maintes contrées, mesme en la Vienne.

6 | Ha ! what pleasure take Forrain Princes ?
Take heed least any should come into thy Countrey,
There should be terrible dangers,
In several Countreys, and chiefly in Vienna.

Century IX

Ans la maison du Traducteur de Boure,
Seront les lettres trouvées sur la Table,
Borgne, roux, blanc, chanu tiendra de cours,
Qui changera au nouveau Connestable.

1

In the House of the Translator of Boure,
The Letters shall be found upon the Table,
Blind of one eye, red white, hoary, shall keep its course,
Which shall change at the coming of the new Constable.

Du haut du Mont Aventin voix ouye,
Vuidez, vuidez de tous les deux costez,
Du sang des rouges sera l'Ire assouvie,
D'Arimin, Prato, Columna debotez.

2

From the top of Mount Aventin, a voice was heard,
Get you gone, get you gone on all sides,
The Choler shall be fed with the blood of the red ones,
From Armini and Prato, the Colonnas shall be driven away.

La magna vaqua à Ravenne grand trouble,
Conduits par quinze enserrez à Fornase,
A Rome naistra deux Monstres à tested double,
Sang; feu, deluge, les plus grands à l'espase,

3

The Magna vaqua great trouble at Ravenna,
Conducted by fifteen, shut up at Foranse,
At Rome shall be born two Monsters with a double head,
Blood, fire, Flood, the greater ones astonished.

L'An ensuivant déscouverts par Deluge,
Deux chefs esleus, le premier ne tiendra,
De fuyr ombre à l'un deux le refuge,
Saccagée case qui premier maintiendra.

4

The year following being discovered by a Flood,
Two Chiefs elected, the first shall not hold,
To fly from shade, to one shall be a refuge
That house shall be plundered which shall maintain the first.

Tiers doigt du pied au premier semblera,
A un nouveau Monarque de bas haut,
Qui Pise & Luiques tyran occupera,
Du precedent corriger le deffault.

5

The third toe of the foot shall be like the first,
To a new high Monarch come from low estate,
Who being a Tyrant shall cease upon Pise and Lucia,
To correct the faults of him that preceded him.

Par la Guyenne infinité d'Anglois,
Occuperont par nom d'Angle Aquitaine,
Du Languedoc. I. palme Bourdelois,
Quils nommeront apres Barboxitaine.

6

There shall be in Guyenna an infinite number of English,
Who shall occupy it by the name of Angle Aquitaine,
Of Languedoc, I by the Land of Bourdeaux,
Which afterwards they shall call Barboxitaine.

Qui ouvrira le Monument trouvé,
Et ne viendra le serrer promptement,
Mal luy viendra & ne poura prouvé
Si mieux doibt estre Roy Breton ou Normand.

7

He that shall open the Sepulchre found,
And shall not close it up again presently,
Evil will befall him, and he shall not be able to prove
Whether is best a Britain or Norman King.

Puisnay Roy fait son pere mettre à mort,
Apres conflict de mort tres in honeste,
Escrit trouvé soupçon, donra remort,
Quand loup chassé pose sur la couchete.

8

A younger King causeth his father to be put
To a dishonest death, after a Battle,
Writing shall be found, that shall give suspicion and remorse,
When a hunted Wolf shall rest upon a truckle bed.

Quand Lampe ardente de feu inextinguible, Sera trouvée au Temple des Vestales, Enfant trouvée, feu, eau passant par crible, Nimes eau perir, Tholonse cheoir les Halles.	**9** When a Lamp burning with unquenchable fire, Shall be found in the Temple of the Vestals, A Child shall be found, Water running through a Sieve, Nismes to perish by Water, the Market hall shall fall at Tholouse.

Moine, Moinesse d'Enfant mort exposé,
Mourir par Ourse & ravy par verrier,
Par Foix & Panniers le Camp sera posé,
Contre Tholose, Carcas, dresser forrier.

10 Monk and Nun having exposed a dead Child,
To be killed by a she Bear, and snatch away by a Glazier,
The Camp shall be set by Foix and Panniers,
And against Tholouse, Carcas shall raise a Harbinger.

Le juste à tort à mort l'on viendra mettre,
Publiquement, & du milieu esteint,
Si grande Peste en ce lieu viendra naistre,
Que les Jugeans fouyr seront contraints.

11 The just shall be put to death wrongfully,
Publickly, and being taken out of the midst,
So great a Plague shall break into that place,
That the Judges shall be compelled to run away.

Le tant d'argent de Diane & Mercure,
Les simulachres au Lac seront trouvez,
Le Figulier cherchant argille neuve,
Luy & les siens, d'or seront abreuvez.

12 The so much Silver of Diana and Mercury
The Statues shall be found in the Lake,
The Potter seeing for new clay,
He and his shall be filled with Gold.

Les Exilez autour de la Sologne,
Conduits de nuict pour marcher en l'Auxois,
Deux de Modene truculent de Bolongne,
Mis discouverts par feu de Burançois.

13 The banished about Sologne,
Being conducted by night to go into Auxois,
Two of Modena, the cruel of Bolonia,
Shall be discovered by the fire of Burancois.

Mis en planure chauderon d'Infecteurs,
Vin, miel en huile & bastis sur Fourneaux,
Seront plongez sans mal dit malfacteurs,
Sept. fum. extaint au Canon des Bordeaux.

14 A Dyers Kettle being put an a Plein,
With Wine, Honey and Oil, and built upon Furnace,
Shall be dipt, without evil, called Malefactors,
Seven, fun. put out at the Canon of Borneaux.

Pres de Parpan les rouges detenus,
Ceux du milieu parfondrez menez loing,
Trois mis en pieces, & cinq mal soustenus,
Pour le Seigneur & Prelat de Bourgoing.

15 Near unto Parpan the red ones detained,
Those of the middle sunk and carried far off,
Three cut in pieces, and five ill backed,
For the Lord and Prelate of Burgoing.

De Castel Franco sortira l'assemblée,
L'Ambassadeur non plaisant fera Scisme,
Ceux de Riviere seront en la meslée,
Et au grand Goulphre desnieront l'entrée.

16 Out of Castel Franco shall come the Assembly,
The Embassador not pleased, shall make a Schisme,
Those of Riviere shall be in the medley,
And shall deny the entry of the great Gulf.

Le tiers premier pis que ne fit Neron,	17	The third first, worse then ever did Nero,
Vuidez vaillant que sang humain respandre,		Go out valliant, he shall spill much humane blood,
Rédifier fera le Forneron,		He shall cause the Forneron to be builded again,
Siecle d'or mort, nouveau Roy grãnd esclandre.		Golden Age dead, new King great troubles.

Le Lys Dauffois portera dans Nanci,	18	Dauffois shall carry the Lillie into Naney,
Jusques en Flanders Electeur de l'Empire,		As far as Flanders the Elector of the Empire,
Neufve obturée au grand Montmorency,		New hinderance to great Montmorency,
Hors lieux prouez delivre a clere peyne.		Out of proved places, delivered to a clear pain.

Dans le milieu de la Forest Mayenne,	19	In the middle of the Forrest of Mayenne,
Sol au Lion la Foudre tombera,		Sol being in Leo the Lightning shall fall,
Le grand Bastard issu du grand du Maine,		The great Bastard begot by the great du Main,
Ce jour Fougeres pointe en sang entrera.		That day Fougeres shall enter its point into blood.

De nuict viendra par la Forest de Reinnes,	20	By night shall come through the Forrest of Rennis,
Deux pars Voltorte Hene, la pierre blanche,		Two parts Voltorte Herne, the white stone,
Le Moyne noir en gris dedans Varennes,		The black Monk in gray within Varennes,
Esleu Cap. cause tempeste, feu, sang tranche.		Elected Cap. causeth tempest, fire, blood cutteth.

Au Temple haut de Blois facre Salonne,	21	At the high Temple of Blois sacred Salonne,
Nuict Pont de Loire, Prelat, Roy pernicant:		In the night the Bridge of Loire, Prelat, King mischevous,
Cuiseur victoire aux marests de la Lone,		A smarting Victory in the Marsh of Lone,
D'ou Prelature de blancs abormeant?		Whence Prelature of white ones shall be abortive.

Roy & sa Cour au lieu de langue halbe,	22	King and his Court in the place of langue halbe,
Dedans le Temple vis a vis du Palais,		Within the Church over against the Pallace,
Dans le Jardin Duc de Montor and Albe,		In the Garden Duke of Montor and Albe,
Albe & Mantor, poignard, langue, en Palais.		Albe and Mantor, dagger, tongue and Pallate.

Puisnay jouant au fresch dessous la tonne,	23	The youngest Son playing under the tun,
Le haut du toit du milieu sur la teste,		The top of the House shall fall upon his head,
Le Pere Roy au Temple Saint Solonne,		The King his Father in the Temple of Saint Soulaine,
Sacrifiant sacrera fum de feste.		Sacrificing shall make festival smoak.

Sur le Palais au Rocher des Fenestres,	24	Upon the Pallace at the Rock of the Windows ;
Seront ravis les deux petits Roiaux,		Shall be carried the two little Royal ones,
Passer Aurelle, Luthece, Denis cloistres,		To pass Aurele, Lutece, Denis Cloisters,
Nonnain, Mallods avaller verts noiaux.		Nonnain, Mollods to swallow green stones of fruit.

Passant les Ponts, venir prez de Roziers,	25	Going over the Bridge, to come near the Rose-trees,
Tard arrivé plustost quil cuidera,		Come late, and sooner then he thought,
Viendront les noves Espagnols a Beziers,		The new Spaniards shall come to Beziers,
Qui icelle chasse emprinse cassera.		Who shall cashiere this new undertaken hunting.

Nice sortie sur nom des Lettres aspres,	26	A silly going out, caused by sharp Letters,
La grande Cappe fera present non sien,		The great Cap shall give what is not his,
Proche de Vultry aux murs des vertes capres,		Near Vultry by the Walls of green Capers,
Apres Plombin levent a bon escient.		About Piombino the wind shall be in good earnest.
De bois la garde vent clos ront Pont sera,	27	The Fence being of Wood, close Wind, Bridge shall be broken,
Haut le receu frappera le Dauphin,		He that's received high, shall strike at the Dolphin,
Le vieux Teccon bois unis passera,		The old Teccon shall pass over smooth Wood,
Passant plus outredu Duc le droit confin.		Going over the right confines of the Duke.
Voile Symacle, Port Massiliolique,	28	Symaclian Sail, Massilian Port,
Dans Venise Port marcher aux Pannons,		In Venice to march towards the Hungarians,
Partir du Goulfre & sinus Illirique,		To go away from the Gulf and Illirick Sea,
Vast a Sicile, Ligurs coups de Canon.		Toward Sicily, the Genoeses with Cannon shots.
Lors que celuy qu à nul ne donne lieu,	29	When he that giveth place to no body,
Abandonner voudra lieu prins non pris,		Shall forsake the place taken, and not taken,
Feu, Nef, par saignes, bietument a Charlieu,		Fire, Ship, by bleeding bituminous at Charlieu,
Seront Quintin, Balez repris.		Then Quintin and Bales shall be taken again.
Au port de Puola & de St. Nicolas,	30	At the Harbour of Puola and of St. Nicholas,
Perir Normande au Gouftre Phanatique,		A Norman Ship shall perish in the Phanatick Gulf,
Cap de Bizance rues crier Helas !		At the Cape of Byzantium the streets shall cry Alas !
Secours de Gaddes & du grand Philippique.		Succours from Cadis and from the great Philippe.
Le tremblement de Terre. a Mortara,	31	There shall be an Earthquake at Mortara,
Caffich, St. George a demy perfondrez,		Cassich, St. George shall be half swallowed up,
Paix assoupie la guerre esueillera,		The War shall awake the sleeping pace,
Dans Temple a Pasques abysmes enfondrez.		Upon Easterday shall be a great hole sunk in the Church.
De fin Porphire profond Collon trouvée,	32	A deep Column of fine Porphyry shall be found,
Dessoubs la laze escripts Capitolin,		Under whose Basis shall be Roman writings,
Os, poil retors, Romain force prouvée,		Bones, haires twisted, Roman force tried.
Classe agiter au Port de Methelin.		A Fleet a gathering about the Port of Methelin.
Hercules Roy de Rome & Dannemark,	33	Hercules King of Rome, and Denmark,
De Gaule trois Gayon surnommé,		Of France three Guyon surnamed,
Trembler l'Italie & l'un de Saint Marc,		Shall cause Italy to quake and one of St. Marck,
Premier sur tous Monarque renommée.		He shall be above all a famous Monarch.

Le part solus Mary sera Mitré;	34	The separated Husband shall wear a Miter,
Retour conflict passera sur le tuille,		Returning, Battle, he shall go over the Tyle,
Par cinq cens un trahir sera tultré,		By five hundred one dignified shall be betrayed,
Narbon & Saulce par coutaux avons d'huile.		Narbon and Salces shall have Oil by the Quintal.
Et Ferdinand blonde sera descorte,	35	And Ferdinand having a troop of faire men,
Quitter la fleur suivre le Macedon,		Shall leave the flower to follow the Macedonian,
Au grand besoing defaillira sa routte,		At his great need his way shall fail him,
Et marchera contre le Myrmidon.		And he shall go against the Myrmidon.
Un grand Roy prins entre les mains d'un jeune,	36	A great King taken in the hands of a young one,
Non loin de Palques confusion, coup cultre:		Not far from Easter, confusion, stroke of a kinfe,
Perpet, cattif temps que foudre en la Hune,		Shall commit, pittiful time, the fixe at the top of the Mast,
Trois Freres lors fe besseront & meurtre.		Three Brothers then shall wound one another and murder done.
Pont & Moulins en Decembre versez,	37	Bridges and Mills in December overturned,
En si haut lieu montera la Garonne:		In so high a place the Garonne shall come,
Meurs, Edifice, Thoulouse reuversez,		Walls, Buildings, Thoulose overturned,
Qu'on ne scaura son lieu coutant matrone.		So that none shall know its plate, so much Matrone.
L'Entrée de Blaye par Rochelle & l'Anglois,	38	The coming in at Blaye by Rochel and the English,
Passera outre le grand Æmathien :		Shall go beyond the great Æmathien,
Non loin d'Agen attendra le Gaulois,		Not far from Agen shall expect the French,
Secours Narbonne deceu par entretien.		Help from Narbonne deceived by entertainment.
En Arbissela, Vezema & Crevari,	39	In Arbissella, Vezema and Crevari,
De nuict conduits pour Savenne atraper,		Being conducted during night to take Savona,
Le vifs Gascon, Giury, & la Charry,		The quick Gascon, Giury and the Charry,
Derrier Mur vieux & neuf Palais grapper.		Behind old Walls and new Pallace to graple.
Pres de Quentin dans la Forest Bourlis,	40	Near Quentin in the Forrest Bourlis,
Dans l'Abbaye seront Flamands tranchez,		In the Abby the Flemmings shall be slashed,
Les deux puisnez de coups my estourdis,		The two younger sons half a stonished with blows,
Suitte appressée & gardes tous hachez.		The followers oppressed, and the Guards all cut in pieces.
Le grand Chyren soy saisir d'Avignon,	41	The great Cheyren shall seize upon Avignon,
De Rome Lettres en miel plein d'amertume,		Letters from Rome shall come full of bitterness,
Lettre, Ambassade partir de Chanignon,		Letters and Embassies shall go from Chanignon,
Carpentras pris par Duke noir, rouge plume.		Carpentras taken by a black Duke with a red Feather.

De Barcelonne, de Gennes & Venise;	42	From Barcelona, from Genoa and Venice,
De la Secile pres Monaco unis,		From Sicily near Monaco united,
Contre Barbare classe prendront la vise,		Against the Barbarian the fleet shall take her aim,
Barbar poulsé bien loing jusqu'a Thunis.		The Barbarian shall be driven back as far as Thunis.

Proche a descendre l'Armee Crucigere,   43   The Crucigere Army being about to Land,
Sera quettée par les Ismaelites, Shall be watched by the Ismaelites,
De tous costez battus par nef Riviere, Being beaten on all sides by the Ship Raviere,
Prompt assailis de dix Galeres d'efflite. Presently assaulted by ten chosen Galleys.

Migrés, migrez de Geneve trestous,   44   Go forth, go forth out of Geneva all,
Saturne d'Orien Fer se changera, Saturn of gold, shall be changed into Iron,
Le contre Raypoz exterminera tous, They against Raypos shall exterminate them all,
Avant l'advent le Ciel signes fera. Before it happeneth, the Heavens will shew signs.

Ne sera soul jamais de demander,   45   He shall never be weary of asking,
Grand Mendosus obtiendra son Empire, Great Mendosus shall obtain his dominion,
Loing de la Cour fera contremander, Far from the Court he shall cause him to be countermanded,
Piemond, Picard, Paris, Tyrhen le pire. Piemont, Picardy, Paris, Tyrhen the worse.

Vuydez fuyez de Tolose les ronges,   46   Get you gone, away from Thoulouse ye red ones,
Du Sacrifice faire expiation, There shall expiation be made of the Sacrifice,
Le Chef du mal dessoubs l'ombre des courges, The chief cause of the evil under the shade of gourdes,
Mort estrangler carne omination. Shall be strangled, a presage of the destruction of much flesh.

Les soubsignez d'indigne deliverance,   47   The underwritten to an unworthy deliverance,
Et de la multe auront contre advis, Shall have from the multitude a contrary advice,
Change Monarque mis en perille pence, They shall change their Monarch and put him in peril,
Serrez en cage se verront vis a vis. They shall see themselves shut up in a Cage over against,

La grand Cité d'Occean Maritime,   48   The great Maritime City of the Ocean,
Environnée de Marests en Crystal, Encompassed with Chrystaline Fens,
Dans le Solstice hyemal & la prime, In the Winter Solstice and in the spring,
Sera tentée de vent espouvental. Shall be tempted with fearful wind.

Gand & Bruxelles marcheoront contre Anvers,   49   Grand and Bruxelles shall go against Antwerp,
Senat de Londres mettront a mort leur Roy, The Senat of London shall put their King to death,
Le Sel & vin luy seront a l'envers, The Salt and Wine shall not be able to do him good,
Pour eux avoir le Regne or desarroy. That they may have the Kingdom into ruine.

Mensodus tost viendra a son haut Regne,	50
Mettant arriere un peu les Norlaris,	
Le rouge blesme, le masle a l'interregne,	
Le jeune crainte & frayeur Barbaris.	

50 | Mensodus shall soon come to his high Government,
Putting a little aside the Norlaris,
The red, pale, the Male at the interreigne,
The young fear, and dread barbarisme.

Contre les rouges Sectes se banderont,
Feu, eau, fer, corde, par paix se minera,
An point mourir ceux qui machineront,
Fors un que monde sur tout ruinera,

51 | Against the red, Sects shall gather themselves,
Fire, water, iron, rope, by peace it shall be destroyed,
Those that shall conspire shall not be put to death,
Except one, who above all shall undo the World.

La paix sapproche d'un costé, & la guerre,
Oncques ne fut la poursuite si grande,
Plaindre homme & femmene sang innocent par
Terre,
Et ce fera de France a toute bande.

52 | Peace is coming on one side, and War on the other,
There was never so great a pursuing,
Man, Woman shall bemoan, Innocent blood shall be spilt,
It shall be in France on all sides.

Le Neron jeune dans, les trois Cheminées,
Fera de Pages vifs pour ardoir ietter,
Heureux qui loin sera de tels menées,
Trois de son sang le feront mort quetter.

53 | The young Nero in the three Chimneys.
Shall cause Pages to be thrown to be burnt alive,
Happy shall he be who shall be far from this doing,
Three of his own blood shall cause him to be put to death.

Arrivera au port de Corsibonne,
Pres de Ravenne, qui pillera la Dame,
En Mer profonde legat de la Ulisbonne,
Sous Roc cachez raviront septante ames.

54 | There shall come into the Port of Corsibonne,
Near Ravenna, those that shall plunder the Lady,
In the deep Sea shall be the Embassador of Lisbonne,
The hidden under the Rock, shall carry away seventy Souls.

L'Horrible guerre qu'en Occident s'appreste,
L'An ensuivant viendra la Pestilence,
Si fort terrible, que jenne, viel, ne beste,
Sang, feu, Mercu. Mars, Jupiter en France.

55 | An horrid War is a preparing in the West,
The next year shall come the Plague,
So strangely terrible, that neither young nor old, nor beast
shall escape.
Blood, fire, Mercu, Mars, Jupiter in France.

Camp prés de Noudam passera Goussanville,
Et a Maiotes laissera son enseigne,
Convertira en instant plus de mille,
Cherchant le deux remettre en chaine & legne.

56 | A Camp shall by Noudam go beyond Goussanville,
And shall leave its Ensign at Maiotes,
And shall in an instant convert above a thousand,
Seeking to put the two parties in good under standing
together.

Au lieu de Drux un Roy reposera,
Et cherchera Loy changeant d'Anatheme,
Pendant le Ciel si tresfort Tonnera,
Portée neufve Roy tuera soy mesme.

57 | In the place of Drux a King shall rest himself,
And shall seek a Law changing Anatheme,
In the mean white the Heaven shall Thunder so strongly,
That a new gate shall kill the King himself.

Au costé gauche a lendroit de Vitry;	58	On the left hand over against Vitry,
Seront quettez les trois rouges de France,		The three red ones of France shall be watched for,
Tous assommez rouge, noir non meurdry,		All the red shall be knockt dead, the black not murdered.
Par les Bretons remis en asseurance.		By the Britains set up again in security.
A la Ferté prendra la Vidame,	59	In the Ferté the Vidame shall take
Nicol tenu rouge quavoit produit la vie,		Nicol, reputed red, whom life hath produced,
La grand Loyse naistra que fera clame,		The great Lewis shall be born, who shall lay claim,
Donnant Bourgongne a Bretons par envie.		Giving Burgundy to the Britains, through envy.
Conflict Barbare en la Cornere noire,	60	A Barbarian fight in the black Corner,
Sang espandu trembler la Dalmatie,		Blood shall be spilt, Dalmatia shall tremble for fear,
Grand Ismael mettra son promontoire,		Great Ismael shall set up his promontory,
Ranes trembler, secours Lusitanie.		Frogs shall tremble, Portugal shall bring succour.
La pille faicte a la Coste Marine,	61	The plunder made upon the Sea Coast,
Incita nova & parens amenez,		Incita nova and friends brought up,
Plusieurs de Malthe par le fait de Messine,		Many of Maltha, for the fact of Messina,
Estroit serrez seront mal querdonnez.		Being close kept, shall be ill rewarded.
Au grand de Cheramonagora,	62	To the great one of Cheramonagora,
Seront croisez par rangs tous attachez,		Shall be crossed by Ranges, all tyed up,
Le Pertinax Oppi, & Mandragora,		The Pertinax Oppi, and Mandragora,
Raugon d'Octobre. le tiers seront laschez.		Raugon the third of October shall be set loose.
Plaintes, & pleurs, cris, & grands hurlemens,	63	Complaints and tears, cries, and great howlings,
Pres de Narbon, a Bayonne & en Foix,		Near Narbonne, Bayonne and in Foix,
O quels horribles, calamitez, changemens,		O what horrid calamities and changes,
Avant que Mars revolu quelquefois.		Before Mars hath made sometimes his revolution.
L'Æmathion passer Monts Pyrenées,	64	The Æmathian shall pass by the Pyrenean Mountains,
En Mas Narbon ne fera resistance,		In March Narbon shall make no resistance,
Par Mer & Terre fera si grand menee,		By Sea and Land he shall make so much ado,
Cap. n'ayant Terre seure pour demeurance.		Cap. shall not have safe ground to live in.
Dedans le coing de Luna viendra rendre,	65	He shall come into the corner of Luna,
Ou sera prins & mis en Terre estrange.		Where he shall be taken and put in a strange Land,
Les fruits immeurs seront a grand esclandre,		The green fruits shall be in great disorder,
Grand vitupere, a l'un grande loüange.		A great shame, to one shall be great praise.
Paix, union, sera & changement,	66	Peace, union, shall be, and mutation,
Estats, Offices, bas hault, & hault bien bas,		States, and Offices, low high, and high low,
Dresser voiages, le fruit premier, tourment,		A journey shall be prepared for, the first fruit, pains,
Guerre cesser, civil proces, debats.		War shall cease, as also civil suits, and strifes.

Du haut des Monts a lentour de Dizere
Port a la Roche Valent. cent assemblez,
De Chasteau-Neuf, Pierrelate, en Donzere,
Contre le Crest, Romans foy assemblez.

67 | From the top of the Mountains about Dizere
Gate at the Rock Valence, a hundred gathered together,
From Chasteau-Neuf, Pierrelate, in Douzere
Against the Crest, Romans, shall be gathered.

Du Mont Aymar sera noble obscurcie,
Le mal viendra au joint de Saone & Rhosne,
Dans bois cachez Soldats jour de Lucie,
Qui ne fut onc un si horrible Throsne.

68 | From Mount Aymar shall proceed a Noble obscurity,
The evil shall come to the joyning of the Saone and Rhosne,
Soldiers shall be hid in the Wood on St. Lucy's day;
So that there was never such an horrid Throne.

Sur le Mont de Bailly & la Bresse,
Seront cachez de Grenoble les fiers
Outre Lyon, Vien eux si grand gresle.
Langoult en Terre n'en cessara un tiers.

69 | Upon the Mount of Bailly, and the Countrey of Bresse,
Shall be hidden the fierce ones of Grenoble,
Beyond Lyons, Vienna, upon them shall fall such a hail,
That laugishing upon the ground, the third part shall not be left.

Harnois trenchans dans les flambeaux cachez,
Dedans Lyon le jour du Sacrement,
Ceux de Vienne seront trestous hachez,
Par les Cantons Latins, Mascon eront.

70 | Sharp Weapons shall be hidden in burning Torches,
In Lyons the day of the Sacrament,
Those of Vienna shall be all cut to pieces,
By the Latin Cantons, after the example Mascon.

Au lieux Sacréz, animaux veus a Trixe,
Avec celuy qui nosera le jour.
A Carcassonne pour disgrace propice,
Sera posé pour plus ample sejour.

71 | In the Sacred places, Animals shall be seen at Trixe,
With him that shall not dare in the day,
In Carcassonne for a favourable disgrace,
He shall be set to make a longer stay.

Encor seront les Saints Temples pollus,
Et expilez par Senat Tholosain,
Saturne deux trois Siecles revolus,
Dans Auril, May, gens de nouveau Levain.

72 | Once more shall the Holy Temples be polluted,
And depredated by the Senate of Thoulouze,
Saturn two three Ages finished,
In April, May, people of a new Leaven.

Dans Foix entrez Roy Gerulée Turban,
Et regnera moins evolu Saturne,
Roy Turban Blanc, Bizance cœur ban,
Sol, Mars, Mercure, pres la Hurne.

73 | In Foix shall come a King with a Blew Turbant,
And shall Reign before Saturn is revolved,
Then a King with a White Turbant shall make Bizance to quake,
Sol, Mars Mercury, being near the top of the Mast.

Dans la Cité de Fertsod homicide,
Fait & fait multe Bœuf arant ne macter,
Retours encores aux honneurs d'Artemide,
Et a Vulcan corps morts sepulturer.

74 | In the City of Fertsod one murdered,
Causeth a Fine to be laid for killing a plowing Oxe,
There Shall be a return of the honours due to Artemide,
And Vulcan shall bury dead bodies.

De l'Ambraxie & du pais de Thrace, Peuple par Mer, Mal, & secours Gaulois, Perpetuelle en Provence la Trace, Avec vestiges de leur Coustumes & Loix.	**75** From Ambraxia, and from the Countrey of Thracia, People by Sea, Evil, and French succours, The Trace of it shall be perpetual in Provence, The footsteps of their Customs and Laws remaining.
Avec le noir Rapax & sanguinaire, Yssu du peaultre de l'inhumain Neron, Emmy deux Fleuves main gauche Militaire, Sera meurtry par Joyn Chaulveron.	**76** With the Black and bloody Rapax, Descended from the paultry of the inhumane Nero, Between two Rivers, on the left Military hand, He shall be murdered by Joyne Caulveron.
Le Regne prins le Roy conviera, La Dame prinse a mort jurez a sort, La vie a Royne Fils on desniera, Et la pellix au fort de la consort.	**77** The Kingdom being taken, the King shall invite, The Lady taken to death, The Life shall be denyed unto the Queens Son, And the Pellix shall be at the height of the Consort.
La Dame Grecque de Beauté laydique, Heureuse faicte de procs innumerable, Hors translatée au Regne Hispanique, Captive prinse mourir mort miserable.	**78** The Græcian Lady of exuisite Beauty, Made happy from innumerable quarrels, Being translated into the Spanish Kingdom, Shall be made a Prisoner, and die a miserable death.
Le Chef de Classe par fraude, stratageme, Fera timides sortir de leurs Galeres, Sortis meurdris chef renieux de Cresme, Puis par l'Embusche luy rendront les saleires.	**79** The Commander of a Fleet by fraud and stratagem, Shall cause the fearful ones to come forth of their Galleys, Come out murdered, chief renouncer of Baptism, After that by an Ambuscado they'l give him again his salary.
Le Duc voudra les siens exterminer, Envoyera les plus forts, lieux estranges, Par tyrannie Bize & Luc ruiner, Puy les Barbares sans Vin feront Vendanges.	**80** The Duke shall endeavour to exterminate his own, And shall send away the strongest of them into remote places, He shall also ruinate Bize and Luc; The Barbarians shall make Vintage without Wine.
Le Roy rusé entendra ses Embusches, De trois quartiers Ennemis assaillir, Un nombre estrange Larmes decoqueluches, Viendra Lemprin du traducteur faillir.	**81** The crafty King shall hear of his Ambuscadoes, And shall asail his Enemies on three sides, A strange number of Friers, mens Tears, Shall cause Lamprin to desert the Traitor.
Par le Deluge & pestilence forte, La Cité grande de long temps Assiegée, La Sentinelle & Garde de main morte, Subite prinse mais de nul outragée.	**82** The great City having been long Besieged, By an Innundation and violent Plague. The Sentinal and Watch being surprised, Shall be taken on a sudden, but hurt by no body.

Sol Vingt de Taurus, fi fort de terre tremblera,
Le grand Theatre remply ruinera,
L'Air, Ciel & Terre, obscurcir & troubler,
Lors l'Infidele Dieu, & Saints voguera.

83 The Sun being in the 20th of Taurus, the Earth shall so quake,
That it shall fill and ruinate the great Theater
The Air, the Heaven, & the Earth shall be so darkened, and troubled,
That the unbelivers shall call upon God, and his Saints.

Roy exposé parfaira l'Hecatombe,
Apres avoir trouve son Origine,
Torrent ouvrir de Marbre & Plomb la Tombe,
D'un grand Romain d'Enseigne Medusin.

84 The King exposed shall fulfill the Hecatombe,
After he hath found out his Offspring,
A Torrent shall open the Sepulcher, made of Marble and Lead,
Of a great Roman, with a Medusean Ensign,

Passer Guenne, Languedoc & le Rhosne,
D'Agen tenants, de Marmande & la Reole,
D'Ouvrir par foy parroy, Phocen tiendra son Throne,
Conflict aupres Saint Pol de Mauseole.

85 They shall pass over Gascony, Languedoc, and the Rhosne,
From Agen keeping Marmande, and the Reole,
To open the Wall by Faith, Phocen shall keep his Throne,
A Battle shall be by St. Paul of Manseole.

Du Bourg la Reyne parviendront droit a Chartres,
Et feront pres du Pont Antony pose,
Sept pour la paix cauteleux comme Martres,
Feront entrée d'Armée a Paris clause.

86 From Bourg la Reyne they shall come straight to Chartres,
And shall make a stand near Pont Antony,
Seven for Peace as crafty as Martres,
They shall enter in Paris besieged with an Army.

Par la Forest du Touphon essartée,
Par hermitage sera posé le temple,
Le Duc d'Estampes par sa ruse inventée.
Du Montlehori Prelat donra exemple.

87 By the Forrest Touphon cut off,
By the Hermitage shall the Temple be set,
The Duke of Estampes by his invented trick,
Shall give example to the Prelat of Montlehery.

Calais, Arras, secours a Theroanne,
Paix & semblant simulera l'escoute,
Soulde d'Allobrox descendre par Roane.
Destornay peuple qui defera la routte.

88 Calais, Arras, shall give succours to Theroanne,
Peace or the like, shall dissemble the hearing,
Souldiers of Allobrox shall descend by Roane,
People perswaded, shall spoil the March.

Sept ans Philipp-fortune prospere,
Rabaissera des Barbares l'effort,
Puis son midy perplex rebours affaire,
Jeune Ogmion abysmera son fort.

89 Philip shall have seven years of prosperous fortune,
Shall beat down the attempt of the Barbarians,
Then in his Noon he shall be perplexed and have untoward business,
Young Ogmion shall pull down his strength.

Un Capitaine de la grand Germanie,
Se viendra rendre par simulé secours,
Au Roy des Roys, aide de Pannonie,
Que sa revolte fera de sang grand cours.

90 | A Captain of the great Germany,
Shall come to yield himself with a fained help,
Unto the King of Kings, help of Hungary,
So that his revolt shall cause a great bloodshed.

L'Horrible peste Perynte & Nicopole,
Le Chersonese tiendra & Marceloine,
La Thessalie naistera l'Amphipole,
Mal incogneu & le refus d'Antoine.

91 | The horrid pestilence shall seize upon Perynthe and Nicopolis,
The Chersonese and Marceloine,
It shall waste Thessalia and Amphipolis,
An unknown evil and the refusal of Antony.

Le Roy voudra dans Cité neufve entrer,
Par ennemis expugner l'on viendra,
Captif libere, faux dire & perpetrer,
Roy dehors estre, loin d'ennemis tiendra.

92 | The King shall desire to enter into the new City,
With foes they shall come to overcome it,
The Prisoner being free, shall speak and act falsly,
The King being gotten out, shall keep far from enemies.

Les ennemis du Fort bien esloignez,
Par Chariots conduits le Bastion.
Par sur les Murs de Bourges esgrongnez,
Quand Hercules battra l'Hemathion.

93 | The enemies being a good way from the Fort,
Shall upon Wagons be conducted to the Bulwark,
From the top of Bourges Walls they shall be cut less,
When Hercules shall beat the Hæmathion.

Foibles Galeres seront unis ensemble,
Ennemis faux, le plus fort en rempart,
Foibles assailies Wratislavie tremble,
Lubeck & Mysne tiendront Barbare part.

94 | Weak Galleys shall be united together,
False enemies, the strongest shall be fortified,
Weak assaults, and yet Breslaw quaketh for fear,
Lubeck and Misne shall take the part of the Barbarians.

Le nouveau fait conduira l'exercite,
Proche apamé jusque aupres du Rivage,
Tendant secours de Melanoise eslite,
Duc yeux privé, a Milan fer de Cage.

95 | The new man shall lead up the Army,
Near Apame, till near the Bank,
Carrying succours of choice Forces from Milan,
The Duke deprived of his eyes, and an Iron Cage at Milan.

Dans Cité entrer exercite desniée,
Duc entrera par persuasion,
Aux foibles portes clam Armée amenée,
Mettront feu, mort, de sang effusion.

96 | The Army being denied the entrance of the City,
The Duke shall enter by persuasion,
To the weak Gates, clam the Army being brought,
Shall put all to fire and sword.

De Mer Copies en trois parts divisées,
A la seconde les Vivres failliront,
Desesperez cherchant Champs Elisées,
Premiers en breche entrez victoire auront.

97 | A Fleet being divided unto three parts,
The victuals will fail the second part,
Being in despaire they'l seek the Elysian Fields,
And entring the breach first, shall obtain victory.

Les affigez par faute d'un seul taint,
Contremenant a partie opposite,
Aux Lygonois mandera que contraint,
Seront de rendre le grand chef de Molite.

98 | The afflicted want of one only died,
Carrying against the opposite part,
Shall send word to those of Lyon, they shall be compelled,
To surrender the great chief of Molite.

Vent Aquilon fera partir le Siege,
Par meurs jetter cendres, chaulx, & poussiere,
Par pluye apres qui leur fera bien piege,
Dernier secours encontre leur Frontiere.

99 | The North wind shall cause the Siege to be raised,
They shall throw ashes, lime, and dust,
By a rain after that shall be a trap to them,
It shall be the last succours against their Frontiere.

Navale pugne nuict sera superée.
Le feu, aux Naves a l'Occident ruine,
Rubriche neuve, la grand néf colorée,
Ire a vaincu, & victoire en bruine.

100 | In a Sea-fight, night shall be overcome,
By fire, to the Ships of the West ruine shall happen,
A new stratagem, the great Ship coloured,
Anger to the vanquished, and victory in a Mist.

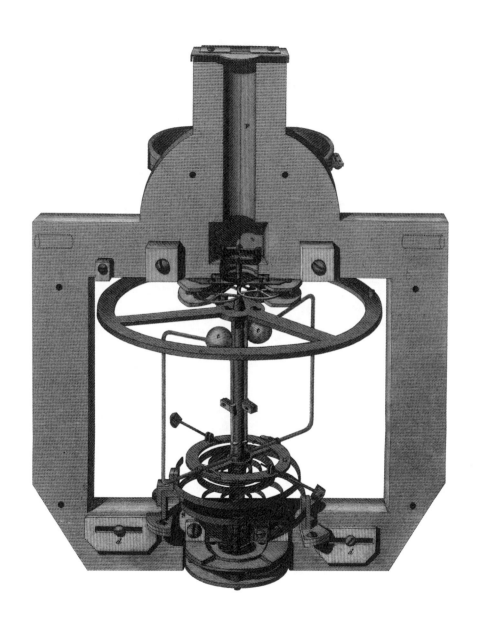

Century X

l'Ennemy, l'ennemy foy promise,
Ne se tiendra, les captifs retenus,
Prins preme mort & le reste en chemise,
Donnant le reste pour estre secourus.

1

To the enemy, the enemy faith promised,
Shall not be kept, the prisoners shall be detained,
The first taken, put to death, and the rest stripped,
Giving the remnant that they may be succoured.

Voile Gallere Voile nef Cachera,
La grand Classe viendra sortir la moindre,
Dix Naves proches le tourneront poulser,
Grande vaincüe, unies a soy joindre.

2

The Galley and the Ship shall hide their Sails,
The great Fleet shall make the little one to come out,
Ten Ships near hand, shall turn and push at it,
The great being vanquished, they shall unite together.

En apres cinq troupeau ne mettra hors,
Un suitif pour Penelon laschera,
Faux murmurer secours venir pour lors,
Le Chef le Siege lors abandonnera.

3

After that, five shall not put out his flock,
He'l let loose a runaway for Penelon,
There shall be a false rumour, succours shall come then,
The Commander shall forsake the Siege.

Sur la minuict conducteur de l'Armée
Se sauvera subit esvanovy,
Sept ans apres la fame non blasmée,
A son retour ne dira oncq ouy.

4

About midnight the leader of the Army,
Shall save himself, vanishing suddenly,
Seven years after his fame shall not be blamed
And at his return he shall never say yea.

Albi & Castres feront nouvelle ligne,
Neuf Arriens, Lisbonne, & Portuguez,
Carcas, Tholouze, consumeront leur brique
Quand chef neuf monstre de Lauraguez.

5

Albi and Castres shall make a new league,
Nine Arriens, Lisbonne, and Portugez,
Carcas, Thoulouse, shall make an end of their confederacy,
When the new chief shall come from Lauragais.

Gardon a Nismes eaux si haut desborderont,
Qu'on cuidera Deucalion renaistre,
Dans le Colosse la pluspart fuiront,
Vesta Sepulchre feu esteint apparoistre.

6

Gardon at Nismes, waters shall overflow so high,
That they'l think that Deucalion is born again,
Most of them will run into the Colossus,
And a Sepulchre, and fire extinguished, shall appear.

Le grand conflict qu'on appreste a Nancy,
L'Æmathien dira tout je soubmets,
L'Isle Britane par Vin Sel en solcy,
Hem. mi. deux Phi. long temps ne tiendra Mets.

7

A great War is preparing at Nancy,
The Æmathien shall say I submit to all,
The British Island shall be put in care by Salt and Wine,
Hem. mi. two Phi. shall not keep Mets long.

Index & Poulse parsondera le front,
De Senegalia le Conte a son Fils propre,
La Myrnamée par plusieurs de plain front,
Trois dans sept jours blessez more.

8

Index and Poulse shall break the forehead,
Of the Son of the Earl of Senegalia,
The Myrnamee by many at a full bout,
Three within seven days shall be wounded to death.

De Castilon figuieres jour de brune,	9	Out of Castilon figuieres upon a misty day,
De femme infame naistra Souverain Prince,		From an infamous woman shall be born a Soveraign Prince,
Surnom de chausses per hume luy posthume,		His surname shall be from Breeches, himself a posthume,
Onc Roy ne fut si pire en sa Province.		Never a King was worse in his Province.
Tasche de murdre, enormes Adulteres,	10	Endeavour of Murder, enourmous Adulteries,
Grand ennemy de tout le genre humain,		A great enemy of all mankind,
Que sera pire qu'ayeulx. Oncles ne Pere,		That shall be worse then Grand-father, Uncle, or Father,
Enfer, feu, eau, sanguin & inhumain.		In Iron, fire, water, bloody and inhumane.
Dessoubs Jonchere du dangereux passage,	11	Below Joncheres dangerous passage,
Fera passer le posthume sa bande,		The posthume shall cause his Army to go over,
Les Monts Pyrens passer hors son bagage,		And his Baggage to go over the Pyrenean Mountains,
De Parpignan courira Duc a Tende.		A Duke shall run from Perpignan to Tende.
Esleu en Pape, d'Esleu sera mocqué,	12	Elected for a Pope, from Elected shall be baffled,
Subit soudain, esmeu prompt & timide,		Upon a sudden; moved quick and fearful,
Par trop bon doux a mourir provoqué,		By too much sweetness provoked to die,
Crainte estainte la nuit de sa mort guide.		His fear being out in the night shall be Leader to his death.
Soubs la pasture d'animaux ruminans,	13	Under the pasture of Beasts chewing the cud,
Par eux conduits au ventre Herbi-polique,		Conducted by them to the Herbi-polique belly,
Soldats cachez, les armes bruit menants,		Souldiers hidden, the Weapons making a noise,
Non loin tentez de Cité Antipolique.		Shall be attempted not from Antipolick City,
Urnel, Vaucile sans conseil de soy mesmes,	14	Urnel, Vaucile, without advice of his own,
Hardy, timide par crainte prins vaincu,		Stout and fearful, by fear taken and overcome,
Accompagné de plusieurs putains, blesmes,		Pale, and in company of many Whores,
A Barcelonne aux Chartreux convaincu.		Shall be convinced at Barcelone by the Charterhouse.
Pere Duc vieux d'ans & de soif chargé,	15	A Father Duke aged and very thirsty,
Au jour extreme fils defniant l'esquiere.		In his extremity, his son denying him the Ewer,
Dedans le puis vif, mort viendra plongé.		Alive into a Well, where he shall be drowned,
Senat au fil la mort longue & legere.		For which the Senate shall give the son a long and easie death.
Heureux au Regne de France heureux de vie,	16	Happy in the Kingdom of France, happy in his Life,
Ignorant sang, mort, fureur, rapine,		Ignorant of blood, death, fury, of taking by force,
Par non flatteurs seras mis en envie,		By no flatterers shall be envied,
Roy desrobé, trop de foy en cuisine.		King robbed, too much faith in Kitchin.

La Reyne Ergaste voiant sa fille blesme,
Par vn regret dans l'estomach enclos,
Cris lamentables seront lors d'Angolesme,
Et au germain mariage forclos.

17 | Queen Ergaste seeing her Daughter pale,
By a regret contained in her Breast,
Then shall great cries come out of Angolesme,
And the Marriage shall be denyed to the Cousin German.

Le rang Lorrain fera place a Vendosme,
Le haut mis bas, & le bas mis en haut,
Le fils d'Hamon sera esleu dans Rome,
Et les deux grands seront mis en defaut.

18 | The House of Lorrain shall give place to Vendosme,
The high pulled down, the low raised up,
The son of Hamon shall be Elected into Rome,
And the two great ones shall not appear.

Jour que sera pour Roine saluée,
Le jour apres le salut, la Priere,
Le compte fait raison & valbuée,
Par avant humble oncques ne fut si siere.

19 | The day that she shall be saluted Queen,
The next day after the Evening Prayer,
All accompts being summoned and cast up,
She that was humble before, never was one so proud.

Tous les amis qu'auront tenu party,
Pour rude en lettres mis mort & saccagé.
Biens publiez par fixe, grand neanty,
Onc Romain people ne fut tant outrage.

20 | All the friends that shall have taken the part
Of the Unlearned, put to death and robbed,
Goods sold publickly by proclamation, a great man seized of them,
Never Roman people was so much abused.

Par le despit du Roy soustenant moindre,
Sera meurdry luy presentant les bagues,
Le Pere & Fils voulant Noblesse poindre,
Fait comme a Perse jadis firent les Magnes.

21 | To spite the King, who took the part of the weaker,
He shall be murdered, presenting to him Jewels,
The Father and the Son going to vex the Nobility,
It shall be done to them as the Magi did in Persia.

Pour ne vouloir consentir au divorce,
Qui puis apres sera cogneu indigne,
Le Roy des Isles sera chassé par force,
Mas a son lien qui de Roy n'aura signe.

22 | For not consenting to the divorce,
Which afterwards shall be acknowledged unworthy,
The King of the Island shall be expelled by force,
And another subrogated, who shall have no mark of a King.

Au peuple ingrat faites les remonstrances,
Par lors l'Armée se saisira d'Antibe,
Dans larc Monech feront les doleances,
Et a Freins l'un l'autre prendra ribe.

23 | The remonstrances being made to the ungrateful people,
At the time the Army shall seize upon Antibe,
In the River of Monaco they shall make their complaints,
And at Freius both of them shall take their share.

Le captif prince aux Itales vaincu
Passera Gennes par Mer jusque a Marseille,
Par grand effort des forens survaincu,
Sauf coup de feu, barril liqueur d'Abeille.

24 | The captive Prince vanquished in Italy,
Shall pass by Sea through Genoa to Marsilles,
By great endeavours of forrain forces overcome,
But that a Barrel of Honey shall save him from the fire.

Par Nebro ouvrir de Brisanne passage,
Bien esloignez el tago fara muestra,
Dans Pelligouxe sera commis l'outrage,
De la grand Dame assise sur l'Orchestra.

25 By Nebro to open the passage of Brisanne,
A great way off, el tago fara muestra,
In Pelligouxe the wrong shall be done,
Of the great Lady sitting in the Orchestra.

Le Successeur vengera son Beau frere,
Occuper Regne soubs ombre de vengeance,
Occis obstacle son sang mort vitupere,
Long temps Bretagne tiendra avec la France.

26 The Successour shall avenge his Brother in Law,
Shall hold by force the Kingdom, upon pretence of revenge,
That hinderance shall be killed, his dead blood ashamed,
A long time shall Brittany hold with France.

Charle cinquiesme & un grand Hercules,
Viendront le Temple ouvrir de main bellique,
Ure Colonne, Julius & Asean reculez,
L'Espagne, clef, Aigle neurent onc si grand
pique.

27 Charles the Fifth, and one great Hercules,
Shall open the Temple with a Warlike hand,
One Colonne, Julius and Ascan put back,
Spain, the Key, Eagle were never at such variance.

Second & tiers qui font prime Musique,
Sera par Roy en honneur sublimée,
Par graffe & maigre presque deny etique
Rapport de Venus faux rendra deprimée.

28 Second and third that make prime Musick;
Shall by the King be exalted to honour,
By a fat one, and a lean one, one in consumption,
A false report of Venus shall pull her down.

De Pol Mansol dans Caverne caprine,
Caché & pris extrait hors par la barbe,
Captif mené comme beste mastine
Par Begourdans amenée pres de Tarbe.

29 From Pol Mansol to a Goats Den,
Hidden and taken, drawn out by the beard
Prisoner, led as Mastiff
By Begourdans shall be brought near to Tarbe.

Nepveu & sang du St. nouveau venu,
Par le surnom soustient arcs & couvert,
Seront chassez mis a mort chassez nu,
En rouge & noir convertiront leur vert.

30 Nephew and blood of the Saint newly come,
By the surname upholdeth Vaults and Covering,
They shall be driven, put to death, and driven out naked.
They shall change their red and black into green.

Le Sainct Empire viendra en Germanie,
Ismaelites trouveront lieux ouverts,
Asnes viendront aussy la Caramanie,
Les soustenans de Terre tous couverts.

31 The Holy Empire shall come into Germany,
The Ismaelites shall find open places,
Asses shall also come out of Caramania,
Taking their part, and covering the Earth.

Le grand Empire chascun en devoit estre,
Un sur les autres le viendra obtenir,
Mais peu de temps sera son Regne & estre,
Deux ans aux Naves se pourra soustenir.

32 The great Empire, every one would be of it,
One above the rest shall obtain it,
But his time and his Reign shall last little,
He may maintain himself two years in his Shipping.

La faction cruelle a Robe longue,
Viendra cacher soubs les pointus Poignards,
Saisir Florence, le Duc & le Diphlongue,
Sa discouverte par Immeurs & Flagnards.

33 The cruel faction of long Robe,
Shall come and hide under the sharp Daggers,
Seize upon Florence, the Duke and the Diphlongue,
The discovery of it shall be Countrey fellows.

Gaulois qu'Empire par Guerre occupera,
Par son Beau-frere mineur sera trahi,
Pour Cheval rude voltigeant trainera,
Du fair le frere long temps sera hay.

34 A Frenchman who shall occupy an Empire by War,
Shall be betrayed by his Brother in Law a Pupil,
He shall be drawn by a rude prancing Horse,
For which fact his brother shall be long hated.

Puisné Roial flagrant d'ardant libide,
Pour se jouir de cousine Germaine,
Habit de femme au Temple d'Artemide,
Allant murdry par incogneu du Marne.

35 The Kingly youngest son heated with burning lust,
For to enjoy his Cosen German,
Shall in womans apparrel go to the Temple of Artemis;
Going, shall be murdered by unknown du Marne.

Apres le Roy du Sod guerres parlant,
L'Isle Harmotique le tiendra a mespris,
Quelques ans bons rongeant un & pillant,
Par tyrannie a l'isle changeant pris.

36 After that the King of the South shall have talked of Wars,
The Harmotick Island despise him,
Some good years gnawing one and plundering,
And by tyranny shall change the price of the Island.

Grande assemblée pres du Lac de Borget,
Se rallieront pres du Montmelian,
Passants plus outre pensifs feront projet
Chambry, Morienne, combat Saint Julian.

37 A great assembly of people near the Lake of Borget,
Will go and gather themselves about Montmelian,
Going beyond, they shall make an enterprize,
Upon Chambery, Moriene, and shall fight at St. Julian.

Amour alegre non loin pose le Siege.
Au Saint Barbar seront les Garnisons,
Ursins, Hadrie pour Gaulois feront plaige,
Pour peur rendus de l'Armée, aux Grisons.

38 Cheerful love doth lay Siege not far,
The Garrisons shall be at Saint Barbar,
Ursini, Hadria shall be sureties for the French,
And many for fear shall go from the Army to the Grisons.

Premier fils veufve malheureux mariage,
Sans nuls enfans deux Isles en discord,
Auant dixhuit incompetant Aage,
De l'autre pres plus bas sera l'accord.

39 Of the first son a widow, an unhappy match,
Without any Children, two Islands at variance,
Before eighteen an incompetant Age,
Of the other lower shall be the agreement.

Le jeune nay au regne Britannique,
Qu'aura le Pere mourant recommandé,
Iceluy mort Londre donra topique,
Et a son fils le Regne demandé.

40 The young man born to the Kingdom of Britanny,
Whom his Father dying shall have recommended,
After his death London shall begot him a topick,
And shall ask the Kingdom from his son,

En la frontiere de Caussade & Charlus,
Non queres loing du fond de la valée,
De Ville Franche Musique a son de Luths,
Environnez Combouls & grand myrtée.

41 Upon the Frontiere of Caussade and Charlus,
Not far from the bottom of the Valley,
Of Ville Franche there shall be Musick of Lutes,
Great dancing and great company of people met together.

Le Regne humain d'Angelique geniture,
Fera son Regne, paix, union tenir,
Captive guerre demy de sa closture,
Long temps la paix leur fera maintenir.

42 The humane Reign of an Angelical brood,
Shall cause his Reign to be in peace and union,
Shall make War, captive shutting it half up,
He shall cause them to keep peace a great while.

Le trop bon temps, trop de bonté Roiale,
Fais & desfaits prompt, subit, negligence.
Legier croira faux, despouse loiale,
Luy mis a mort par sa benevolence.

43 The time too good, too much of Royal bounty,
Made and unmade, nimble, quick, negligence,
Fickle shall believe false o' his loyal Spouse,
He shall be put to death for his good will.

Par lors qu'un Roy sera contre les siens,
Natifs de Blois subjuguera Ligneres,
Mammel, Cordube, & les Dalmatiens,
Des sept puis l'ombre a Roy estrennes & Lemures,

44 At that time that a King shall be against his own,
One born at Blois shall subdue the Ligures,
Mammel. Cordua and the Dalmatians,
After that the shadow of the seven shall be to the King a
  new years gift and Hoggoblins.

L'ombre du Regne de Navarre non vray,
Fera la vie de sort illegitime,
La veu promis incertain de Cambray,
Roy d'Orleans donra mur legitime

45 The shadow of the Reign of Navarre not true,
Shall make the life of illigitimate chance,
The uncertain allowance from Cambray,
King of Orleans shall give a lawfull Wall.

Vis sort mort de l'or vilain indigne,
Sera de Saxe non nouveau Electeur,
De Brunsvick mandra d'amour signe,
Faux le rendant au peuple seducteur.

46 The living receives his death from Gold, infamous slut!
Shall be of Saxony not the new Elector,
From Brunswick shall come a sign of love,
Falsly persuading the people that he is a seductor.

De Bourze Ville a la Dame Guyrlande,
L'on mettra sur par la trahison saite
Le grand Prelat de Leon par Formande,
Faux Pellerins & Rauisseurs deffaite.

47 From Bourze City belonging to the Lady Garlant,
They shall impose by a set treason,
The great Prelate of Leon by Formande,
False Pilgrims and Ravishers destroyed.

Du plus profond de l'Espagne ancienne,
Sortants du bour & des fins de l'Europe,
Troubles passant aupres du Pont de Laigne,
Sera deffaits par bande sa grand troppe.

48 From the utmost part of old Spain,
Going out of the extremities of Europe,
He that troubled the travellers by the Bridge of Laigne,
Shall have his great Troop defeated by another.

Jardin du Monde aupres de Cité neufve,
Dans le chemin des Montaignes cavées,
Sera saisi & plongé dans la Cuve,
Beuvant par force eaux Soulphre envenimées.

49 Garden of the World, near the new City,
In the way of the digged Mountains,
Shall be seized on, and thrown into the Tub,
Being forced to drink Sulphurous poisoned waters.

La Meuse au jour Terre de Luxembourg,	50	The Maes by day in the Land of Luxembourg.
Descouvrira Saturne & trois en Lurne,		Shall discover Saturn, and three in the Lurne,
Montaigne & pleine, Ville, Cité & Bourg,		Mountain and plain Town, City, and Countrey Town,
Lorrain Deluge, trahison par grand hurne.		A Lorrain flood, treason by a great hurne.
Des lieux plus bas du Pais de Lorraine,	51	The Lowest of places in the land of Lorraine,
Seront des basses Allemagnes unis,		With the Lower Germans will be united,
Par ceux du Siege Picards, Normans, du Maine,		Through those of Picards, Normans, of Main,
Et aux Cantons se seront reunis.		And to the Cantons they will be joined.
Au lieu ou Laye & Scelde se marient,	52	In the place where Laye and Scelde are united,
Seront les Nopces de long temps mamée,		Shall the Nuptials be, that were long a doing.
Au lieu d'Anvers ou la grappe charient,		In the place of Antwerp where they draw the grape,
Jeune vieillesse consorte intamnée.		The young unspotted will comfort the old Age.
Les trois Pellices de loing s'entrebatront,	53	The three Concubines shall fight one with another a far off,
La plus grand moindre demeurera a l'ecoute,		The greatest less shall remain watching,
Le grand Selin n'en sera plus patron,		The great Selin shall be no more their Patron,
Le nommera feu, pelte, blanche, route.		And shall call it fire, pelte, white, route,
Née en ce Monde par Concubine furtive,	54	Born in this world from a stollen Concubine,
A deux hault mise par les tristes nouvelles,		Set up at two heights by the sad news,
Entre Ennemis sera prinse Captive,		Shall be taken Prisoner among the Enemies,
Et amenée a Malines & Bruxelles.		And brought to Malines and Bruxelles.
Les malheureuses Nopces celebreront	55	The unhappy Nuptials shall be celebrated,
En grande joye mais la fin malheureuse,		With great joy, but the end shall be unhappy,
Mary & Mere Nore desdaigneront,		Husband and Mother shall scorn Nore
Le Phibe mort, & Nore plus piteuse.		The Phybe dead, and Nore more pitifull.
Prelat Royal soy baissant trop tiré,	56	Royal Prelate bowing himself too much,
Grand Flux de Sang sortira par sa bouche,		A great flood of Blood shall come out of his mouth,
Le Regne Anglicque par Regne respire,		The English Reign by Reign respited,
Long temps mort vis en Tunis comme souche.		A great while dead, alive in Tunis like a Log.
Le sublevé ne cognoistra son Sceptre,	57	The exalted shall not know hit Scepter
Les enfans jeunes des plus grands honnira,		He shall put to shame the young Children of the greatest,
Oncques ne fut un plus ord cruel estre,		Never was one more dirty and cruel,
Pour leur Espouses a mort noir bannera.		He shall banish to Black death their Spouses.

Au temps du dueil que le Selin Monarque	58	In the time of mourning, when the Monarch Selin,
Guerroiera la jeune Æmathien,		Shall make War against the young Æmathien,
Gaule bransler, pericliter la barque,		France shall quake, the Ship shall be in danger,
Tenter Phocens au ponant entretien.		Phocens shall be attempted, the business shall be in the West.
Dedans Lion vingt & cinq d'une haleine,	59	In Lyons five and twenty of a breadth
Cinq Citoyens Germains, Bressans, Latins,		Five Citizens Germans, Bressans, Latines,
Par dessous Noble conduiront longue traine,		Under Nobleman shall conduct a long Train,
Et descouvers par abboy de Mastins.		And shall be discovered by the barking of Mastiffs.
Je pleure Nice, Monaco, Pise, Genes,	60	I bewail Nice, Monaco, Pisa, Genoa,
Savone, Sienne, Capoue, Modene, Malthe,		Savona, Sienna, Capoua, Madena, Maltha,
Le dessus sang & glaive par estrenes,		Upon them blood and sword for a new years-gift,
Feu, trembler Terre, eau, malheureuse nolte.		Fire, Earth-quake, water, unhappy nolte.
Betta, Vienne, Comorre, Sacarbance,	61	Betta, Vienna, Comorre, Sacarbance,
Voudront livrer aux Barbares Pannone,		Shall endeavour to deliver Pannone to the Barbarians,
Par picque et feu, enorme violence,		By Pike, and fire, extraordinary violence !
Les conjurez d'escouverts par Matrone.		The Conspirators discovered by a Matron.
Pres de Sorbin pour assaillir Hongrie,	62	Near Soribn to assail Hungary,
L'Heraut de Bude le viendra advertir,		The Herald of Brudes will warn,
Chef Bizantin, Sallon de Sclavonie,		Chief of the Byantines, Salona of Slavonia,
A Loy d'Arabes les viendra convertir,		The law of the Arabs to which they will convert.
Cydron, Raguse, la Cité au Sainct Hieron,	63	Cydron, Raguse, the City of Saint Hieron,
Reverdira le medicant secours,		Shall make green again the Physical help,
Mort fils de Roy par mort de deux Heron,		The Kings Son dead, by the death of two Herons,
L'Arabe, Hongrie, feront un mesme cours.		Arabia and Hungary shall go the same way.
Pleure Milan, pleure Lucques, Florence,	64	Weep Milan, weep Lucques, and Florence,
Que ton grand Duc sur le Char montera,		When the great Duke shall go upon the Chariot,
Changer le Siege pres de Venise s'advance,		To change the Siege near Venice he goeth about,
Lors que Colonne a Rome changera.		When Colonne shall change at Rome.
O vaste Rome ta ruine s'approche,	65	O great Rome thy ruine draweth near,
Non de tes Murs, de ton sang, & substance,		Not of they Walls, of thy blood and substance,
L'aspre par lettres fera si horrible coche,		The sharp by Letters shall make so horrid a notch,
Fer pointu mis a tous jusques au manche.		Sharp Iron thust in all to the hast.

Le Chef de Londres par Regne l'Americh,	66	The Chief of London by Reign of America,
L'Isle d'Escosse tempiera par gelée,		The Island of Scotland shall catch thee by a frost,
Roy, Reb. auront un si faux Antechrist,		King and Reb. shall have so false an Antichrist,
Que les mettra tretous dans la meslée.		As will put them altogether by the ears.

66 The Chief of London by Reign of America,
The Island of Scotland shall catch thee by a frost,
King and Reb. shall have so false an Antichrist,
As will put them altogether by the ears.

Le Chef de Londres par Regne l'Americh,
L'Isle d'Escosse tempiera par gelée,
Roy, Reb. auront un si faux Antechrist,
Que les mettra tretous dans la meslée.

67 The Earth-quake shall be so great in the month of May,
Saturn, Caper, Jupiter, Mercury in the Bull,
Venus also, Cancer, Mars in Nonnay,
Then shall fall Hail bigger then an Egge.

Le tremblement si fort au mois de May,
Saturne, Caper, Jupiter, Mercure au Bœuf,
Venus aussi, Cancer, Mars, en Nonnay,
Tombera gresle lors gresse qu'un œuf.

68 The Fleet shall stand before the City,
Then shall go away for a little while,
And then shall take a great troop of Citizens on Land,
Fleet shall come back and recover a great deal.

L'Armée de Mer devant Cité tiendra,
Puis partira sans faire longue allée,
Citoyens grande proye en Terre prendra,
Retourner classe reprendre grand emblée.

69 The bright actions of new old exalted,
Shall be so great through the South and North,
By his own Sister great forces shall be raised,
Running away he shall be murdered near the bush of Ambellon.

Le fait luysant de neuf vieux eslevé,
Seront si grands par Midy Aquilon,
De sa sœur propre grandes alles levé,
Fuyant meurdry au buisson d'Ambellon.

70 The eye by the object shall make such an excrescency,
Because so much, and so burning shall fall the Snow,
The Field watered shall come to decay,
Insomuch that the Primat shall fall down at Rhege.

L'œil par objet fera telle excroissance,
Tant & ardente que tombera la Neige,
Champ arrousé viendra en decroissance,
Que le Primat succombera a Rhege.

71 The Earth and the Air shall freeze with so much water,
When they shall come to worship Thursday,
That which shall be never, was so fair,
From the four parts they shall come to honour him,

La Terre & l'Air geleront si grand eau,
Lors qu'on viendra pour Jeudy venerer,
Ce qui sera jamais ne fut si beau,
Des quattre parts le viendront honorer.

72 In the year a thousand nine hundred ninety nine, and seven months,
From Heaven a great terrible King,
To raise again the great King of Angoulesme,
Before and after, Mars shall Reign luckily.

L'an mil neuf cent nonante neuf, sept mois,
Du Ciel viendra vn grand Roy d'effrayeur,
Resusciter le grand Roy d'Angoumois,
Avant apres, Mars regner par bonheur.

73 The time present, together with the past,
Shall be judged by a great Jovialiste,
The World shall at least be wear of him,
And he shall be thought unfaithful by the Cannon-Law Clergy.

Le temps present auecque le passé,
Sera jugé par grand Jomaliste,
Le Monde tard luy sera lassé,
Et desloyal par le Clergé juriste.

Au revolu du grand nombre septiesme,	74	The year of the great number seven being past,
Apparoistra au temps jeux d'Hecatombe,		Shall be seen at that time the sports of Hecatombe,
Non esloignez du grand age milliesme,		Not far from the great age thousand,
Que les entrez sortiront de leur Tombe.		That the Buried shall come out of their Graves.

74 The year of the great number seven being past,
Shall be seen at that time the sports of Hecatombe,
Not far from the great age thousand,
That the Buried shall come out of their Graves.

Au revolu du grand nombre septiesme,
Apparoistra au temps jeux d'Hecatombe,
Non esloignez du grand age milliesme,
Que les entrez sortiront de leur Tombe.

75 So long expected shall never come
Into Europe, in Asia shall appear,
One come forth of the line of the great Hermes,
And shall grow above all the Kings in the East.

Tant attendu ne reviendra jamais,
Dedans l'Europe, en Asie apparoistra,
Un de la ligne yssu du grand Hermes,
Et sur tous Roys des Orient croistra.

76 The great Senate will decree a Pomp,
To one who after shall be vanquished and expelled,
The goods of his partners shall be
Publickly sold, and the enemy shall be driven away.

Le grand Senat decernera la Pompe
A un qu'apres sera vaincu chassé,
Des adhærans seront a son de trompe,
Biens publiez, ennemy dechasse.

77 Thirty associated of the Order of Quirettes,
Banished, their goods shall be give to their adversaries,
All their good deeds shall be imputed to them as crimes,
The Fleet scattered, they shall fall into the hands of Pyrates.

Trente adhærans de l'Ordre des Quirettes,
Bannis, leurs biens donnez ses adversaires,
Tous leurs bienfaits seront pour demerites,
Classe espargie, delivrez aux corsaires.

78 Sudden joy shall turn into a sudden sadness,
At Rome to the embraced graces,
Mourning, cries, weeping, tears, blood excellent joy,
Contrary Troops surprised and carryed away.

Subite joye en subite tristesse,
Sera a Rome aux graces embrassees,
Dueil, cris, pleurs, larm, sang, excellent liesse,
Contraires bandes surprises & troulsées.

79 The old ways shall be made all fair,
There shall be made a passage to Memphis Somentrées,
The great Mercury of Hercules Flower de luce,
Making the Earth, the Sea, and the Counteys to quake.

Les vieux chemins seront tous embellis,
L'on passera a Memphis somentrées,
Le grand Mercure d'Hercules fleur de lys,
Faisant trembler Terre, Mer, & Contrées.

80 In the great Reign, of the great Reign Reigning,
By force of Arms the great Brass Gates,
He shall cause to be open, the King being joyned with the Duke,
Haven demolish'd, Ship sunk on a fair day.

Au Regne grand, du grand Regne Regnant,
Par force d'armes les grands Portes d'airain,
Fera ouvrir, le Roy & Duc joignant,
Port demoly, nef a fonds jour serain.

81 A Treasure put in a Temple by Hesperian Citizens,
In the same hid in a secret place,
The hungry bonds shall cause the Temple to be open,
And take again and ravish, a fearful prey in the middle.

Mis Tresor Temple, Citadins Hesperiques,
Dans iceluy retire en secret lieu,
Le Temple ouvrir, les liens fameliques,
Repris, ravis proye horrible au milieu.

Cris, pleurs, larmes viendront avec couteaux,
Semblant faux donront dernier assaut,
L'entour parques planter profons plateaux,
Vifs repoussez & meurdris de plin saut.

82 | Cries, weeping, tears, shall come with daggers,
With a false seeming they shall give the last assault,
Set round about they shall plant deep,
Beaten back alive, and murdered upon a sudden.

De batailler ne sera donné signe,
Du Parc seront contraints de sortir hors,
De Gasp l'entour sera cogneu l'enseigne,
Qui fera mettre de tous les siens a morts.

83 | There shall no sign of battle be given,
They shall be compelled to come out of the Park,
Round about Gasp. shall be known the Ensign,
That shall cause all his own to be put to death.

La Naturel a si haut, haut non bas,
Le tard retour fera marris contens.
Le Recloing ne sera sans debats,
En emploiant & perdant tout son temps

84 | The Natural to so high, high not low,
The late return shall make the sad contented,
The Recloing shall not be without strife,
In employment and looking all his time.

Le vieil Tribun au point de la Trehemide
Sera presse, Captif ne delivrer,
Le vueil non vueil, le mal parlant timide,
Par legitime a ses amis livrer.

85 | The old Tribun, at the point of the Trehmide,
Shall be much intreated not to deliver the Captain,
They will not will, the ill speaking fearful,
By legitimate shall deliver to his friends.

Comme un Gryphon viendra le Roy d'Europe
Accompagne de ceux d'Aquiloa,
De rouges & blancs conduira grand Troupe,
Et Iront contre le Roy de Babylon.

86 | As a Griffin shall come the King of Europe,
Accompanied with those at the North,
Of red and white shall conduct a great Troop,
And they shall go against the King of Babylon.

Grand Roy viendra prendre port pres de Nice,
Le grand Empire de la mort si en fera,
Aux Antipodes posera son genisse,
Par Mer la Pille tout esvanouira.

87 | A great King shall land by Nice,
The great Empire of death shall interpose with it.
He shall put his Mare in the Antipodes,
By Sea all the Pillage shall vanish.

Pieds & Cheval a la seconde veille,
Feront entrée vastiant tout par Mer,
Dedans le Port entrera de Marseille,
Pleurs, cris & sang, onc nul temps si amer.

88 | Foot and Horse upon the second Watch,
Shall come in destroying all by Sea,
They shall come into the Harbour of Marseilles,
Tears, cryes and blood, never was so bitter a time.

De Bricque en Marbre seront les Murs reduits,
Sept & cinquante annees pacifiques,
Joye aux humains renevé l'aqueduct,
Santé, grands fruits, joye and mellisluous time.

89 | The Walls shall be turned from Brick into Marble,
There shall be peace for seven and fifty years,
Joy to mankind, the Aqueduct shall be built again,
Health, abundance of fruit, joy and mellifluous time.

Cent fois mourra le Tyran inhumain,
Mis a son lieu scavant & debonnaire,
Tout le Senat sera dessoubs sa main;
Fasche sera par malin temeraire.

90 | The inhumane tyrant shall die a hundred times,
In his place shall be put a Learned and mild man,
All the Senate shall be at his command,
He shall be made angry by a rash malicious person.

Clergé Romain l'an mil six cens & neuf, *Au chef de l'an fera Election,* *D'un gris & noir de la Compagne yssu,* *Qui oncques ne fut si malin.*	**91** The Roman Clergy in the year a thousand six hundred and nine, In the beginning of the year shall make choice Of a gray and black, come out of the Countrey, Such a one as never a worse was.
Devant le Pere l'Enfant sera tué, *Le Pere apres entre cordes de jonc,* *Genevois peuple sera esvertué,* *Gisant le Chef au milien comme un tronc.*	**92** The Child shall be killed before the Fathers eyes, The Father after shall enter into ropes of rushes, The people of Geneva shall notably stir themselves, The Chief lying in the middle like a log.
La Barque neuve recevra les Voiages, *La & aupres transfereront l'Empire,* *Beaucaire, Arles, retiendront les Hostages,* *Pres deux Colomnes trouvées de Porphyre.*	**93** The new Ship shall make journeys Into the place, and thereby where they shall translate the Empire, Beaucaire, Arles, shall keep the Hostages, Near them shall be found two Columns of Porphyry.
De Nismes d'Arles, & Vienne contemner, *N'obeyront a ledict Hesperique,* *Au Labouriez pour le grand condamner,* *Six eschapez en habit Seraphique.*	**94** From Nismes, d'Arles and Vienna contempt, They shall not obey the Spanish Proclamation, To the Labouriez for to condemn the great one, Six escaped in a Seraphical habit.
Dans les Espagnes viendra Roy trespuissant, *Par Mer & Terre subjugant au Midy,* *Ce ma fera rabaissant le croissant,* *Baisser les aisles a ceux du Vendredy.*	**95** A most potent King shall come into Spain, Who by Sea and Land shall make great Conquests towards the South, This evil shall beat down the horns of the new Moon, And slack the Wings of those of Friday.
Religion du nom des Mers viendra, *Contre la Secte fils Adaluncatif,* *Secte obstinée deplorée craindra,* *Des deux blessez par Aleph & Aleph.*	**96** Religion of the name of the Seas shall come, Against the Sect son Adaluncatif, Obstinate Sect deplorate shall be afraid, Of the two wounded by Aleph and Aleph.
Triremes pleines tout aage captifs, *Tempsbon a mal, le doux pour amertume,* *Proye a Barbare trop tost seront hastifs,* *Cupid de voir plaindre au vent la plume.*	**97** Triremes full of Captives of all Age. Time good for evil, the sweet for bitter, Pray to the Barbarian, they shall be too hasty, Desirous to see the feather complain in the wind.
La splendeur clairëa Pucelle ioicuse, *Ne luira plus, long temps sera sans Sel,* *Avec Marchans, Ruffiens, Loups, odieuse,* *Tous pesle mesle monstre universel.*	**98** The clear splendour of the merry Maid, Shall shine no more, she shall be a great while without Salt, With Merchants, Ruffians, Wolves, odious, All promiscuously, she shall be an universal Monster.

A la fin le Loup, le Lion, Oxe and asse,
Timide dama seront avec Mastins,
Plus ne cherra a eux la douce Manne,
Plus vigilance & custode aux Mastins.

99 | At last the Wolf, the Lion, Oxe and Asse,
Fearful Doe, shall be with the Mastiffs,
The sweet Manna shall no more fall to them,
There shall be no more watching and keeping of Mastiffs.

Le grand Empire sera par l'Angleterre,
Le Pempotam des ans plus de trois cens,
Grandes Copies passer par Mer & Terre,
Les Lusitains n'en seront pas contens.

100 | The great Empire shall be in England,
The Pempotan for more then three hundred years,
Great Armies shall pass through Sea and Land,
The Portugueses shall not be contended therewith.

ADJOUSÉ DUPUIS L'IMPRESSION DE *1568*.

Quand le fourchu sera soustenu de deux paux,
Avec six demy cors, & six sizeaux ouvers :
Le trespuissant Seigneur, heritier des crapaux,
Alors subjuguera, sous soy tout l'univers.

Century XI

eysnier, Manthi, & le tiers qui viendra,
Peste & nouveau insult, enclos troubler.
Aix & les lieux fureur dedans mordra,
Pius les Phocens viendront leur mal
doubler.

91 Meysinier, Manthi, and the third that shall come,
Plague and new attempt shall trouble them enclosed,
The fury of it shall bite in Aix and the places there about,
Then they of Phocens shall come and double their misery.

Par Ville Franche, Mascon en desarroy,
Dans les Fagots seront Soldats cachez.
Changer de temps en prime pour le Roy,
Par de Chalon & Moulins tous hachez.

97 By Ville Franche, Mascon shall be put in disorder,
In the Faggots shall Souldiers be hidden,
The time shall change in prime for the King,
By Chalon and Moulins they shall be all bewed to pieces.

Century XII

Eu, flamme, faim, furt, farouche fumée,
Fera faillir, froissant fort, foy faucher,
Flis de Deité! toute Provence humée,
Chassé de Regne, enragé sans crocher.

4/5   Fire, flame, hunger, theft, wild smoak,
Shall cause to fail, brusing hard, to move Faith,
Son of God ! all Provence swallowed up ?
Driven from the Kingdom, raging mad without
spitting.

Le grand secours venu de la Guyenne,
S'arrestera tout aupres de Poitiers,
Lion rendu par Montluel en Vienne,
Et saccagez par tout gens de Mestiers.

24   The great succours that came from Gascony,
Shall stop hard by Poitiers,
Lion surrendred by Montluel and Vienna,
And ransacked by all kinds of Tradesmen.

Assault farouche en Cypre se prepare,
La larme a l'œil de ta ruine proche,
Byzance Classe Morisque si grand tare,
Deux differens le grand vast par la Roche.

26/   A cruel assault is preparing in Cyprus,
36   Tears in my eye, thou art near thy ruine,
The Fleet of Constantinople and the Morick so great
damage.
Two differents the great wast shall be by the Rock.

Deux corps un chef, champs divisez en deux,
Et puis respondre a quattre non ouys,
Petits pour grands a pertius mal pour eux,
Tour d'Aigues foudre, pire pour Eussovis.

52/   Two bodies, one head, fields divided into two,
4   And then answer to four unheard ones,
Small for great ones, open evil for them,
The Tower of Aigues beaten by Lightning, worse for
Essovis.

Tristes Conseils, desloiaux, cauteleux,
Aduis meschant, la loy sera trahie,
Le peuple esmeu, farouche, querelleux,
Tant Bourg que Ville toute la paix haie.

55/   Sad Councels, unfaithful, malicious,
5   Ill advice the Law shall be betrayed,
The people shall be moved, wild & quarrel'ome,
Both in Countrey and City the peace shall be hated.

Roy contre Roy, & le Duc contre Prince,
Haine entre iceux dissension, horrible,
Rage & fureur sera toute Province,
France grand guerre & changement terrible.

56/   King against King, and Duke against a Prince,
6   Hatred between them, horrid dissension,
Rage and fury shall be in every Province,
Great War in France, and horrid changes.

L'accord & pache sera du tout rompue,
Les amitiez pollues par discorde,
L'haine enviellie, toute foy corrompue,
Et l'esperance, Marseilles sans concorde.

59/   The agreement and contract shall be broken in pieces,
7   The friendships polluted by discord,
The hatred shall be old, and faith corrupted,
And hope also, Marseilles without concord.

Guerre & debats, a Blois guerre & tumulte,
Divers aguets, adveux inopinables,
Entrer dedans Chasteau Trompette, insulte,
Chasteau du Ha, qui en seront coulpables.

62/   War and strifes, at Blois war and tumult,
8   Several lying in wait, acknowledgment unexpected,
They shall get into the Chasteau Trompette by assault,
And into the Chasteau du Ha, who shall be guilty of it.

A tenir fort par fureur contraindra,
Tout cœur trembler, Langon advent terrible,
Le coup de pied mille pieds te rendra,
Guirond. Garon, ne furent plus horribles.

65 | He shall by fury compel them to hold out,
Every heart shall tremble, Langon shall have a terrible event,
The kick shall return to thee a thousand kicks,
Girond. Caron. are no more horrid.

Eiovas proche, esloigner, Lac Leman,
Fort grand apprests, retour confusion,
Loin des Nepueux, du feu grand Supelman,
Tous de leur suyte.

69 | Eiovas near, yet seemeth to be far from the Lake Leman,
Very great prepardtives, return confusion,
Far from the Neveux of late great Supelman,
All of their train.

Fleuues, riuieres de mal seront obstacles,
La vielle flame d'ire non appaisée:
Courir en France. cecy comme d'oracles,
Maisons, manoirs, Palais, secte rasée.

71 | Brooks and Rivers shall be a stopping to evil,
The old flame of anger being not yet ceased,
Shall run through France, take this as an Oracle,
Houses, Mannors, Palaces, Sect shall be raced.

FIN.